Managerial Accounting
FOR Libraries
& OTHER
Not-for-Profit Organizations

SECOND EDITION

G. Stevenson Smith

AMERICAN LIBRARY ASSOCIATION

Chicago   2002

Cover and text design by Dianne M. Rooney

Project editor, Eloise L. Kinney

Composition by the dotted i in Times and Helvetica Condensed using QuarkXpress 4.1 on a Macintosh platform

Printed on 50-pound white offset, a pH-neutral stock, and bound in 10-point coated cover stock by McNaughton & Gunn

The paper used in this publication meets the minimum requirements of American National Standard for Information Sciences—Permanence of Paper for Printed Library Materials, ANSI Z39.48-1992. ∞

Library of Congress Cataloging-in-Publication Data
Smith, G. Stevenson.
   Managerial accounting for libraries and other not-for-profit organizations /
  G. Stevenson Smith.—2nd ed.
     p.   cm.
   Includes bibliographical references and index.
   ISBN 0-8389-0820-9 (alk. paper)
   1. Library finance. 2. Libraries—Accounting. 3. Nonprofit organizations—Accounting. 4. Managerial accounting. I. Title.

  Z683 .S63 2002
  025.1'1—dc21   2001056162

06 05 04 03 02   5 4 3 2 1

*This book is dedicated
to my wife, Carol,
a former librarian,
who truly understands
the value of patience.*

CONTENTS

FIGURES

CHAPTER 1

Introduction to Nonprofit Managerial Accounting

The purpose of this book is to explain techniques of accounting analysis that will help managers within a library make better management decisions. These techniques will assist the library manager in making decisions about selecting equipment and determining whether costs are being efficiently incurred, monitoring financial and nonfinancial performance measures, and developing strategic plans. By using this book, questions such as the following can be answered:

- How do I efficiently plan for the future?
- How do I decide which computer system to purchase?
- How do I know if today's decision fits within our mission and vision?
- Can I save money by buying more expensive equipment?
- How do cash flows affect my purchase decisions?

Budget development, although important in library management, is not one of the topics discussed in this book. The techniques described in this book allow the manager to identify costs that make a difference in planning future decisions. In addition, the reader will see that some typically stated financial reports are only extraneous information to managerial decision making.

To understand the focus of the book, one must first be aware of differences between managerial and financial accounting. These two areas of specialization need to be distinguished from one another. Second, decision making in nonprofit and for-profit organizations needs to be contrasted to highlight the reasons for-profit analytical methods may not be used in a standardized fashion in the nonprofit environment. The environment in which decision making occurs affects the application of these analytical methods. Therefore, if the reader has previously seen these techniques applied in a for-profit organization, he or she needs to understand that the applications here are being specifically adapted to the nonprofit environment.

MANAGERIAL ACCOUNTING

Managerial accounting, which is the focus of this book, has a different orientation than financial accounting. Managerial accounting is directed at the internal users of accounting information. Library directors, department heads, and other supervisors represent this group. Unlike financial accounting statements, managerial accounting reports are not required to follow any prescribed accounting formats. Instead, managerial reports provide useful information to the manager so that efficient and accurate decisions can be made. These reports can show financial information such as the shelved cost per book or nonfinancial information such as levels of patron satisfaction with the collection.

Unlike financial accounting, where statements are usually issued at the end of yearly or quarterly periods, managerial reports are issued as they are needed. Therefore, some reports may be issued on a monthly basis, and others may be issued bimonthly. The purpose of financial reports is to show what happened in the *past* year. These reports are not forward looking. With managerial reports, the purpose is to help change or influence decisions occurring in the future. Unlike the aggregated organizational information in financial reports, managerial reports contain specific and detailed information about subunits within the organization. This detailed data allow the manager to focus more accurately on the changes occurring within an organizational subunit. Aggregated financial statement data or budget information cannot take the place of properly prepared managerial reports, nor can the former provide the manager with the information required to make proper cost-control or strategic decisions.

The information in managerial reports goes beyond the reporting found in financial statements. For example, managerial reports can (1) help in analyzing variances from cost standards; (2) trace future cost flows, such as maintenance costs, to help in equipment selection decisions; (3) aid in equipment purchasing versus leasing decisions; and (4) determine the break-even level of a service (the point where costs equal support or revenues). Many of the techniques used in for-profit managerial accounting are similar to those used in nonprofit decision making, but these methods cannot be wholly transferred into a nonprofit context without carefully considering whether they are truly applicable to the analysis.

FINANCIAL ACCOUNTING

Financial accounting must follow set accounting standards or guidelines when preparing the organization's financial statements. The three financial statements that are prepared under these guidelines are (1) the balance sheet, (2) the income statement, and (3) the statement of cash flows. These financial statements are prepared under prescribed guidelines called generally accepted accounting principles (GAAP). In the nonprofit area, the Financial Accounting Standards Board (FASB) or the Governmental Accounting Standards Board (GASB) establishes GAAP. These boards are responsible for prescribing accounting principles for external reporting by nonprofit organizations. Libraries are one such organization.[1]

If financial statements are prepared for a nonprofit organization on a basis other than that prescribed by the boards, and these statements are audited by an independent certified public accountant (CPA), the CPA or auditor will not provide what is known as a "clean" opinion. The CPA's opinion consists of a statement regarding the fairness of presentation of the financial statements. An opinion usually contains boilerplate language about the financial statements, but if material problems occur in the audit, these difficulties need to be reflected in the CPA's opinion. An opinion of this nature is called a *qualified opinion,* and it is not a clean opinion. Such an opinion would highlight the fact that the audited financial information may be misleading in some manner, such as following unprescribed accounting methods.

In other words, financial accounting places restrictions on the manner in which information can be presented for external reporting. It also provides a means to enforce these reporting standards with the auditor's opinion. Of course, there is a reason for this. If prescribed accounting standards are not followed, the consistency and comparability of the financial statements from period to period cannot be assured.

Financial accounting's external orientation and requirements for following specifically prescribed practices make it different than managerial accounting because only managerial accounting practices are directly oriented toward decision-making issues.

MANAGERIAL ACCOUNTING IN FOR-PROFIT AND NONPROFIT CONTEXTS

In planning for a business project, a comparison is made between a periodic series of revenue inflows and expense outflows. The first objective is to ascertain, as best as possible, if the cash inflows from the activities will exceed the outflows. The second objective is to select the project with the highest net inflow. Generally, if cash inflows exceed outflows on a project, the decision criteria will allow for acceptance of the project as a viable investment. The profit premise is basic to the managerial analysis that is performed in a for-profit context.

In nonprofit organizations, earning a profit has limited applications. In most nonprofit operations, managerial emphasis is placed on the level of services provided to patrons. If costs are not recovered, the service may be provided anyway and funded from other sources. Therefore, the techniques of for-profit analysis cannot be adopted in nonprofit organizations without modifications.

To better understand these differences, it is important to view nonprofit decision making in a more holistic perspective. A very efficient method to develop such a view is with the balanced scorecard.[2] The balanced scorecard is a method that clearly and concisely relates performance goals among diverse organizational activities, and it will be discussed in a nonprofit context later. The balanced scorecard is the underlying mechanism that makes a systemwide business plan successfully function and continue adapting to a rapidly changing external environment as it ties together financial and non-financial techniques.

Briefly, the *balanced scorecard* evaluates performance targets through the perspectives of the customer, finance, learning and growth, and internal business processes. The development of interrelated performance goals among these four areas begins with the organization's vision and mission statements. Those statements guide all other activities and measures. The purpose of a fully implemented balanced scorecard is to link short-term goals into a long-term strategy. Consequently, this method is particularly important for nonprofit organizations whose activities are not solely related to the "bottom line."

In nonprofit organizations, the objective is not to ensure that the revenues, if any, exceed the costs of a service activity. A nonprofit operation may generate cash outflows that will always exceed cash revenue inflows. For example, the operating costs of zoological or botanical parks have always exceeded any fee revenues charged to the users of these parks. The profit objective is not paramount in a nonprofit organization. Many services are provided without recovery of their costs. Therefore, in nonprofit managerial analysis, the revenue side of the analysis is usually not as relevant as it is in for-profit organizations.

Furthermore, the monetary support provided to a nonprofit organization is not always directly related to the services provided, as patrons are not directly charged for services. This lack of a relationship is in marked contrast with a for-profit business, where the products sold and the revenues received are closely tied together.[3] The methods of analysis applied in a business organization closely relate revenues and their corresponding costs. Measures of nonprofit success, however, are not recorded by the highest monetary profit. Rather, success is measured by the quality of economically costed services.

This measure of success indicates that decision making in a nonprofit organization is at variance with decision making in a for-profit company. As an example, consider depreciation expense in for-profit and nonprofit contexts. *Depreciation expense* is an accounting allocation where the purchase price of an asset with a life of more than one year is assigned to the time periods over which the asset is used. This allocation procedure assigns the asset's purchase price in a "reasonable" manner to the time periods of estimated asset use, but no cash outflows arise from this allocation procedure. The only cash outflow that might have occurred took place when the asset was originally purchased.

Depreciation expense in a for-profit context is important because it reduces the taxes that a corporation pays; depreciation is a tax-deductible expense. Without a reduction of revenues from depreciation expenses, higher taxes result in larger cash outflows to the Internal Revenue Service. Therefore, depreciation expenses are important in making managerial decisions in a for-profit business. But, in organizations that do not pay taxes, the importance of depreciation expense to decision making is reduced. In fact, recording depreciation may be a nuisance to managerial decision making because noncash depreciation allocations must be added back to cash received as contributions and budget allocations to determine the total cash flowing into an organization. The managerial importance of depreciation expense in a nonprofit context is restricted to making a determination about the extent to which facilities have been depreciated. The amount of accumulated depreciation may provide insights into the status of the infrastructure.

For a nonprofit organization, a more important asset question than depreciation-related issues is, How well have the assets been maintained? For any organization, but especially for a nonprofit entity, the amount spent to maintain assets is more important information than knowing the amount of accumulated depreciation of an asset. The level of normal preventive maintenance on an asset can be established by manufacturer's guidelines within a fairly specific range. If these preventive maintenance procedures are not followed, the expected life of the asset is reduced prematurely. It is fairly common to see public infrastructures literally collapsing because of curtailed maintenance. In these instances, maintenance was stopped in an attempt to save budget dollars. Without proper maintenance of facilities, public funds in excess of projections will have to be used to replace prematurely deteriorated facilities or to fund above-normal maintenance repairs. Even though maintenance expenditure information is not specifically reported in the financial statements, it can be recorded in managerial reports. Information about the amount of deferred maintenance can be more important to a nonprofit manager than depreciation expense information. This illustrates a basic difference between managerial decision making in for-profit and nonprofit organizations.

Care should be taken to separate the analytical techniques that are used in for-profit organizations from those that are used in nonprofit organizations. This means that the methods used by for-profit organizations must be thoughtfully adopted by nonprofit organizations. The approach taken in this book is oriented toward the *nonprofit managerial accounting* view. A subdivision of the area generally described as managerial accounting, this view adapts those methods for nonprofits to use.

THE NORMATIVE MODEL VERSUS
THE DESCRIPTIVE MODEL
IN THE NONPROFIT ENVIRONMENT

A primary nonprofit managerial accounting objective is to provide the greatest amount of cost-efficient services to the largest number of people. The best nonprofit managerial accounting techniques are used to achieve this objective. Often, however, when the final decision for a course of action is chosen, it may be different than the recommended solution arrived at through the use of financial analysis. In fact, the final decision may have been made without considering or reviewing the analysis. Why does this occur?

Financial analysis provides a *normative* illustration of what should be done in analyzing a problem. These financial techniques show how a problem can best be analyzed to arrive at the optimum solution. If the normative model considered all factors, the best solution to a problem would always be the action taken, but it is not. The normative model incorporates the best analytical techniques to a managerial problem, but it does not incorporate the political and behavioral factors that are very real influences in nonprofit organizations. Unlike the normative model, a descriptive model incorporates political and behavioral factors into the model. A descriptive model that is particularly pertinent to nonprofit organizations has been described in *agency theory.*[4]

The basic premise in agency theory is that someone other than the owner of the organization (i.e., the agent) manages the organization. In nonprofit organizations, this manager is the director, and the owners are either the groups that provide monetary resources or, in some cases, the groups that are receiving services. In a library, relationships exist between the director and the board, the director and the governmental entities providing funding, and the director and the service groups. Agency theory relationships are present any time decision-making authority has been delegated to a subordinate. A basic assumption of agency theory is that the managers are out to maximize benefits to themselves. The agent is chiefly concerned with satisfying his or her own self-interests without regard to the needs of the owners or the organization. Agency theory is applied as a method of formalizing contractual relationships between the agent and owners to optimize the welfare of the organization and the groups it serves.

Under agency theory, consideration is aimed at overcoming the self-interest or opportunism of the managers in charge of departments within the organization. *Opportunism* occurs when a manager selects solutions to a problem that are in the best interests of that manager but not necessarily in the best interests of the organization or the groups the manager serves. For example, the best solution for a manager may mean exercising the least amount of effort or shirking regardless of the outcome. The lack of congruence between the manager's goal and the service goals of the organization should be a concern in nonprofit managerial accounting. Personal ambition or the rewards of prestige that come from a position may be factors in a manager's decision-making process that determine whether he or she will accept higher levels of career risk in order to provide better services.

A great deal of the hard data in managerial accounting is based on *estimates,* and estimates are often biased because of a managerial manipulation of information. The manager, in direct control of an operation, usually is assumed to have the best information about its operation. Therefore, it may be difficult for others to determine if an estimate is unbiased or if it is biased to further the manager's interests. A manager may be asked to makes estimates of such things as the time it takes to finish a project, personnel requirements, or the amount of use a new service will receive once it is offered. The estimate that is received from the manager is used to prepare an internal accounting report, to evaluate the feasibility of a project, or to develop a grant proposal. Any bias introduced into the manager's estimate is often difficult to detect because evaluative information is only received after the action has been implemented. Therefore, the accuracy of managerial estimates can be determined only on the basis of historically collected information. Agency theory is directed at correcting the causes of these managerial contrivances.

As an example, assume a library director is on an upward career path. In accepting a new position, this person is mainly concerned with how personal accomplishments in the new job will have an impact on his or her next job. For a manager, establishing a track record of accomplishments is important. This track record is oriented toward the short term because a director is usually expected to remain at a particular job for a maximum of three years. The director will approve those decisions that contribute positively to his or her three-year record of performance. Some of these decisions may not be in the best interests of the library. For example, the director might install computers in the library in order to list a computer initiative in the library on his or her vita. In implementing this initiative, the cheapest computers are purchased, with little technical support, no maintenance agreement, and hardly any software. In this example, the computers will have to be completely discarded within a four-year period, after providing little public service. The limited four-year life of these computers is not important to the manager because he or she is likely to have found another better-paying job before the limitations of the initiative become apparent. Additionally, if the cheaper computers are purchased, funds may be left over so that the director can start another "initiative" that will make his or her résumé even more impressive. Agency theory is concerned with establishing contractual relationships to prevent this type of behavior from occurring.

One particularly difficult nonprofit managerial accounting problem is how to monitor an individual's performance to prevent nonproductive behavior. In a for-profit organization, a worker's performance can be easily seen and evaluated, but in most nonprofit organizations, it is particularly difficult to evaluate performance. How can a nonprofit organization determine if the director of a library is not interested in an upward career path but instead is more interested in expending a minimum amount of effort?

These examples illustrate the special problems that may arise when traditional managerial accounting methods are introduced into the nonprofit organization. Nonprofit organizations have been criticized for not adopting the modern methods of business; however, these methods have not been properly modified for the context of the nonprofit organization and do not take into consideration the managerial behavioral characteristics described in agency theory. It is possible to correct for this behavior in several ways, as is explained later.

WHAT IS NONPROFIT MANAGERIAL ACCOUNTING?

With the differences between nonprofit and for-profit entities in mind, what is nonprofit managerial accounting? Nonprofit managerial accounting adapts the techniques of for-profit analytical analysis to a nonprofit environment to find solutions to managerial problems. Whenever possible, nonprofit managerial accounting uses for-profit analysis within an agency theory framework. It adapts the best analytical techniques in the corporate world to the special environment of nonprofit organizations.

The major emphasis in business is for profits to exceed costs by as much as possible. In nonprofit managerial accounting, cost containment is important if the nonprofit organization is to remain viable. Cost performance needs to be evaluated to determine how efficiently services are being provided. Without cost control, the resource base of capital within the organization erodes to a level that prevents the organization's service activities from continuing. A minimum resource level is needed if the organization is to perform its mission. Therefore, providing services, not making a profit, is the major reason for controlling costs in a nonprofit organization.

In addition to adopting analytical techniques from for-profit business, nonprofit managerial accounting uses techniques unique to the nonprofit organization. For example, greater emphasis is placed on developing nonfinancial performance measures in addition to financial performance measures.

WHO WILL BENEFIT FROM THIS BOOK?

Library cost control, project evaluation, and strategic planning are the primary concerns of this book. Managers within a library system who are required to control costs or make choices between service levels as budgets are curtailed will find this book useful. Library boards interested in controlling costs can use the illustrations in the book to request that similar reports be prepared within their organizations. In a period of budget reductions and cost curtailment, the importance of an efficient and cost-effective organization requires serious attention. Therefore, it is important to be familiar with the analytical techniques described in this book. The book uses these financial techniques within a framework that allows nonprofit managers to determine whether the defined organizational mission is being accomplished.

Although the material is specifically directed at libraries and the financial questions that arise within them, many of the illustrations apply in other nonprofit organizations as well. For example, cost concerns that face a library manager also face administrators in museums, civic organizations, professional associations, performing arts organizations, and fraternal organizations. Readers who are likely to benefit from the material in this book are those individuals who have operating responsibility within a nonprofit organization.

SUMMARY

The purpose of this book is to illustrate to those who have operating responsibility within a nonprofit organization that a number of techniques can be used successfully to evaluate projects and make long-term managerial decisions. These techniques must be carefully used on the specific event facing the library manager.

Managerial accounting, project analysis, and long-term planning in a nonprofit setting cannot unhesitatingly adopt the managerial accounting techniques used by for-profit organizations without awareness of their limitations in the nonprofit environment. The director of a library should thoroughly question reports that are prepared using for-profit accounting techniques. In addition, the director of a library should not expect to make managerial decisions by using the financial statements and reports prepared for external use. These are historical documents that are not prepared for internal use and may not provide the information critical to decisions oriented toward the future.

Notes

1. The Governmental Accounting Standards Board (GASB) sets accounting standards for state and local governments, and the Financial Accounting Standards Board (FASB) and

the American Institute of Certified Public Accountants (AICPA) set accounting standards for business organizations. The organizations set standards with the issuance of statements and with audit guides. When a library is part of a state and local government, its financial statements are not prepared separately from those of the state and local government, and the library is considered to be part of the state or government organization. Usually, the only separate financial reports this type of library receives are related to budgetary numbers. If a library is not considered to be part of a government organization, its financial statements must be prepared using a different method of accounting than used by the state and local government. In those cases, the accounting rules are prescribed by the FASB and the AICPA, not the GASB. In 1999 the GASB issued Statement No. 34, *Basic Financial Statements—and Management's Discussion and Analysis—for State and Local Governments* (Norwalk, Conn.: GASB, 1999). This statement changed financial reporting under the state and local government model as it reduced the importance of funds and placed more emphasis on a total government financial perspective.

2. The balanced scorecard has been described in a number of books and articles. For example, *see* R. S. Kaplan and D. P. Norton, "The Balanced Scorecard—Measures That Drive Performance," *Harvard Business Review* 70 (January-February 1992): 71–79; R. S. Kaplan and D. P. Norton, *The Balanced Scorecard: Translating Strategy into Action* (Boston: Harvard Business School Press, 1996); R. S. Kaplan and D. P. Norton, "Using the Balanced Scorecard as a Strategic Management System," *Harvard Business Review* 74 (January-February 1996): 75–85; and N. Olive, J. Roy, and M. Wetter, *Performance Drivers: A Practical Guide to Using the Balanced Scorecard* (West Sussex, England: John Wiley & Sons, 1999).

3. *See* the classic article by R. K. Mautz, "Monuments, Mistakes, and Opportunities," *Accounting Horizons* 2 (June 1988): 123–28.

4. For an introduction to agency theory, read D. B. Thornton, "A Look at Agency Theory for the Novice: Part 1," *CA Magazine* (November 1984): 90–97; and D. B. Thornton, "A Look at Agency Theory for the Novice: Part II," *CA Magazine* (January 1985): 93–100. For applications of agency theory, *see* R. J. Indejejikian, "Performance Evaluation and Compensation Research: An Agency Perspective," *Accounting Horizons* 13 (June 1999): 147–57; and R. M. Wiseman and L. R. Gomez-Mejia, "A Behavioral Agency Model of Managerial Risk Taking," *Academy of Management Review* 23 (January 1998): 133–53.

2

Cost Concepts and Decision Making

Although it may initially appear that the only decision to be made about costs is related to their incurrence, cost behavior patterns make any cost decision more complex. For example, curtailing library operations without properly analyzing cost patterns may result in overstating any anticipated cost savings.

This chapter describes most of the cost terms that are introduced in this book and provides examples of why *cost analysis* is important in nonprofit managerial decision making. Managerial decision making encompasses both future costs and historical costs. Future costs are most important in making decisions about equipment purchases, whereas historical costs are important in evaluating past performance.[1]

Before beginning an analysis of cost concepts, a definition must be provided for the term *cost* and distinctions made among *assets, costs,* and *expenses.* The term *cost* is defined as net resources used or consumed to achieve specific organizational objectives. *Net resources* are the cash or other assets remaining after those amounts owed are paid. Although the resources consumed may consist of assets, it is not always necessary for assets to be consumed to incur costs, as costs can increase when liabilities are incurred.

We are all faced with the choice between asset consumption or liability incurrence when we choose how to pay our monthly credit card bill. If we pay with cash, we experience the expiration of an asset. If we don't pay a credit card bill at the end of the month, we increase the amount we owe—

our liability. The effect of a decrease in assets or an increase in liabilities is the same—it is a reduction of net resources available for future use.

Expired or consumed assets are assigned to the proper fiscal periods for financial reporting purposes and are called *expenses* on an income statement. *Expenses* are costs incurred with no recognizable future benefit beyond the current time period, and therefore they become deductions on a current income statement. In other words, expenses are the costs of operating a library in a time period when specific library services are rendered. Yet the incurrence of some costs does not always create an immediate increase in expenses in the current time period. Expense recognition can be deferred to later time periods. For example, when cash is expended on a new library building, the building's cost is not an immediate expense, but it is still referred to as the cost of the building. The cost becomes part of the cost of a property or an asset that will provide a future benefit to the organization.[2] For that reason, the costs of a building are recorded as the building's services are received.

The term *cost* is referred to when net resources are either used to construct a building or to pay for photocopying services, for example. Although both cases involve cost incurrence, photocopying services are considered an expense of the current time period; building costs result in a long-lived asset that expires and turns into an expense as the building is used. The building has the potential to provide services for a long time, but the photocopying services are received in the immediate time period.

In some cases, costs that are usually considered an expense of the current period may not be recorded as such because of special circumstances. For example, if a large percentage of a library manager's work time was devoted to planning and supervising the construction of a new library building, charging a portion of that manager's salary to the cost of the building, as overhead, might be appropriate. This action is justified because the library manager's efforts are contributing to the future value of the building, and the cost of the effort should not be recorded as an expense of the current period. This manager's contribution will provide services for a long-term period in the same manner as other construction costs. Thus, the amount of salary expense recorded in the current period is reduced, and the asset value of the building is increased by an equal amount.

To expand on this recognition concept, consider how the cost of a building is handled. The building's cost is not immediately recorded as an expense because it has a useful value that is assumed to benefit a number of future periods. Instead, the costs of the building are reasonably allocated to the future periods that will receive benefits from building use. The process of allocating the building's costs to future time periods is called *recording depreciation expense.* Depreciation expense is an allocation procedure that assigns the costs of a long-term asset to future fiscal periods based on the *assumed estimated* wear or obsolescence of that asset. Figure 2-1 highlights the relationship between assets, costs, and expenses.

As costs are incurred, they either become expenses or create property— an asset or a productlike asset. Over time this property is turned into an expense as it loses its usefulness.[3] Depreciation gradually transfers property values into an expense by the allocation of cost to time periods.[4]

COST CONCEPTS FOR MANAGERIAL DECISION MAKING

In a review of cost concepts, a time period for analysis needs to be assumed. Without a time-period assumption, it is difficult to develop concise cost definitions. For example, in a long-run time frame all costs vary, but as time periods become shorter, some costs begin to vary less. For this review of cost concepts, a twelve-month time period is assumed.

As initially stated, it may not be a simple matter of eliminating departmental functions in order to cut costs. Some costs may behave in a manner that shows little change even when departmental services are reduced. An organization chart for a typical medium-sized public library is shown in Figure 2-2. This organization chart will be used to illustrate the cost concepts highlighted here.

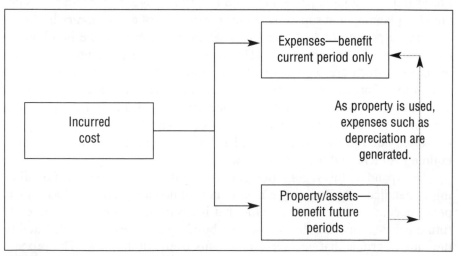

FIGURE 2-1   The expense-cost cycle

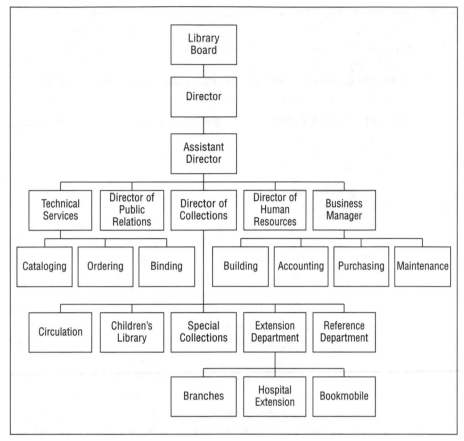

FIGURE 2-2 Organization chart for a medium-sized public library

Actual Cost

What are the actual costs involved in decision making? Actual costs are costs incurred at the time a transaction takes place. A service is received or goods are purchased, and in return the organization either incurs a debt or makes a payment. The usefulness of this information for managerial decision making depends on the analysis under way. For some managerial decisions, cash flow is the only information that is important. The importance of cash flows will be explained in chapter 6. For other managerial decisions, however, actual costs need to be used together with other data to arrive at the correct decisions. For example, will the actual cost of operating a bookmobile determine the total cost per unit of services—miles traveled or books loaned—provided by the vehicle? The answer is, not with actual costs alone. It is only when a portion of actual costs are mingled with costs that must be allocated over time that the full cost of services can be determined on a per-unit basis.[5] Of course, a number of limitations to intermingling these costs need to be understood, and they are discussed later.

Note that the actual costs provide the raw data for the accounting system, the basis for financial reports. These financial reports are only one part of managerial reports that are used for decision making. Accounting rules must be followed for external reporting purposes, but the only reporting rule that has to be used for managerial decision making is to provide reports that are useful to management.

Allocated (Indirect) Costs

For cost data to be useful for managerial decision-making purposes, *service objectives* must be identified. The library's service objectives are related to the various departmental units, such as those shown in Figure 2-2. The services provided directly to the public by the library are found in Circulation, Children's Library, Special Collections, the Extension Department, and the Reference Department. These departments have direct contact with patrons, and for that reason they are called *program departments.* The rest of the activities performed within the library support the library's program departments. Departments that provide supporting services are called *service departments.*

The costs of the service departments are usually allocated to the program departments. Examples of allocated service department costs are depreciation on service department equipment, salaries and wages paid in the service department, and the cost of materials used there. This allocation procedure, which will be discussed in chapter 3, determines the full cost of operating each program department, as well as the per-unit cost of the service objectives within a program department. For example, in determining the unit cost of specific service objectives, the full cost of program operations are divided by a service unit, such as the number of books loaned, to determine the per-unit cost of this service. Allocation procedures are followed because service department costs are difficult to trace directly to specific patron services provided by the library.

In the organization chart, Technical Services, Human Resources, Public Relations, the Business Department, and the salaries being paid to the library director and assistant director represent service department operating costs. These costs, also referred to as indirect or overhead costs, are allocated in a "reasonable" manner to the program departments in order to determine the full costs of operating each program. The main benefit from collecting this information is that full-cost comparisons can be made on a year-to-year basis within a library, as well as with annual periods. Additionally, full-cost data may be required to receive reimbursements on work performed under grant agreements.[6]

Yet, the question remains: How useful is allocated cost information to managerial decision making? Before answering, several problems with allocated cost should be noted. First, the methods for allocating overhead costs will vary widely from one library to another. Even within the same system, different individuals could select different allocation methods. This variation occurs because allocation methods are usually required to be "reasonable" rather than "uniform." A number of reasonable methods can be adopted to allocate costs. Therefore, full-cost data calculated on a per-unit basis should only be used to make intralibrary cost comparisons because comparable or uniform full-cost data are not likely to be available among libraries.

A second problem with full-cost data from a managerial perspective is its misleading effect on the performance evaluations of managers. Allocated costs have little bearing on actual manager performance because the manager has no managerial control over costs allocated to his or her unit. Therefore, there is little relationship between actual performance and full costs. In fact, performance evaluation based on full costs can hide poor performance if the reported results are strongly influenced by the *method* used to allocate overhead costs rather than actual performance. For this reason, full-cost data should not be used for making performance evaluations.

Therefore, the answer to the question of how useful allocated cost information is to managerial decision making can only be answered within the context of the circumstances in which it is used. Generally, the usefulness of allocated cost information to managerial decision making is somewhat limited. Clearly, it must be used with caution whenever it is employed for analysis purposes as it can easily lead to incorrect conclusions.

Exercise 2-1

Thinking about Overhead Costs

In the Moreover Library, the Human Resources Department is responsible for handling hiring, promotion packages, and health and other benefit issues that relate to the entire library.

1. How do you think the costs of running the Human Resources Department should be allocated to the Reference Department? (All answers to the exercises are found in appendix C, at the end of the book.)

Standard Costs

Unlike allocated costs, *standard costs* can be useful in evaluating efficient performance. Standard costs are predetermined future costs set at efficient levels that are attainable by employees. Through past experience or the use of time and motion studies, it is possible to determine how long it should take to efficiently perform many routine activities. Activities such as shelf reading and book processing readily lend themselves to the determination of time/cost standards. The standards for time spent or materials used are established as cost performance criteria to be met by employees. The evaluation of efficient operations requires that actual cost be at least equal to standard costs. It is also possible to evaluate service objectives and determine if they are being achieved efficiently. If actual costs do not meet the attainable standard, the differences need to be investigated so that corrections can be made to reach efficient levels of operations.

An example of standard costs is the standard labor cost per book processed, which can be established based on attainable time and labor rates. These costs include the standard labor costs per hour for activities such as sorting, affixing labels, stamping and attaching pocket and date due slip, inserting Tattle Tape Strips, and sorting for distribution. The standard labor costs allow for determining if there is a dollar variance between the number of books actually processed and the number of books that should have been processed within the standard labor hours allowed for the task. In other words, for the number of books processed, how many hours should have been used? This number should be compared with the actual number of hours used. It is assumed that these tasks or activities are similar from one library to another; therefore, work standards allow for more comparability between libraries as well as within the same library system.

It may appear that the dollar variances between actual work performed and standards are similar to the differences between actual dollars expended and budget appropriations, but they are not. When standard costs are determined, efficiency is the primary consideration. With standards, an attempt is being made to determine if the staff is performing work at an efficient level. This comparison is used to evaluate management performance.

When the differences between budget appropriations and actual expenditures are determined, efficient work performance is not a concern. The difference between budget and actual expenditures is made to highlight deviations from board-approved spending levels only, which is a quasi-legal concern, not an efficiency consideration per se.

Controllable and Noncontrollable Costs

For managerial decision-making purposes, it is important to separate controllable and noncontrollable costs. Without this cost separation, managers may be held accountable for costs over which they have no control or responsibility, such as allocated costs. A *controllable cost* is a cost that can be changed by a specific manager taking a specific action. An example of a controllable cost is the amount of overtime incurred within a manager's department. If such costs are not controllable by a manager, they are called *noncontrollable costs.*

The definition of a controllable cost will vary at different organizational levels within a library. For example, in the organization chart in Figure 2-2, the business manager may be directly responsible for the incurrence of maintenance costs, but to the department head of the children's library, any maintenance costs allocated to that department are not controllable. As another example, consider the costs that are controllable by the library board. One cost controllable by the board is the library director's salary, but if a portion of that salary is allocated to departments within the library in determining the full costs of their operations, those individual department heads will view that allocated cost as noncontrollable.

Cost responsibility and cost controllability for a manager should coincide. Therefore, a manager's performance evaluation should include consideration of how well controllable costs are kept within cost limits. If a cost is noncontrollable, however, a manager's performance should not be evaluated based on its incurrence.

Although allocated costs are generally associated with noncontrollable costs, unallocated costs may also be noncontrollable. For example, the price of supplies is an unallocated cost. Although the technical services manager does have control over the efficient use of supplies, he or she is likely to have little control over the price paid for those supplies by the business office. The price of supplies is an unallocated cost that is noncontrollable by the manager of technical services, but it is likely to be directly traced to the department. This example illustrates that care must be exercised in determining who has responsibility for costs.

When full costs, including allocated costs, are determined, it is helpful to separate controllable costs from noncontrollable costs in managerial reports. Managers need to realize that they are responsible only for those costs over which they exercise control. The separation of costs into controllable and noncontrollable classifications will highlight this fact.

Exercise 2-2

Why Am I in Trouble?

As head of the Reference Department, you are presented with the following Cost Report from accounting.

Nicer Library
Reference Department
Annual Cost Report
January 1, 20xx

Personnel	$ 95,000
Equipment purchases	100,000
Telephone	6,000
Supplies	10,000
Building	15,000
Administration	15,000
Total Cost	$241,000

You are shocked to find out that the one phone in the Reference Department is costing $500 per month and that your section of the library is charged $15,000 in building charges. Finally, you also do not understand why you are charged $15,000 of the director's salary when the director has only talked to you during nonlibrary events.

Explain why the Reference Department's Cost Report is showing charges for telephone, building, and administration costs.

Fixed, Variable, and Mixed Costs

The separation of costs into fixed, variable, or mixed costs is important in analyzing cost behavior patterns and in making managerial decisions. Cost behavior patterns affect decisions about the savings or cost increases that are likely to occur from changes in activities or service levels. Remember that the time period under which these costs are being defined is one year. This somewhat arbitrary designation of a one-year time frame means that care should be exercised when separating fixed and variable costs in this manner. For example, a cost recognized as a fixed cost in a one-year time frame may be the most rapidly changing, or variable, cost in a two-year time frame.

A *fixed cost* is a cost that does not change as the level of services within a library changes. Rent and insurance are examples of fixed costs. The salaries of all contract employees are fixed and will not change directly with the level of library services provided. If a cost changes as the volume of services provided changes, it is a *variable cost*. Some costs may vary, but they must vary directly with volume levels to be considered a variable cost. Supplies used in the Technical Services Department in Figure 2-2 are an example of a variable cost. Hourly salaries are another example of variable costs because as service levels increase, so do hours worked and wage costs.

Some costs, however, may be variable or fixed depending on how they are calculated. For example, depreciation on a bookmobile may be a fixed amount every year, or the expense could vary with the number of miles logged on the bookmobile. Depreciation expense may vary with time periods, but unless it varies directly with services—hours of use and mileage—it is not a variable cost.

Figure 2-3 provides three illustrations of variable costs. Graph A in Figure 2-3 is the typical example of a variable cost—a 45-degree line between total variable cost and volume or level of services. Graphs B and C are also examples of variable costs, but they change at decreasing and increasing rates, respectively, with volume of service. Both graph B and graph C are illustrations of variable costs because they vary with the volume level of services provided. If the horizontal axis were changed to a measure of time instead of a volume level, none of these costs would be considered a variable cost.

Although it may be useful to separate all costs into fixed and variable costs, this practice may ignore actual cost behavior. Some costs do not exhibit all the characteristics of either a fixed or variable cost. These costs can be called *mixed costs* because they have characteristics of both variable and fixed costs. An example of a mixed cost is found in the way total salaries for supervisors behave when the span of control is taken into consideration. One supervisor can efficiently handle a specific number of employees, but as employees are added beyond a certain number, other supervisory personnel

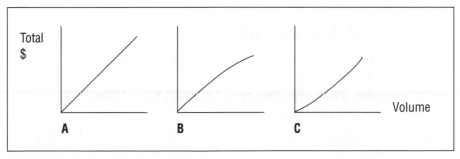

FIGURE 2-3   Illustrations of variable costs

must be added to help with the supervision tasks. The salary cost pattern for total supervisors' salaries behaves as illustrated in Figure 2-4, graph A. As the end of an efficient span of control is reached, a new supervisor is added and total salary costs increase in a stair-step fashion. This mixed cost remains fixed for only a limited change in volume of service. Therefore, it is not fixed per se, but it does not exhibit all the characteristics of a variable cost either.

Another example of mixed costs is illustrated in Figure 2-4, graph B. This cost pattern begins as a fixed cost and changes to a variable cost after a specific volume level is reached. Utility rates that begin with a flat charge and change to a variable rate per unit after a certain usage figure is reached are an example of this cost pattern.

These cost patterns show that it is important to know cost behavior before assumptions about future cost reductions can be made. In a library facing budget curtailments, knowledge of cost behavior patterns assist the library manager in initiating cost cuts with a minimum reduction in services. The decision involves more than simply curtailing activities or instituting across-the-board percentage budget cuts.

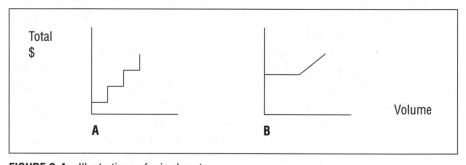

FIGURE 2-4   Illustrations of mixed costs

Exercise 2-3

Some Simple Cost Patterns

For each of the following descriptions, develop a cost pattern similar to those shown in Figures 2-3 and 2-4.

1. Assuming a budget purchase plan is not in effect, draw the seasonal cost pattern of electrical cost usage for a library in Minnesota.

2. At the initial change, draw the cost pattern, to the library, of switching from printed periodicals to online periodicals.

Direct and Indirect (Allocated) Costs

Direct costs are directly traceable to the cost of a service or department. Examples of direct cost are the cost of labor and materials that go into a library's in-house bookbinding operations, the labor costs of running branch libraries, or the labor and material costs of processing interlibrary loans. Indirect costs or allocated costs cannot be easily traced to an organizational objective, program, or department. Allocated costs have already been described, but they need to be compared here with direct costs.

A direct cost is a controllable cost if a specific manager can control it; however, identification as a direct cost does not necessarily mean that cost is controllable by a department manager. Indirect costs are similar to noncontrollable costs. But, again, a cost may be controllable by a manager even though it is an indirect cost. Therefore, these definitions may overlap, but they do not implicitly overlap.

Only direct costs can be eliminated. Therefore, separation of direct costs from indirect or allocated costs is important if future costs savings from curtailing department operations are to be accurately determined. If the library director reviews full costs in determining the future cost savings from curtailing activities, the amount of savings will be overestimated because a high percentage of indirect or allocated costs is likely to remain when service is reduced. An analysis of direct and indirect costs to determine the cost savings from reducing services is important to sound managerial decision making.

Discretionary Costs, Sunk Costs, and Differential Costs

Distinctions between *discretionary costs, sunk costs,* and *differential costs* are important because only differential costs have an effect on managerial decision making.

The decision to incur discretionary costs is usually made as part of the annual appropriation. Discretionary costs are expenditures based on the discretion of management rather than on managerial analysis. These costs are easy to change; managers need only change their minds about the expenditures to increase or decrease amounts expended.

Management may believe that discretionary expenditures are important, but their value to the organization is difficult to measure. Examples of discretionary costs are seminar training for employees in technical services, training for reference personnel on a new database, setting aside amounts for travel to professional meetings, and promoting library programs. It is difficult to determine the direct increase in service to the library that is being received from making these expenditures.

Another cost classification is *sunk cost.* Unlike discretionary costs, sunk costs are costs that cannot be changed. The organization has made a commitment to their continuation. Examples of these costs are depreciation, long-term contract payments, and liability insurance payments. Identifying these costs will allow them to be separated from those costs that influence managerial decisions. As an example of a sunk cost, consider the calculation of depreciation. Depreciation is calculated by assigning the cost of an asset to the time periods in which the asset is used. Although the future amount to be paid for an asset is an important consideration in decision making, after the purchase price has been paid, its accounting disposition is of little importance to managerial decision making. The yearly depreciation charges based on the price paid for an asset are not useful for future decision making as long as the asset is in use. For this reason, the sunk cost or purchase price of an asset acquired yesterday has no bearing on the decision to replace that asset today. Many managerial decision-making questions are oriented toward the future, not the past, and historical cost allocations have no effect on those decisions.

Differential costs are another cost classification. Unlike discretionary or sunk costs, differential costs are important for managerial decision-making purposes. Differential costs are sometimes called *incremental costs.* These costs are the dollar differences between the costs of alternative future actions that can be taken by a manager. For example, if the purchase prices of two vehicles are $10,800 and $10,000, the differential or incremental cost is $800. If the cost of license plates for each vehicle is $35, this is not a differential because the charge is the same. Therefore, the cost of license plates should not be a consideration in determining which of the two vehicles to purchase.

Consider the decision to close a branch library as another example of differential cost analysis. The costs of operating the branch are shown in Figure 2-5. The total cost of operating the branch is $36,500, and initially it may appear that this is the amount saved if the branch is closed.

However, to determine the actual amount of savings that will occur if the branch is closed, the costs of operating the branch need to be individually analyzed. The salary of an administrator within the Extension Department is allocated to this branch based on the time spent assisting with branch functions. As shown in Figure 2-5, $6,500 of the administrator's salary is allocated to the branch. This is an example of an indirect or allocated cost. The administrator would not be released if the branch were closed; therefore, this

Cost Item	Full Costs	Differential Costs
Administrative salary	$ 6,500	—
Technician wages	10,000	$10,000
Utility charges	3,000	3,000
Annual rent payments	9,000	9,000
Book purchases, exhibits, videos, and movie rental	8,000	4,000
Totals	$36,500	$26,000

FIGURE 2-5   Full costs and differential costs for a branch library

administrative salary would not be reduced. A technician working at the branch who receives a salary of $10,000 would be laid off if the branch were closed. Approximately one-half of the book purchases and video rental costs would still have to be paid for by the main library. The differential cost savings from closing the branch are $26,000—the costs that change as a result of closing the branch, not the total costs of operating the branch. Figure 2-5 shows that the cost savings from closing the branch are less than the branch's full operating cost—costs of $10,500 will continue to be incurred regardless of whether the branch is closed ($36,500 – $26,000). These costs are unavoidable and should not enter into the decision-making process. Only costs that will differ as a result of alternative future choices—the differential costs—should be allowed to influence such a decision.

Exercise 2-4

Budget Cuts

Use the Cost Report from Exercise 2-2 to answer the questions below.

   To save money, the director of the Nicer Library has been forced to cut the budget by 10 percent. As head of the Reference Department, your portion of the reduction is equal to $24,100 (.10 × 241,000).

1. Can you explain to the director why the level of this reduction may not be possible without seriously curtailing reference services?

2. And, further, can you explain how much of the 10 percent across-the-board budget cut should be taken out of your department?

Life Cycle Costs

Costs associated with an asset over its entire life or life cycle are called *life cycle costs.* These costs are used in determining which of several similar assets to purchase. Life cycle costing goes beyond the initial acquisition price in selecting which asset to purchase; it includes a projection of the asset's operating and maintenance costs over its entire life. This information may have to be estimated from a number of sources. Besides the future operating and maintenance costs, another factor in this analysis is the estimated salvage value of the asset at the end of its useful life. All these variables affect the overall cost of asset ownership. A complete discussion of this topic is presented in chapter 6.

Future operating and maintenance costs are not reflected in the acquisition price and may differ significantly between two assets. Therefore, in making asset purchase decisions, total ownership costs need to be compared. These costs are important because maintenance costs of an asset may equal more than half the asset's original cost, and with an aging asset, these costs tend to increase.

For management to select the most cost-effective asset for use in the organization, the total ownership costs of an asset must be estimated. If the initial acquisition price is the major criteria used for the selection of an asset, the asset acquisition process is likely to be misguided. This is especially true with assets that have longer lives.

Historical Costs and Current Costs

The *historical cost* of an asset is the price that was originally paid for that asset and is recorded in the accounting records when that asset is acquired. This is the only cost that can be shown directly on the financial statements.

Yet, as inflation continues, the purchase cost of the same type of asset increases. For example, a desk may have cost $225 ten years ago, and today the market price of that same desk is $650. This amount is not recorded in the books, but for managerial decision making, the current cost of $650 is more important because it shows the resources that will have to be used to acquire a new desk. Current cost adjustments will be used in chapter 3.

SUMMARY

This chapter provides a background to specific cost terms and concepts that will be used in later chapters. It is not the purpose of this chapter to deal in great detail with these concepts or to cover all the cost terminology that will be introduced in the book but, rather, to provide an overview of cost concepts and indicate how these concepts affect managerial decision making.

The chapter has highlighted cost terms that are useful to managerial decision making. A total of sixteen cost terms were introduced: *actual, allocated, standard, controllable, noncontrollable, fixed, variable, mixed, direct, indirect, discretionary, sunk, differential, life cycle, historical,* and *current.*

Gaining a familiarity with these cost definitions is important because they will be used throughout the remainder of the book. Terms such as *controllable, noncontrollable,* and *allocated costs; variance analysis* and *variable* and *fixed costs;* and *life cycle costing techniques* and *differential cost analysis* will be covered in future chapters.

In managerial decision making, there is an emphasis on making future-oriented decisions, and therefore the anticipated costs associated with these decisions are also important. In evaluating managerial performance, historical cost information provides a measure of feedback on past performance.

The cost classifications described in this chapter are not available in budget reports. Budget reports classify all costs together on budget lines to ensure that appropriated budget dollars have not been exceeded. As a result, budget reports cannot be used for most managerial decision-making issues. Also, most budget reports do not provide for cost control except on a total expenditure basis.

Additionally, the cost classifications described here cannot be found on the financial statements prepared for a library. As constructed, financial statements do not provide cost information that is required by operating managers for decision making. Therefore, library managers have a special need for the preparation of managerial reports containing this specific cost information.

Notes

1. It was stated in chapter 1 that it is more useful for a manager to know the amount of deferred maintenance on an asset than the amount of accumulated depreciation on that asset. This is still true. Many managerial decisions have a future orientation, and for those decisions only costs that affect the future are important. Historical cost information does have a place in managerial decision making, but the allocated purchase price of an asset does not. A manager is responsible for the costs that he or she can control, and managerial performance is evaluated on that basis. But, in neither decision making nor performance evaluation is depreciation expense important.

2. For managerial decision making, it is not important how these costs are assigned to the financial statements. From a managerial decision-making perspective, the primary concern is when the cash flow related to the transaction occurs, not how it was allocated on the financial statements. Cash flow analysis will be discussed in chapter 6.

3. In a corporation, product costs are eventually recorded on the income statement as the cost of units sold. Libraries usually do not record the cost of sales on their financial statements.

4. The terms *costs* and *expenses* are based on accrual accounting methods. The term *expenditures* is based on modified accrual accounting methods. Cash accounting methods do not record true expenditures, expenses, or costs, but they record disbursements instead. For additional explanations of these accounting methods, *see Accounting for Libraries and Other Not-for-Profit Organizations* (Chicago: American Library Association, 1999), by G. Stevenson Smith. As the financial report for nonprofits becomes similar to corporate financial reporting (a current trend), the terms *costs* and *expenses* will replace the term *expenditures* more commonly found in modified accrual methods.

5. The term *allocated cost* is often used as a synonym for indirect costs or overhead costs.

6. Under federal grants where costs may be reimbursed, the allocation of overhead is closely regulated.

CHAPTER

3

Responsibility Accounting and Methods of Managerial Cost Control

Responsibility accounting is a system that assigns cost-control responsibility to a specific functional manager in the library. Cost information is accumulated for that manager's area of responsibility. A widely used traditional approach to responsibility accounting is discussed in this chapter. Under this approach, costs are accumulated in responsibility centers. A newer cost-control approach, called activity-based costing, relates costs to the activities performed and is explained in chapter 4. Both cost approaches are concerned with controlling and assigning responsibility for cost control to specific operating managers within a library. Therefore, both methods can be used with responsibility accounting.

Responsibility centers within an accounting system are centers of accountability established around organizational objectives. Traditionally, organizational objectives are centered on the organization's structure, with each department representing a responsibility center. A manager who has the authority to make operating decisions on a day-to-day basis controls these responsibility centers. The assignment of one manager to a responsibility center makes that manager clearly responsible for the cost performance of that unit. Significant deviations from agreed-upon spending levels are clearly traceable to the manager. In the organization chart of a public library (*see* Figure 2-2), responsibility centers can be represented by the directors of Technical Services, Public Relations, and Human Resources; the Business

Manager; and the department heads of Circulation, the Children's Library, Special Collections, the Extension Department, and the Reference Department. All these departments may be considered responsibility centers headed by managers who are assigned responsibility for cost control. Essentially, responsibility centers are established as a way of monitoring cost control and managerial performance.

Once it is determined that a responsibility center approach is to be used for cost control, and that a manager will be responsible for each center, a decision has to be made as to how to evaluate performance in such a responsibility center. Although "cost" evaluations are usually used, evaluations can be based on profits or a rate of investment return.

PERFORMANCE BASIS FOR RESPONSIBILITY CENTERS

In a library, performance measures are usually based on a *cost-center* structure. In a cost center, the direct costs of operations are accumulated. The direct costs are the costs that a manager is assumed to be able to control. These costs are important because one measure of successful managerial performance can be the comparison between the direct cost budgeted and the direct cost actually incurred. Incurring more costs than the amount budgeted may indicate a problem that needs to be investigated.

It is common practice to accumulate costs in cost centers based on departmental structures. In some libraries, a different accumulation base may be better for establishing responsibility centers. As stated, a responsibility center may be considered a profit or investment center as well as a cost center. If a library has the good fortune to have a sales center on its premises that sells books or prints, for example, then this unit can be evaluated as either a profit center or investment center. Profit and investment centers are discussed later in the chapter. However, as previously indicated, responsibility accounting in a library usually focuses on cost-center accountability.

The cost-center approach is closely related to the budget process in nonprofit organizations. Comparing actual costs with budgeted amounts is already an established library procedure, and that process fits well into the cost-center format for responsibility accounting. Yet, in making these dollar comparisons, caution needs to be exercised. In a budget, all costs can be compared, but when using a cost-center approach to evaluate managerial performance, only costs controllable by a manager should be evaluated. The evaluation of managerial performance with the use of costs not controllable by a manager does not provide any indication of how well that manager is actually performing.

TRADITIONAL COST CENTERS

The traditional cost analysis in a cost-center format separates controllable and noncontrollable costs from one another in order to evaluate managerial performance properly. The manager in charge of the department, project, or operation can control a controllable cost—the manager can increase or decrease the expenditure. A comparison between controllable costs and total board-authorized amounts can be one aspect of the manager's performance evaluation.

In a different approach, actual expenditures may be compared with acceptable expenditures for actual volume levels. If yearly budget appropriations are simply divided by twelve months to show monthly expenditure levels, no consideration is being given to variation in actual patron usage that may occur over the year—for example, summer versus winter usage. Expenditures for actual volume levels can be calculated by multiplying the actual number of patrons who used a department's services by a predesignated charge per library patron. This predesignated charge is estimated ahead of time and is based on the past year's cost data and this year's budget as a reasonably estimated charge to incur for each patron using the department. If actual library expenditures were significantly more than indicated by using the predesignated charge, the manager's performance would be rated unfavorably.

The predesignated charge is similar to a standard applied cost used by a manufacturing firm. In a manufacturing firm, actual costs of a period are compared to the standard cost that should have been incurred for a particular volume of activity. A manufacturing firm's standards are based on the level of successfully completed units, or unspoiled production volume, during a period. When a budget is calculated based on standard cost and production volume, it is called a *flexible budget*. Nonprofit organizations do not usually use standards; comparisons are more commonly made between the actual expenditures and budget-approved spending levels.[1]

In this analysis, it is assumed that most costs are controllable by someone within the organization. For example, a department manager, such as the head of the Children's Library, can control the cost of photocopying, equipment rental agreements, travel, training, and publicity. At higher organizational levels, more costs become controllable. For example, the director of a library may have the authority to increase or decrease departmental budgets within the library.

On the other hand, there are also noncontrollable costs. Noncontrollable costs for a department head include such items as utilities, insurance, depreciation on equipment, database charges, and certain administrative salaries set by the board. When the full cost of operating a department such as the Children's Library is calculated, it is necessary to allocate these types of costs to the departmental level.

The purpose of allocating overhead costs to a department is to extend managerial control over all costs. A major argument supporting the allocation of overhead is that if no one sees the overhead costs, no one will be responsible for these costs. The logic of this argument is questioned in chapter 4, where activity-based costing is discussed. It should be noted that it is common practice to request grant funding on a full-cost basis, and that practice is not being questioned here.

Figure 3-1 provides an example of how actual and budgeted costs for the month of April are analyzed for the Technical Services Department. The costs are classified by objects of expenditure—human resources, which are salaries and wages, as well as supplies and travel, for example.

Prior to preparing the performance report in Figure 3-1, each *budgeted* cost is analyzed to determine if it is a controllable cost. Therefore, the report may be somewhat different from a governmental budget report that analyzes monthly or year-end variances by accumulating *all* costs incurred, not just controllable costs. Under traditional responsibility accounting, the manager is only responsible for costs that he or she can directly control.

In Figure 3-1, the Controllable Cost Performance Report recognizes controllable costs as human resources services, supplies, travel, membership dues, maintenance and repairs, and training. The budgeted costs are compared to actual costs incurred to determine favorable or unfavorable variances. For example, supplies had an unfavorable variance of $200 for the month just ended. In other words, amounts in excess of the monthly budget appropriation were spent. Another unfavorable variance exists for maintenance and repairs of $500 for the monthly period.

The performance report also shows the year-to-date totals for budgeted amounts and actual amounts incurred. The last column shows the year-to-date variance. Although this is similar to a budget report, all costs would appear on the budget report, whereas on a performance report only controllable costs are reviewed. This difference arises because the budget document is used to account for all board-approved expenditures. The purpose of the budget document is to ensure that approved spending levels have not been

Department: **Technical Services**

Controllable Cost Performance Report
for the Month Ended April 30, 20xx

Controllable Cost by Object of Expenditure	Monthly Budgeted	Monthly Actual	Variance (U) or F*	Year-to-Date Budgeted	Year-to-Date Actual	Variance (U) or F*
Human resources	$ 6,200	$ 6,200	$ 0	$18,500	$18,500	$ 0
Supplies	1,200	1,400	(200)	3,600	4,400	(800)
Travel	0	0	0	0	0	0
Membership dues	410	410	0	210	210	0
Maintenance and repairs	2,000	2,500	(500)	2,200	2,700	(500)
Training	0	0	0	1,600	0	1,600
Total controllable costs and variances	$ 9,810	$10,510	$ (700)	$26,110	$25,810	$ 300

*(U) Unfavorable; F Favorable

FIGURE 3-1 Report on controllable costs for the Technical Services Department

exceeded. In many cases, budget reports are not related to specific department spending levels but only to total library spending.

Unlike a budget document, the report in Figure 3-1 is directly related to evaluating managerial performance within a department. It shows controllable spending levels and variances for the Technical Services Department, and only *its* manager is responsible for the variances in that department. To further analyze the performance being reported upon, it would be possible to add ratios to this document that highlight the level of budget spending. For example, ratios could be based on "year-to-date budgeted" and "year-to-date actual" dollars shown in Figure 3-1. The resulting ratios quickly show the overspent budget lines (supplies and maintenance and repairs).

The Percent of Budgeted Dollars Expended

	Actual/ *Budgeted $*
Human resources	100%
Supplies	122%
Travel	n/a
Membership dues	100%
Maintenance and repairs	123%
Training	0%

Figure 3-2 illustrates a responsibility accounting report prepared for the director of the library and shows only director controllable costs incurred by all departments in the library. This report is prepared as a performance report, not a budget report, for the library director. Total budgeted costs for the entire library will be shown in a budget report typically aggregated by objects of expenditure such as supplies, books, salaries, and wages.

The format of the Controllable Cost Performance Report in Figure 3-2 is the same as that shown in Figure 3-1. This example illustrates one format that may be used in reporting controllable costs. The departments listed in the first column are based on the organizational structure for a medium-sized library (*see* Figure 2-2). Each department's controllable costs are the responsibility of the director. Total controllable cost for Technical Services, shown in Figure 3-1, is reported in the second row of Figure 3-2. This report allows the director to review exceptions—cost variances—within departments in greater detail. For example, public relations has a $1,200 unfavorable monthly variance that may be considered significant enough to be investigated in more detail to determine its exact cause. In addition, public

Department: Director's Office

Controllable Cost Performance Report
for the Month Ended April 30, 20xx

Controllable Cost by Object of Expenditure	Monthly Budgeted	Monthly Actual	Variance (U) or F*	Year-to-Date Budgeted	Year-to-Date Actual	Variance (U) or F*
Administration	$ 5,600	$ 5,900	$ (300)	$ 15,000	$ 15,700	$ (700)
Technical Services	9,810	10,510	(700)	26,110	25,810	300
Public Relations	6,800	8,000	(1,200)	7,500	8,800	(1,300)
Human Resources	2,200	2,200	0	6,600	6,600	0
Business Office	5,000	4,500	500	15,000	14,500	500
Circulation	6,000	6,100	(100)	20,000	19,000	1,000
Children's Library	3,000	3,000	0	9,000	8,000	1,000
Special Collections	3,000	3,000	0	2,000	3,000	(1,000)
Extension Department	7,000	7,400	(400)	21,000	18,000	3,000
Reference Department	6,000	5,900	100	22,000	24,000	(2,000)
Total control able costs and variances	$54,410	$56,510	$(2,100)	$144,210	$143,410	$ 300

*(U) Unfavorable; F Favorable

FIGURE 3-2 Report on controllable costs for the library director

relations is $1,300 over budget on year-to-date controllable costs ($8,800 – $7,500). The director can request the detailed performance report from public relations at this time. This report does not show all budgeted dollars. For responsibility reports, it may be acceptable to stop at this point with the separation of controllable and noncontrollable costs. But, for some cases, in which reports with full-cost information are desired, departmental reports are prepared with overhead allocated to departments.

Exercise 3-1

Calculate Performance Ratios Based on Cost Data

1. Using the information in Figure 3-2, calculate the percent of budget dollars expended by Administration, Technical Services, Public Relations, and Human Resources.

2. Why are Human Resources costs (wages and salaries) not likely to be overexpended? And if they are overexpended, what is it likely to indicate?

Full Costs and Performance Reports

If the full costs of operations are to be determined, overhead costs must be allocated to *program* departments. If the primary objective of a library is related to providing patron services, then a program department can be defined as any department whose major function involves direct contact with patrons. If the primary objective of a library were different than patron services, then the definition of a program department would have to be redefined. Allocated overhead cost includes all program department noncontrollable costs as well as overhead incurred by service departments. An example of a noncontrollable program department charge that becomes part of the general overhead is the department head's salary.

Overhead costs not directly traceable to program departments are found in the library's *service* departments. Like a program department, a service department provides services, but the services it provides are internal services for the program departments. For example, the Technical Services Department catalogs books for program departments. As a result, the costs incurred by Technical Services are considered to be general library overhead. Service departments help the program departments achieve their patron service objectives; therefore, service department overhead is allocated to program departments in a reasonable fashion. The Children's Library, Reference

Department, and Circulation are program departments, whereas Technical Services, Human Resources, Administration, and the Business Office are service departments. The costs in service departments cannot be easily traced to the services provided to patrons through the library's programs. For example, how much of a janitorial salary should be part of the cost of operating the Circulation Department? To overcome this allocation problem, rational methods are consistently used to allocate overhead to programs. Yet, these allocation methods are likely to vary widely among different libraries.

One method of allocating overhead to program departments is the use of a predetermined overhead rate. Because actual overhead for a library cannot be calculated until the fiscal year has ended, a predetermined rate, estimated at the beginning of the year, provides a means for allocating overhead to program departments. Using a predetermined overhead rate stands as a measure that allows managers to take quick corrective actions if costs are becoming excessive.

One or two overhead rates are usually sufficient for allocating overhead to program departments and branch libraries. Ferdinard F. Leimkuhler and Michael D. Cooper, Robert M. Hayes, and Richard M. Dougherty and Fred J. Heinritz provide examples of libraries applying this technique.[2] In a library setting, overhead is typically allocated based on the amount of direct labor hours or dollars incurred in a department. The argued purpose of overhead allocation is to allow for better control over all costs. Also, full-cost data are useful in making comparisons of per-unit cost data among departments.[3]

In the Leimkuhler and Cooper illustration of using overhead allocation in a library, a charge of $5 per square foot is used to assign a portion of the overhead costs. The $5 overhead charge represents the costs of depreciation, utilities, and maintenance. Once this predetermined charge is calculated, each program department and branch in the library system is allocated overhead based on this $5-per-square-foot rate. The remaining overhead is more closely related to administrative functions and is allocated based on the *direct labor* in each program department. Therefore, two librarywide allocation bases are used.

In Figure 3-3, these two overhead rates are used to prepare a Full-Cost Performance Report for the circulation department. When this report is prepared during the year it contains *estimates* of overhead costs because total *actual* overhead costs will not be accumulated until after the fiscal year is completed. Although full costs are shown for the circulation department, its manager is held accountable only for those costs that he or she can actually control, which do not include any allocated overhead costs.

Yet, it is useful to estimate the full cost of operations for making cost comparisons within a library. In Figure 3-3, allocated overhead charges are

Department: Circulation
Statistics: Sq. footage, 2,700 sq. ft.
Actual number of direct labor hours per month, 480 hours

Full-Cost Performance Report
for the Month Ended March 31, 20xx

Controllable Cost by Object of Expenditure	Monthly Budgeted	Monthly Actual	Variance (U) or F*	Year-to-Date Budgeted	Year-to-Date Actual	Variance (U) or F*
Human resources	$6,000	$ 6,000	$ 0	$18,000	$18,000	$ 0
Supplies	1,200	1,400	(200)	3,600	4,400	(800)
Travel	0	0	0	0	0	0
Membership dues	210	210	0	210	210	0
Maintenance and repairs	2,000	2,500	(500)	2,200	2,700	(500)
Training	0	0	0	1,600	0	1,600
Total controllable costs and variances	$9,410	$10,110	$(700)	$25,610	$25,310	$ 300
Noncontrollable cost						
1. Space allocation†		13,500			40,500	
2. Direct labor cost allocation‡		1,080			3,150	
Full Cost of Operations		$24,690			$68,960	
Books circulated:						
Monthly		3,000				
Year-to-date		—			9,000	
Full cost per book processed		$ 8.23			$ 7.66	

*(U) Unfavorable; F Favorable; †$5 per square foot; ‡$2.25 per direct labor hour

FIGURE 3-3 Cost report on full costs for books circulated

added to the monthly and the year-to-date actual controllable costs. The square footage occupied by the circulation department is shown at the top of the report along with the number of direct hours worked this month. The 2,700 square feet and the 480 labor hours are multiplied by their respective application rates to determine the overhead charges.

In this report, all controllable costs are listed by object of expenditure at the top of the report. After the total controllable costs are determined, overhead is allocated to circulation. As stated, two predetermined overhead rates are used to charge overhead to this department. The square footage allocation is for overhead items such as utilities, maintenance, insurance, depreciation, and other space utilization charges. This space utilization rate is determined by dividing the total projected overhead costs for the current year by the entire square footage space of the library's facilities. The result is a predetermined charge of $5 per square foot. This overhead rate is multiplied times the square footage in circulation to arrive at a total overhead charge of $13,500 ($5 × 2,700). In determining the three-month charge of $40,500 for space utilization, the one-month charge is multiplied by three ($13,500 × 3). *See* Year-to-Date Actual column.

The second predetermined overhead rate is for the administrative overhead of the library. Administrative overhead is charged at the rate of $2.25 per direct labor hour, and it is equal to $1,080 ($2.25 × 480) for circulation. The $2.25 overhead charge is multiplied by the total direct labor hours worked during the three-month period (1,400 hours) to determine the charge as of March 31 in the Year-to-Date Actual column of Figure 3-3.[4] The rate of $2.25 is not a wage rate; it is an allocation charge that includes salaries and benefits paid to administrators not in a program department and other non-controllable administrative salaries. In calculating the rate of $2.25 per direct labor hour, the total projected administrative costs for the year are divided by the total number of direct labor hours estimated to be worked in all program departments in the coming year. This cost is an estimate projected on trends of past years and the current year's budget.

Once all controllable and noncontrollable costs are totaled, the full cost of operating the circulation department for the one-month and the three-month periods are $24,690 and $68,960, respectively. These full-cost figures are based on the estimated overhead rates. Actual overhead costs cannot be determined until the end of the fiscal year, when all overhead costs can be accumulated.

Of course, there are a number of reasons for developing full-cost data during the year. Some of these reasons have already been mentioned, but another reason is the attempt to exercise cost control over *all* costs incurred, which would be difficult to do if only controllable costs are shown. If the full costs of a program department are determined to be significantly above estimates, it may mean that corrective actions are necessary.

The Full-Cost Performance Report in Figure 3-3 shows the monthly full cost per unit of circulating 3,000 books ($8.23) and the per-unit cost of processing books for the three-month period ending March 31, 20xx ($7.66).[5] Per-unit information is useful in determining cost trends of providing services within a program department, particularly when this information is compared to prior periods. The report in Figure 3-3 should be compared with data from the prior year to help determine the trend of per-unit costs. If a full-cost report were prepared for the director's office, it would show each department in the library with its portion of allocated overhead separated from controllable costs. This report can also include per-unit measures based on the full cost of operations, for example, the cost per book cataloged or circulated or the cost per reference question answered. The full-cost per-unit information allows for comparisons to be made among departments performing similar functions.

Determining Overhead Cost-Allocation Rates

Cost-allocation procedures attempt to find some way to allocate the costs of services to programs. Traditional costing systems assign allocated costs to producing departments by first allocating all service overhead costs to producing departments. After the entire service department's overhead costs have been allocated, it is possible to determine per-unit full cost of the items or activities completed by the producing department. In this way, the $2.25 per direct labor hour overhead charge was determined in Figure 3-3. In this section, it will be shown in detail how such overhead rates are determined.

Often it is not possible to find a direct relationship between the general overhead found in services and programs and an allocation base. However, an allocation procedure should be based on at least a logical relationship between overhead costs and the allocation base. Figure 3-4 illustrates several allocation bases that can be used to allocate service overhead costs to programs. The first column in Figure 3-4 lists five overhead cost "pools." A first step in the cost-allocation procedure is to divide the service department overhead costs into cost pools. The cost pools are used to accumulate the overhead costs of similar activities before they are assigned to programs.

The second column in Figure 3-4 lists the allocation bases that could be used to allocate the costs in the cost pools. For example, the building depreciation expenses are allocated to the programs based on the percentage of direct expenses in each program. This is one allocation method that can be used.

Overhead Cost Pool	Allocation Base
Depreciation—Building	Direct Expenses or Area Usage
Maintenance and Cuotodial	Square Footage of Space
Accounting Department	Direct Expenses
Administration	Number of Full-Time Equivalent Employees
Technical Services	Books Cataloged to Programs

FIGURE 3-4   Examples of allocation bases for cost pools

The depreciation expense on equipment used in a specific program is not considered to be an allocated overhead cost but, rather, a direct cost of that program. Only when equipment is used by general program areas should its cost be allocated.

In Figure 3-4, maintenance and custodial overhead is allocated to the programs based on the square footage used by each program. The relationship between the cost of maintenance and custodial services and the square footage is fairly well accepted. (The underlying assumption is that it takes more time to maintain larger areas.) Accounting service costs are allocated to each program on the direct expenses in each program. (This allocation assumes that more time is involved in record keeping for programs with more direct expenses.) Another way of allocating these overhead costs could be based on the number of full-time-equivalent (FTE) employees.[6] FTE is used to allocate the administrative costs to the various programs. It is assumed that more administration time is devoted to programs with more FTE employees. Finally, the method used to allocate the overhead costs of Technical Services is based on the number of books cataloged for each program.

The allocation method should be based on data that are already being collected by the library. Allocation methods should not require the collection of information not already available in the system. For example, it would be possible to allocate the costs of the accounting department based on the number of documents processed for each program, but the additional work involved in collecting this information is not justified.

The Step-Down Method of Overhead Allocation

Several methods can be used to allocate the indirect costs to programs.[7] The first method illustrated here is the *step-down* method of cost allocation. It begins by allocating one service department's costs to all other service departments and programs. This procedure continues, with reallocation through each of the other service departments and programs, until all service costs have been allocated to the programs. With this method, it is important to realize that all overhead costs are allocated *forward* to departments and programs that have not previously received a cost allocation from a service department. This process continues until all the costs in all service departments have been completely reallocated to programs. Overhead costs are never allocated back to a service department that has already assigned its costs to another service department.

In the following section, the step-down method is illustrated for the Harriet Fairchild Library. The first step in this cost-allocation procedure is to determine the allocation bases. For example, the number of square feet (an allocation base) in each program area needs to be determined. The information on the allocation bases for the Harriet Fairchild Library is recorded in Figure 3-5, where the amount of direct expenses, square footage, number of FTE employees, and number of books cataloged or recataloged are shown for the four service departments and four programs in the library.

The second step in this cost-allocation process is to determine the order in which the service overhead costs are to be assigned. The order of allocation is important because a different pattern will result in a different cost for each program. In the Harriet Fairchild Library, the following order of cost allocation and basis of allocation was selected:

1. Depreciation: direct costs base
2. Maintenance and custodial: square footage base
3. Accounting: direct costs base
4. Administration: number of FTE employees base
5. Technical Services: number of books cataloged base

Generally, the order of cost allocation varies from one organization to another. In this instance, the reason for selecting depreciation expense as the first cost to be allocated is because it relates to all other activities, and direct costs (the allocation base) for the service departments and programs are readily available. The reason for picking Technical Services last is because if it were chosen first, some of its costs would have to be allocated to service departments lower on the allocation list where little relationship existed, such as maintenance and custodial services.

Once the order of allocation is chosen and the basis for allocating the overhead costs has been determined, the allocation process can begin. It distributes costs by using a simple percentage of the total allocation base. The percentages are computed from the "Totals" column in Figure 3-5, and the amounts in this column are computed by adding across each of the four rows.

Allocation Base	Service Departments				Programs				Totals
	Maintenance & Custodial	Accounting	Administration	Technical Services	Circulation	Reference	Children's Library	Regional History	
Direct cost	$12,000	$18,000	$26,000	$22,000	$57,000	$32,000	$25,000	$18,000	$210,000
Square footage	—	1,750	2,600	3,000	117,000	30,000	57,000	5,000	216,350
No. of FTE employees	5	3	6	5	6	3	4	2	34
Books cataloged or recataloged	—	—	—	—	60,000	13,000	20,000	8,000	101,000

Total Depreciation Expense = $89,000

FIGURE 3-5 Information about the allocation bases for the Harriet Fairchild Library

The percentage allocation to each service department and program is shown in Figure 3-6, where the second column is the "Base," which represents the denominator in determining the percentages of cost allocated. The "Base" is taken from the "Totals" column summations in Figure 3-5.

Note that although the service costs are allocated forward, they are never allocated backward. The process of forward allocation is apparent when the costs in the Accounting Department are allocated. Accounting overhead is allocated forward to Administration, Technical Services, Circulation, Reference, Children's Library, and Regional History, using the same base (direct costs) as was used to allocate depreciation expense. Unlike the depreciation expense, the dollar amount of that direct costs allocation base is equal to $180,000, rather than $210,000. A base of $180,000 is used because accounting expenses must be allocated forward. Therefore, the Maintenance and Custodial Department as well as the Accounting Department receive no allocation of accounting overhead. When the direct costs of these two departments, $30,000, is eliminated from the total direct costs, the base becomes $180,000.[8] By dividing $180,000 into the remaining direct costs for each department and program, the percentages in Figure 3-6 for the distribution of accounting expenses (in the third row) are determined.

The process of forward allocation can also be seen when the number of FTE employees is used as an allocation base for distributing the costs of Administration to Technical Services, Circulation, Reference, Children's Library, and Regional History. Although the number of FTE employees in the Harriet Fairchild Library is equal to thirty-four, the numbers of FTE employees in the departments to which the costs are going to be allocated are equal only to twenty; therefore, the base must also be equal to twenty. The percentages in the fourth row of Figure 3-6 are based on twenty employees, divided into the number of employees in each department and program to which the costs of Administration are allocated.

The first allocated expense, depreciation expense, is based on the direct costs in each service department and program. The "Base" for depreciation expense is equal to the total of all direct operating expenses in the library, or $210,000.[9] The percentages for the service departments and programs are computed by dividing this "Base" into the direct costs for each department and program. In this manner, 5.7 percent of the depreciation expense is allocated to the Maintenance and Custodial Department, and 8.6 percent of the depreciation expense is allocated to the Accounting Department. The same procedure is followed for each of the other departments and programs to determine their allocation percentages.

Service or Activity	Allocation Base Total	Service Departments				Programs			
		Maintenance & Custodial	Accounting	Administration	Technical Services	Circulation	Reference	Children's Library	Regional History
Depreciation	$210,000	.057*	.086	.124	.105	.271	.152	.119	.086
Maintenance & Custodial	216,350	—	.008⁻	.012	.014	.541	.139	.263	.023
Accounting	180,000	—	—	.144‡	.122	.317	.178	.139	.10
Administration	34	—	—	—	.25§	.30	.15	.20	.10
Technical Services	101,000	—	—	—	—	.594**	.129	.198	.079

*12,000/210,000; †1,750/216,350; ‡2,600/180,000; §5/20; **60,000/101,000

FIGURE 3-6 Determining the percentage allocations for the Harriet Fairchild Library

This procedure will result in an initial allocation, with a subsequent re-allocation, until all service department overhead is allocated to the programs. The allocation is shown in Figure 3-7, where it can be seen that depreciation expenses are allocated once, across all departments and programs, and then reallocated four times. Reallocation is clearly apparent in the Maintenance and Custodial Department. Depreciation expense of $5,703 is first allocated to the Maintenance and Custodial Department; it is then reallocated to all the other departments and programs when the $17,073 total in the Maintenance and Custodial Department costs is reallocated. This process continues until all overhead costs in the service departments have been allocated to the program departments. Once this allocation procedure is completed, the amounts accumulated in each program represent its full cost of operation.

The allocation procedure in Figure 3-7 is based on the percentages that were computed in Figure 3-6. For example, to assign depreciation expenses to the various departments and programs in the library, the percentages based on the direct costs in Figure 3-6 are multiplied by the total depreciation expenses of $89,000. This multiplication results in the overhead costs allocated to the other departments and programs in the library. At the time of reallocation, the column containing depreciation expenses is reduced to a zero balance ($17,073.00 – $17,073.00).

The allocation of Administration costs is another example of this process. To assign the costs in Administration to the other departments and programs in the Harriet Fairchild Library, we need to know the percentage breakdowns on the number of employees in the departments and programs (to the right of "Administration" in Figure 3-6). The percentages shown in Figure 3-6 (25 percent, 30 percent, 15 percent, 20 percent, and 10 percent) are multiplied by the total costs in Administration ($40,954.72) to determine the amount of these costs to allocate to the respective departments and programs.[10] Once these amounts are computed, the $40,954.72 is deducted from the total direct and allocated costs in Administration. This deduction reduces the costs in Administration to zero. At the same time, the allocation is made to the other departments and programs.

In the same manner, the total costs in Technical Services are assigned to the programs based on the percentages of books cataloged in Figure 3-6. These percentages are equal to 59.4, 12.9, 19.8, and 7.9 percent. Multiplying these percentages times $44,969.15 total cost in Technical Services results in the amounts allocated to each of the programs.[11] The cost total in Technical Services is reduced to zero when the costs of this department are allocated to the remaining programs.

Step No.	Service Departments' Costs					Program Costs and Allocated Overhead				
	Depreciation	*Maintenance & Custodial*	*Accounting*	*Administration*	*Technical Services*	*Circulation*	*Reference*	*Children's Library*	*Regional History*	*Totals Allocated*
	$89,000.00*	$12,000.00	$18,000.00	$26,000.00	$22,000.00	$57,000.00	$32,000.00	$25,000.00	$18,000.00	
1	(89,000.00)	+5,073.00	+7,654.00	+11,036.00	+9,345.00	+24,119.00	+13,528.00	+10,591.00	+7,654.00	$89,000.00
		$17,073.00								
2		(17,073.00)	+136.58	+204.88	+239.02	+9,236.49	+2,373.15	+4,490.20	+392.68	$17,073.00
			$25,790.58							
3			(25,790.58)	+3,713.84	+3,146.45	+8,175.61	+4,590.72	+3,584.89	+2,579.06	$25,790.58†
				$40,954.72						
4				(40,954.72)	+10,238.68	+12,286.42	+6,143.21	+8,190.94	+4,095.47	$40,954.72
					$44,969.15					
5					(44,969.15)	+26,711.68	+5,801.02	+8,903.89	+3,552.56	$44,969.15
Full Cost of Programs:						**$137,529.20**	**$64,436.10**	**$60,760.92**	**$36,273.77**	

Per-unit cost data (based on full costs):

	Circulation	Reference	Children's Library	Regional History
Number of general library books checked out (100,000)	$1.38	—	—	—
Number of reference questions answered (400,000)	—	$0.16	—	—
Number of children's books checked out (150,000)	—	—	$0.41	—
Number of regional history books checked out (18,000)	—	—	—	$2.02
Number of persons checking out books (Circulation 60,000; Children's Library 30,000; Regional History 15,000)	$2.29	—	$2.02	$2.42

*Given in Figure 3-5; †Caused by rounding differences

FIGURE 3-7 Allocating service departments' overhead costs to programs and calculating per-unit cost data

The objective of the cost-allocation procedure in Figure 3-7 is to determine the full costs of each of the four programs in the Harriet Fairchild Library. The full costs are shown in Figure 3-7 under each of the programs. The full cost for Circulation is $137,529.20, and it is composed of $57,000 of direct costs (i.e., costs charged directly to this program) and $80,529.20 of costs allocated from the various service departments. This makes the Circulation Department twice as expensive to operate as any of the other programs. This cost difference is not as apparent when the direct costs of operation are compared across programs (top line in Figure 3-7).

The full costs of programs should be viewed from a *per-unit* perspective. For example, a per-unit cost for checked-out books can be determined. This per-unit cost provides an indication of the expense in providing these services to the public. In addition, it provides a comparison between the three programs as to the cost per unit of services provided. Whenever per-unit costs are computed, care should be exercised in their interpretation. For example, in Figure 3-7 the Children's Library has the lowest per-unit checkout cost in any of the three programs where per-unit cost is calculated, but when books are checked out of the Children's collection, usually a large number of books are checked out by each person. This effect may unduly reduce the per-unit cost. Although the same number of people may use the collection in the Children's Library as in Circulation and Regional History, the larger number of children's books checked out by each person may favorably (and unjustifiably) influence the Children's Library per-unit costs.

If the per-unit figures are changed to the number of patrons checking books out from the three collections, the unit costs are much closer, as can be seen in the last row in Figure 3-7. The costs for Circulation, Children's Library, and Regional History are $2.29, $2.02, and $2.42, respectively. These unit costs, clearly, are not out of line with one another. The favorability toward one department when per-unit cost is based on a per-book basis disappears. The point is not that there should be no disparity existing between per-unit costs but that the underlying reasons for differences should be investigated before any managerial decisions are made.

Per-unit cost information can be very useful in making decisions about the operations of a program. In making comparisons between per-unit costs, decisions can be made as to whether the costs of operating one program are out of line with the other programs. If this appears to be the case, analysis can focus on determining the reasons for this apparent difference, with the objective of lowering these high costs. The full costs of these programs and the unit costs are likely to lead to conclusions as to which programs, from a cost perspective, should be providing the maximum level of benefits to the patrons of a library.

Cost-allocation procedures provide information about the full costs of operating programs as well as unit cost information. The process of allocation can also provide information about the cost of eliminating a program or department. The costs that can be eliminated when a program or department is dropped are the direct costs that are associated with that department. If overhead costs are included in the program expenses on the financial statement, it cannot be assumed that elimination of the program will eliminate all costs associated with the program (as shown on the financial statements). This may lead to the statement, "I thought we were going to save more!" Overhead costs are allocated costs, and they need to be examined separately from direct costs in a program to determine if the elimination of a program will have any effect on them. If the Regional History Department (Figure 3-7) were eliminated, the direct costs that would be saved would be $18,000—the unallocated costs. The allocated costs, $18,273.77, are not likely to be affected by elimination of the department because these costs relate to service departments, which are expected to continue functioning in the same manner. As these allocated costs remain, they will be reallocated to the remaining three programs, which means that the costs of $18,273.77 would now be allocated among Circulation, Reference, and Children's Library. Through development of a cost schedule, as in Figure 3-7, it is possible to determine very clearly the costs that can be saved by eliminating or cutting back a particular program. This information cannot be assumed to be available from the amounts shown under program expenses on a financial statement prepared for the public.

Other considerations besides cost concerns always need to be taken into account when making decisions about cutbacks in programs. There may be a particular need for a program that overrides cost considerations, but per-unit and full-cost data can provide administrators with additional information for making a decision. Whether cost considerations are of primary or secondary importance to an administrator, they should be considered in making these kinds of decisions.

The development of full-cost reports requires planning. Summarization of accounting data for financial reporting purposes is usually different from summarization for internal cost reporting. To prepare different reports based on the same data, the accounts have to be coded in such a fashion to make it easy to generate this information for both purposes.

Exercise 3-2

Cost Allocations

The Sherman Hanks County Library is attempting to determine the full cost of its programs for the year ended June 30, 20xx. Three programs have been identified in the library, and there are three service departments. The service departments are Administration, Custodial, and Technical Services. It has been decided that service department costs will be allocated to the programs using the step-down method. Information about the costs in each department and program follows. Administration costs are to be allocated first and Technical Services last.

Program or Department	Cost of Operations	Allocation Base	No. of Employees	Square Feet	Cataloged Books
Program 1	$60,000	——	4	4,000	11,000
Program 2	18,000	——	2	1,500	3,000
Program 3	65,000	——	4	3,500	7,000
Administration	60,000	No. of employees	3	1,500	——
Custodial	16,000	Square feet	2	—	——
Technical Services	23,000	No. of books cataloged	2	800	——

1. Determine the full costs of each of the three programs. Allocation of Administration cost is based on the number of employees, Custodial cost allocation is based on square footage, and Technical Services costs are allocated on the number of books cataloged for each program.

2. Using the full costs of the three programs determined in question 1, answer the following questions.

   (a) What is the per-unit cost of the books cataloged in the programs?

   (b) Assume that the numbers of patrons checking books out of the collections in the three programs during the fiscal year ended June 30, 20xx, are as follows:

   Program 1—12,000
   Program 2—15,000
   Program 3—16,000

What is the per-unit cost of patrons using the collection in the three programs?

(c) What do the different per-unit results in (a) and (b) indicate about the programs?

(d) Which of these per-unit measures would be more useful to the library in determining whether its objectives are being met?

3. Using the data in Figures 3-5 and 3-6 for the Harriet Fairchild Library, assign the costs in the service departments to the programs, based on the following order (rather than the order in the chapter).

> Depreciation
> Administration
> Maintenance and Custodial
> Accounting
> Technical Services

(a) What is the total cost of each program?

(b) Do the differences in program costs in question 3 and the costs shown in the chapter mean that cost allocation is inaccurate and should not be used?

Profit and Investment Centers

Responsibility accounting from the viewpoint of costs centers has been reviewed, but a library may also have a responsibility center that operates as a revenue center. Two common ways to review the performance of a revenue center is as either a profit or investment center. In a profit or investment center, both the cost of operations and the revenues from sales are accumulated. If a profit center is established, costs are deducted from the revenues in determining a profit for the operation.

If it is decided that the sales center (e.g., gift shop or any service for which user fees are charged) is to be evaluated as an investment center, then the amount of resources committed to run the operation is compared to the profit earned. In essence, the manager's performance is evaluated by comparing the level of profits with the resources used to earn that profit. This rate of return may be a good measure of evaluation if the center's operations require significant levels of library resources to perform its function. In most cases, a profit center will provide sufficient information about the operations to evaluate performance.

In a profit or investment center, both the cost of operations and the revenues from sales are accumulated. If a profit center is established, costs are deducted from the revenues in determining a profit for the operation. One way to measure successful managerial performance is to compare a target profit goal established at the beginning of the period to the actual profit earned. If it is decided that the sales operation is to be evaluated as an investment center, then the amount of resources committed to run the operation is compared to the profit earned. In essence, the manager's performance is evaluated by comparing the level of profits with the resources used to earn that profit.

With revenue centers, there is still the question, Should overhead cost allocation be part of the costs that are deducted from sales to determine profit?

It is recommended that only those costs that are directly controllable by the manager of the revenue center be used in calculating its profits. Although overhead costs such as utilities and maintenance can be traced to the revenue center, only direct costs of operations should be used to calculate the revenue center's profits.

In some nonprofit organizations, the profits earned through a revenue center may be transferred to another portion of the organization. For example, the profits earned within a gift or coffee shop run by a library may be required to be transferred to the city or state government of which the library is a part. Where such transfers are required, there is a tendency to charge the revenue center with fees and other expenses that reduce the center's profits to zero. Fees of this nature may be simply the rent charged the revenue center by the library for operating within the library building. As the revenues increase, so do the rental charges, thus keeping profit transfers out of the library to zero. Of course, there are numerous methods for obtaining the same result, such as the way that overhead costs are charged, but in the examples that follow, it is assumed that this is not an issue.

When rates of return or profits are calculated for a revenue center, it is assumed that only direct costs are charged against the center's operations and that all charges are fairly determined. Figure 3-8 provides an illustration of profit determination and rate of return calculations for the Coffee Stop, a revenue center run within the Jessie Lynne Library. The Coffee Stop provides a place for patrons to read books and drink various types of coffee within the library.

In the example, the direct costs are deducted from the Coffee Stop's revenues. This provides an easy measure of profitability for the revenue center. The profit in terms of dollars can be compared with projected profits made at the beginning of the period. The annual profit can be compared with the previous year's profits to trace upward or downward trends.

The second illustration (Part B) in Figure 3-8 illustrates how the rate of return is calculated. In this illustration the previously calculated profit is divided by the library's investments in the Coffee Stop. These investments are the direct costs of remodeling this portion of the library, purchase of coffee and expresso machines, inventory of coffee beans, and additional furniture and other assets purchased to develop the atmosphere in the Coffee Stop. Except for the short-lived inventory, other assets will be decreased in value as they are depreciated in value. As the present time, the book value of the assets is $137,000.[12]

In Figure 3-8, the rate of return is determined to be 30 percent on the investments invested in the Coffee Stop. The annual return rates need to be compared to determine the direction of any changes that are occurring. The rate of return for revenue centers can be set as a performance level to be achieved by the manager in charge of operations.

PART A: Revenue Center Profit Calculation

Coffee and gift sales	$130,000
Less: inventory costs	70,000
Gross profit	$ 60,000
Directly traceable costs	25,000
Profit	$ 35,000

PART B: Rate of Return Based on Investment in Revenue Center

$$\text{Rate of return} = \frac{\text{revenue center profit (\$35,000)}}{\text{investment in center* (\$117,500)}} = 30\%$$

---

*Investments = equipment ($60,000) + coffee inventory ($7,500) + gift inventory ($25,000) + remodeling ($25,000)

FIGURE 3-8 Determining revenue center profit and rate of return for the Jessie Lynne Library

---

Exercise 3-3

Determine Returns on Revenue Centers

The Hawthorne Library was originally built in 1962 at a cost of $5,000,000. Today, city architects have estimated that the cost to rebuild the 100,000-square-foot library would cost $25,000,000.

Recently a gift shop has been opened in an enclosed section of the foyer that encompasses 2,500 square feet. The library director is happy about the $25,000 in profits that were earned in the last year, but she would like an indication of the level of performance. The investment for new equipment in the shop cost $125,000.

1. Assuming only the new equipment is considered as the total investment cost of the shop, determine the rate of return on the library's investment.

2. Assuming that the new equipment and a reasonable charge for the space occupied by the gift shop are both considered as the total investment cost of the shop, determine the rate of return on the library's investment.

3. Explain which is the better measure of the return on investment.

SUMMARY

A number of difficulties can develop as overhead is allocated to program activities, and they should be remembered. In the overhead allocation process, all service department costs are allocated to program departments. This makes it difficult to determine if service departments such as Technical Services, the Business Office, Human Resources, and Maintenance and Repairs are operating efficiently. Allocations are made because expenditures of the service departments are assumed to be made for the benefit of the programs; these programs have requirements that demand the particular services. But without additional analysis, it is unknown whether the service departments are operating efficiently. Under a full-cost reporting system, where the program manager is only responsible for departmental controllable costs, no one is really responsible for ensuring that service departments are cost-efficient operations. Service departments may be operating inefficiently and simply passing their excessive costs on to the program departments. One method of overcoming this problem is to use standard costs in service departments. Standard costs are discussed extensively in chapter 5. Another approach to ensure service departments are operating efficiently is to establish strategic goals for the entire library that encompass efficient performance for all departmental units.

Another problem with the allocation of overhead occurs when overhead costs are tied to direct labor in the allocation process. This relationship makes it appear that direct labor is the cause of overhead costs, which is not the case. If cost reduction is stressed in a library, it may appear that by eliminating direct labor, overhead costs can be reduced, but this assumption is incorrect. The total allocated overhead costs usually remain unchanged when direct labor hours—human resources—are dropped from a program department. The costs of utilities, insurance, depreciation, and higher administrative salaries within a library remain constant. The effect of a program reduction—for example, cutting staff—only changes the way overhead is allocated among program departments, but the total overhead costs to be allocated remain constant.

Finally, under traditional cost accounting, overhead carries a negative connotation, but this is too simple an approach. Overhead costs need to be analyzed to determine whether they are contributing value to the organization by meeting organizational objectives. Overhead contributes value if it aids in meeting the service objectives of a department. When overhead is allocated in the traditional way, no effort is made to determine the value received from overhead. Again, value determination may become apparent as this goal becomes a performance measure tied to the library's long-term goals.

Notes

1. If it is assumed that appropriations are calculated based on volume levels, the budgeted amounts can be assumed to be the same as the amounts shown on a flexible budget. In chapter 5, this topic and standard costing are covered in more detail.

2. F. F. Leimkuhler and M. D. Cooper, "Cost Accounting and Analysis for University Libraries," *College and Research Libraries* 32 (November 1971): 449–64; R. M. Hayes, "Cost of Electronic Reference Resources and LCM: The Library Costing Model," *Journal of the American Society for Information Science* 47 (March 1996): 228–34; R. M. Dougherty and F. J. Heinritz, *Scientific Management of Library Operations* (Metuchen, N.J.: The Scarecrow Press, 1982).

3. P. Rosenburg, in *Cost Finding for Libraries* (Chicago: American Library Association, 1985), used full-cost data to calculate per-unit data such as the annual cost per item circulated and the per-item cost of identifying and processing overdue materials.

4. The direct labor hours worked during the three-month period did not add to 1,440 hours (3 × 480) because of sick leave taken.

5. Once this rate is calculated, it can be used as a means to effectively reduce the cost of processing each book. For example, a performance goal might be a 1 percent reduction in the cost of book processing within a specified time period. Such a goal should not be an isolated goal but rather one that is related to the organization's overall strategic objectives.

6. The term *full-time-equivalent employees* is important when there are part-time employees. For example, when two part-time employees are working for the organization, they are the equivalent of one full-time employee for cost-allocation purposes. All part-time

employees' working hours must be summed to determine their contribution in terms of full-time equivalents.

7. These methods are the direct allocation method, the step-down method, and a cost-allocation method using simultaneous equations. For an explanation of these methods, refer to a cost-accounting textbook.

8. The $30,000 is composed of $12,000 in maintenance and custodial and $18,000 in accounting expenses.

9. Also, *see* the "Totals" column in Figure 3-5.

10. It can be seen in Figure 3-7 that the amount allocated to Technical Services is $10,238.68, which is equal to 25 percent of $40,954.72.

11. Of the total costs in Technical Services ($44,469.15), $10,238.68 had just been allocated from Administration.

12. Book value of an asset is equal to the original price paid for the asset less the depreciation that has accumulated on the asset since it was purchased. Each year, additional depreciation is recorded on the asset as it ages.

Bibliography

Hilton, R. W., M. W. Maher, and F. H. Selto. *Cost Management: Strategies for Business Decisions.* Boston: McGraw-Hill, 2000.

CHAPTER

4

Activity-Based Accounting and Management

Chapter 3 explained the use of responsibility accounting management methods and the allocation of overhead to responsibility centers using traditional methods of cost allocation. In chapter 4, *activity-based costing* (ABC) and *activity-based management* are explained and suggestions are made for the use of these methods as an alternative to traditional costing methods. The method that is best for a specific library must be determined by the managers of that library, so familiarity with both of the traditional methods based on the concept of responsibility centers and the ABC method is important.

Responsibility accounting is a system that assigns cost-control responsibility to a specific functional manager in the library. ABC is also a system that can align the cost-control and managerial responsibility, but under ABC methods, there is a more detailed tracing of costs to the various activities performed within the library.

ACTIVITY-BASED COSTING: AN ALTERNATIVE TO TRADITIONAL COST REPORTING

Under traditional responsibility accounting and cost-analysis methods, the focus is on using organizational departments as cost centers and separating costs into controllable costs, such as labor and materials, and noncontrollable overhead. Under activity-based cost accounting, the cost centers can still be organizational units, but cost allocation is focused on the activities performed within those cost centers. An activity-based cost accounting system relates cost accumulation to the activities necessary to achieve program or service objectives rather than accumulating costs by allocating overhead based on such general measures as square footage or direct labor hours. Activities are repetitive actions that are performed by specialized organizational groups to achieve the goals and mission objectives of the library. With activity-based accounting, it is necessary to determine which activities are the most direct cause of costs. Then, by analyzing activities, costs can be reduced and the cross-functional coordination among different responsibility centers increased. Under traditional cost accounting, little analysis is directed at the activities performed; emphasis is placed on the level of resources consumed, for example, personnel, supplies, and training to provide the services.

Activities can be divided into a specific series of tasks required to complete the activity. For example, the acquisition of library materials can be considered one activity area; within that activity area, there are a number of tasks, such as ordering and receiving. The task of receiving library materials can be further separated into unpacking books, matching invoices with materials, matching purchase orders with invoices, returning unordered or damaged materials, corresponding with vendors, recording cancellations, reviewing standing orders, and distributing books to proper work areas for further processing and shelving.

In traditional cost accounting, there is a large pool of overhead costs that cannot be directly identified with a specific program department's objectives. Therefore, these costs must be allocated to the various program departments using a basis such as square footage, number of employees, or direct labor hours in a department. Under activity-based accounting, one purpose for identifying the activities of the organizational units is to provide a way to trace overhead costs to an activity and, consequently, to a department. When specific activities, such as those in receiving, are identified and overhead costs are traced directly to these activities, the large pool of general overhead starts to shrink. More detailed identification of activities requires that department managers accept more responsibility for traceable overhead costs, whereas in traditional cost accounting, the department manager generally believes that allocated overhead can be ignored because it is not controllable. Responsibility for traceable overhead is a managerial improvement; the entire organization benefits from this additional overhead cost scrutiny.

Exercise 4-1

Identifying Cost-Creating Activities

Max Streeter is the director of the Florence Library. He has heard about activity-based costing methods, but he feels that it would be difficult to assign costs to the various library departments based on activity measures because there is no clear-cut description of staff work activities. There is a manual of job descriptions, but everyone knows it is out of date. Can you make some suggestions to help him out?

Under activity-based accounting, it is the department manager's initial responsibility to accept or reject how activity costs are traced to his or her department. The acceptance of the method carries with it the responsibility for the costs. Initial acceptance must be mutually agreed upon within the organizational hierarchy and carefully considered to ensure that activities and decisions in another department are not driving up the costs of a second department to which these costs are traced. With the emphasis on activities, the interrelatedness of costs will be easier to identify, and interdepartmental cost activities will become easier to control.

There are costs associated with collecting information according to activity patterns. These additional costs are not incurred under traditional cost methods. The higher costs of data collection in activity-based accounting need to be balanced against the benefits expected to be received from the information to ensure that the additional expense is worthwhile.

Figure 4-1 is an example of an activity cost report for technical services. Unlike traditional cost performance reports that are separated into controllable costs and allocated overhead, the activity cost report in Figure 4-1 has three separate cost categories. The first cost section, department activity, lists the cost of the primary activities within the department, and although not shown, each of these activities can be further subdivided into tasks. For example, the tasks in withdrawing a book include locating and removing a book from the collection, pulling the card from the catalog or making the entries into the online catalog, and updating all records to reflect the change in the collection. Naturally, variations in the activities of departments from library to library can be expected. For illustrative purposes, it is assumed in Figure 4-1 that only books are being processed, but in another library with a multimedia-processing environment, the activities should be redefined.

Department: **Technical Services**
Mission Objective: To assist users in easily locating library materials

Activity Cost Report
for the Month Ended March 31, 20xx

	Monthly Estimate	Monthly Actual	Variance (U) or F*
PART 1: Department activity			
Bibliographic checking	$ 2,450	$ 2,500	$ (50)
Card procurement	125	130	(5)
Book distribution	500	575	(75)
Original book cataloging	4,200	4,000	200
Original periodical cataloging	3,300	3,400	(100)
Recataloging books and periodicals	600	500	100
Withdrawing materials	400	375	25
Online catalog maintenance	525	525	0
Shelf list maintenance	525	600	(75)
Personnel services	6,975	6,975	0
Administrative duties	4,300	4,500	(200)
Training	800	880	(80)
Total cost of department activities	$24,700	$24,960	$(260)
PART 2: Nondepartment traceable costs			
Technology†	2,500	3,000	(500)
Order initiation	4,300	4,000	300
PART 3: Nontraceable overhead	3,200	3,200	0
Total department cost	$34,700	$35,160	$(460)

*(U) Unfavorable; F Favorable; †Includes purchase price, start-up cost, and current cost

FIGURE 4-1   Activity cost report for Technical Services Department

The second cost section of the activity cost report, nondepartment traceable costs, deals with costs that are directly traceable to the Technical Services Department. An objective of activity cost reporting is to trace a large portion of the traditional overhead to specific departmental activities.[1] The two traceable costs charged to technical services are technology and order initiation costs (explained later in this chapter). The manager in charge of technical services is assigned usage responsibility for these nondepartment traceable costs.

The third cost division on the activity report is nontraceable overhead. Although an objective of activity-based accounting is to directly trace as much overhead as possible to departments, all overhead is not traceable; therefore, each department will still be charged with nontraceable overhead. But, the amount of nontraceable overhead (general overhead, for example) will generally be a smaller percentage of the total department's operating costs than under traditional cost-accounting methods. Even though the manager of technical services is not responsible for nontraceable overhead charges, the manager is responsible for the department's activity costs and the traceable overhead.

Several other aspects of the activity cost report should be noted. First, cost classification takes place within a department structure, such as technical services, but these costs are broken down even further to determine the costs of individual activities performed within the department, such as the monthly book distribution costs. This is reflected by the change in the heading on the full-cost performance reports from "Monthly Budgeted," shown in Figures 3-1, 3-2, and 3-3, to "Monthly Estimate" on the activity cost reports. The monthly estimate is based on the actual activity level for that month times the cost per unit of the activity. For example, the monthly book distribution costs are determined by multiplying the actual number of books distributed by a standard cost per book. This results in a monthly estimate that is based on efficient standards. After the monthly estimate is computed, it is compared with the actual book distribution costs to determine the variance. In a traditional cost report, the "Monthly Budgeted" column may be based on the total library budget appropriation for the year divided into twelve equal monthly portions rather than on a standard cost per unit. In such a traditional report, efficiency of operations is not highlighted.

With the activity cost report, the analysis can be extended to determine the specific cause of variances. For example, the card procurement activity (where it is still used) includes the tasks of (1) obtaining catalog cards and (2) processing the cards. These two tasks are the cause of cost generation in card procurement. If the unfavorable variance, shown in Figure 4-1, needs to be investigated, the costs of the two tasks can be analyzed in detail to determine the actual cause of the variance. If an online catalog is used, cards are not ordered and updating the catalog involves such activities as scanning the bar code on the book. In this case, the Technical Services Department is responsible for a reduced level of activity in the book distribution process. As this change in processing activity caused by adoption of an online catalog is recognized, it would be important for library managers to reevaluate the entire responsibility range of activities within the Technical Services

Department. Such a review would determine if the performance of activities needed to be realigned within the library.

In activity-based accounting, the focus for cost reduction is on those activities that are not directly related to the department's mission objective. The mission objective for technical services is listed at the top of the activity cost report in Figure 4-1. If an activity is not contributing directly to the mission objective of technical services, it is called a *nonvalue-added activity.* An example of a nonvalue-added activity is the book distribution activities where books are moved about and stored before they are completely cataloged for shelf placement. Book distribution is a handling activity that is indirectly related to the department's mission objective. If this activity can be reduced, more resources can be spent on activities that are directly related to the department's mission.

With activity-based accounting, activities are assumed to be the cause of costs; therefore, through an analysis of activities, costs can be reduced. Under traditional cost accounting, little analysis is directed at the activities performed; instead, emphasis is placed on the level of resources consumed to provide services, for example, supplies. With activity-based accounting, tracing costs to departments allows more thought to be applied to the interaction of costs between departments. In Figure 4-1, one of the nondepartmental traceable costs is an order initiation charge. A portion of the cost of ordering materials that is incurred by program departments is charged back to technical services because the latter department is responsible for the order initiation of many library materials. This charge back makes the manager of technical services more conscious of and committed to accepting this program department cost and, it is hoped, more helpful in finding ways to reduce program department ordering costs. Under traditional cost accounting, order initiation costs are part of the organization-wide overhead allocated on the basis of direct labor hours or square footage. The focus on specific activities in Figure 4-1 allows for more detailed analysis of departmental cost and activity interrelationships.

The service departments, previously discussed in chapter 3, support program departments that have direct contact with patrons. Figure 4-2 provides an example of an activity cost report for one such program department—Circulation.

This activity cost report is formatted in the same manner as the report in Figure 4-1. In the Circulation Department, all the activities shown can be further subdivided into tasks. For example, the term *Circulation* in column one refers to tasks such as charging out books and periodicals, issuing library cards, answering questions, shelving books in the stacks, checking for holds, and accepting and updating records for returned books.

Department: **Circulation**

Mission Objective: To maximize the availability of library materials to patrons

Activity Cost Report
for the Month Ended March 31, 20xx

	Monthly Estimate	Monthly Actual	Variance (U) or F*
PART 1: Department activity			
Copy machine maintenance	$ 600	$ 500	$ (100)
Search holds	400	425	25
Circulation	4,000	3,700	(300)
Fines and billings	315	300	(15)
Exit control	85	68	(17)
Stack maintenance	1,150	1,100	(50)
Exhibit preparation	115	125	10
Personnel services	5,600	5,625	25
Administrative duties	2,100	1,900	(200)
Training	475	400	(75)
Total cost of department activities	$14,840	$14,143	$ (697)
PART 2: Nondepartment traceable costs			
Technology†	3,700	3,000	(700)
PART 3: Nontraceable overhead	1,200	1,200	0
Total department cost	$19,740	$18,343	$(1,397)

---

*(U) Unfavorable; F Favorable; †Includes purchase price, start-up cost, and current cost adjustment less residual value of the technology

FIGURE 4-2   Activity cost report for Circulation

The only nondepartment cost shown as traceable to this department is a technology charge. The technology charge is for the use of computers, computer software, or other new technology systems that are traceable to this department by usage rates. Under traditional cost accounting, the costs of technology are part of the organization-wide overhead charge based on square footage. Therefore, the department with the largest amount of space would be allocated the highest charge for technology, regardless of whether that department used the technology. Under activity-based accounting, the department generating the technology costs would be responsible for those costs.

Both the Technical Services and Circulation Departments have a charge for technology. In activity-based accounting, this charge is directly traceable to those departments. As shown in the footnotes to the activity cost reports, the technology charge is composed of the initial cost of the asset, the start-up costs, and a current cost adjustment, which is an incremental cost for inflation. Any estimated salvage value is deducted from these charges. Start-up costs are the costs incurred to get the asset working at full capacity, and these charges include the costs of testing the system, debugging it, and training personnel to use it properly.

The effects of inflation on costs are incorporated by the current cost adjustment in order to reflect true cost in an environment where technologies are rapidly replaced. The current cost adjustment represents an adjustment based on the estimated replacement (market) price the organization will have to pay for a new, similar asset. The difference between the historical cost paid for the asset and the market price is used as a current cost adjustment in determining the technology charge. This charge is allocated over the life of the asset and increases the per-unit cost of items processed within circulation. All these costs are reduced by the estimated salvage value, which is the projected value of the asset when the library disposes of it at the end of its useful life. With most information systems, the salvage value is usually zero. Figure 4-3 shows how a technology charge is calculated in an activity-based accounting system. Under traditional cost accounting, only the net purchase price of the asset and its start-up costs are charged to program departments as a portion of the general overhead.

Exercise 4-2

Interlibrary Loans and Activity-Based Accounting Methods

The director of Essex University Library is considering using activity-based costing (ABC) methods to more accurately determine which activities are creating cost increases within the Interlibrary Loan (ILL) Department. The ILL Department is staffed with one professional librarian, Alice Ward, and two staff members who spend 90 percent of their time working on departmental activities. The librarian has indicated that 60 percent of her time is devoted to interlibrary loan activities, and the other 40 percent of her time is devoted to activities such as reference committee assignments, meetings, and other non–ILL Department activities such as special projects and training. Salaries for the department total $92,000. The librarian receives an annual salary of $45,000. Mailing costs in the department equal $35,000 per year, and on-campus mailing costs are minimal.

It is estimated that the mailing costs are divided between requested materials from Essex University Library's patrons and materials being requested by outside ILL Departments at 70 and 30 percent, respectively. The department has collected the following information about its activities.

- Ten percent of the interlibrary loans are for materials that are already in the library's collection.
- The average number of ILL Department requests sent to patrons to get circulated materials back into the ILL are as follows: faculty (5), undergraduates (1), and graduate students (2).
- The average number of requests needed to successfully receive materials is 1.2 requests from loaning libraries.
- The average number of interlibrary loans is 9,750 (books, 6,000; articles, 3,750).
- The average number of annual external requests for library materials is 5,500 (books, 4,500; articles, 1,000).

The director has asked Alice, the head of the ILL Department, to outline the activities that are performed within the department related to both loaning materials to other libraries as well as borrowing materials per patron requests. Alice is unfamiliar with ABC methods, but she developed the following outline about her department's activities.

Interlibrary Loan Activities

PROCESSING PATRON REQUESTS FOR MATERIALS
FROM OTHER LIBRARIES

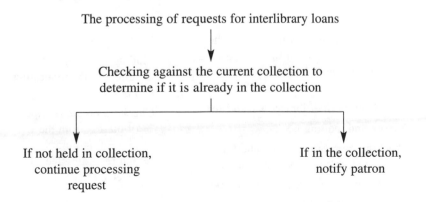

Books

Mailing request to loaning library

Checking receipt of item or initiating follow-up

Notifying patron (e-mail, campus mail)

Recording pickup by patron

Return of book after loan period or follow-up on unreturned material

Return and recording return of book to loaning library

Articles

Mailing request to loaning library

Checking receipt of item or initiating follow-up

Notifying patron (e-mail, campus mail)

Recording pickup by patron

PROCESSING MATERIALS REQUESTED BY OTHER LIBRARIES

Processing requests for materials by other libraries

Checking against current collection for location of requested materials

If requested materials are in the collection, continue processing

If not in collection, notify the requesting library (this occurs infrequently)

Books

Locating book and pulling it from shelves or checking to see if in circulation, then requesting circulation to place a hold on book

Documenting interlibrary loan and fee

Boxing and mailing book

Checking on return of book and fee charged; follow-ups as necessary

Recording the receipt of returned book

Reshelving returned book

Articles

Photocopying the article

Mailing the copy of the article to the requesting library

Checking on the receipt of the fee from the requesting library and recording fee received

The director and the head of the Interlibrary Loan Department have been meeting for an hour and a half trying to determine how to assign costs to the various activities performed within the department. Can you help them find the unit cost of activities?

In Figure 4-3, the yearly market values of a new and similar computerized circulation system are assumed to change as shown in each of the five years. If an integrated computer system is used for the library, market values

---

A new computerized circulation system was purchased for the Hanover Library on January 1, 20xx. Assume the following facts about this system:

Total number of books to be processed:

By this system over its life:	2,500,000
Purchase cost of the system:	$130,000
Estimated life of system:	5 years
Salvage value:	zero

Straight-line depreciation: $130,000/5 years = $26,000

Market value, incorporating inflation, at the end of each year is shown below. In other words, the cost to purchase the system would be as follows at the end of each of the next five years. This represents a total increase of $70,000 from the purchase price over the five-year period:

Year 1	$138,000
Year 2	150,000
Year 3	165,000
Year 4	180,000
Year 5	200,000

Traditional cost system: under this system, a charge of $26,000 equal to the straight-line depreciation will be allocated among all departments in the library.

Activity cost system: under this system, a charge of $.028 ($70,000/2,500,000) per book circulated in the Circulation Department will be charged to that department as the current cost adjustment along with the $26,000 technology charge for depreciation expense. Therefore, if 500,000 books are circulated in one year, the technology charge is $40,000 ($26,000 + $14,000).

FIGURE 4-3   Illustration of a current cost adjustment

can still be assigned to the Circulation Department for its portion of the cost of the system. In this example, the computer system does not have a salvage value at the end of its useful life, and start-up costs are assumed to be insignificant. The difference between the purchase price and final market value of the system at the end of five years is used to determine the amount of the current cost adjustment. The difference is divided by the estimated number of books processed in the circulation department over the five years and the result ($.028) is charged on a per-book-circulated basis to the Circulation Department as the current cost adjustment in the technology charge. This method can also be adapted to incorporate present value analysis.[2]

Technology costs are traced directly to the process using the technology. When this technology tracing occurs, a distinction needs to be made between technologies used in commonality by the entire library and those specifically purchased for departmental use. Business software such as Excel, for example, is used to prepare financial and managerial reports for all departments within the library. Software and equipment of this nature can remain part of the general overhead charged to all departments. On the other hand, software that is used specifically by technical services to order or catalog books should be charged directly to that department as a technology charge. If circulation has purchased a new computerized circulation system, any equipment and software included in the purchase should be part of that department's technology charge. Under activity-based accounting systems, a major distinction is made between systems used in commonality and those systems specifically used by one department.

Two methods can be used to charge a department for its use of technology. One method was illustrated in Figure 4-3. Another technique establishes a per-hour rate for using the technology, and then charges a department for its hourly use regardless of the number of units processed.

With a per-hour charge, the objective is to stress efficient usage of the technology, often causing a department to become concerned with its rate of processing. Regardless of the method adopted, the head of a department must accept responsibility for the incurrence of the charge.

Exercise 4-3

Applying Activity Accounting in Acquisitions

The Acquisitions Department in the Quill Library has classified its activities into ordering, processing suppliers' invoices, accession/processing, and cancellations. The costs of these activities on a per-hour basis follow. In addition, a technology charge as a percent of the hourly cost of activities is charged against departmental activities. For ordering, this charge would be $0.75 per hour ($15 × .05 = $0.75).

Activities	Hourly Cost per Activity	Tech Charge	No. of Units This Year
Ordering	$15	5%	500 purchase orders
Processing invoices	12	5%	1,000 invoices
Accession/processing*	32	7%	400 accessions
Cancellations	20	5%	50 cancellations

---

*Processing includes maintaining periodicals after initial purchase

The on-average time required to acquire new books and periodicals follows:

	New Book	New Article
Ordering	0.50 hours	0.80 hours
Processing invoices	0.50 hours	0.50 hours
Accession/processing	0.30 hours	0.80 hours
Cancellations	0.10 hours	1.00 hour

1. Determine the cost of activities on a per-unit level for ordering books and articles.
2. Using the following actual costs incurred during the year, determine the variances between actual costs incurred and activity costs.

Activity	Actual Cost Incurred
Ordering	$ 7,500
Processing invoices	13,000
Accession/processing	14,000
Cancellations	1,500
Total	$36,000

In using activity-based accounting, managerial efforts are devoted to reducing the costs of activities that do not directly help to accomplish the library's mission objectives. The costs of activities that do not directly assist in mission accomplishment are called nonvalue-added costs. There is little emphasis directed at reducing nonvalue-added costs in traditional cost accounting because these costs are part of the general overhead, making them very difficult to analyze. Under traditional cost accounting, it is difficult to pinpoint the specific overhead activity that is not making a contribution to meeting organizational objectives, and as a result, it is more common to use across-the-board cost-cutting measures to curtail costs. Under activity-based accounting, it is possible to take a more surgical approach to cost cutting by curtailing the specific nonvalue activity.

Therefore, in activity-based accounting, costs are subdivided into costs that contribute to meeting service objectives (i.e., value-added costs) and those costs that do not (i.e., nonvalue-added costs). The primary service objectives of a specific library will vary. Therefore, differences will exist in the definition of value-added activities, activities that contribute to achieving mission objectives. If an activity does not *directly* contribute to the achievement of a mission objective, it is considered to be a nonvalue-added activity. Examples of nonvalue-added activities are reporting, moving library materials, sorting, storing, counting, recording, or checking. The costs of these activities generate nonvalue-added costs. They reduce the service level to the patrons of the library because, with an increase in these activities and costs, less time and resources are available for patron services. Other examples of nonvalue-added activities are the time spent for departmental parties, jury duty, docked time not reported, activities involving promotion or the tenure process, university-wide committee meetings, recruiting, compiling workload statistical summaries, administrative personnel performing tasks that should be assigned to lower-level personnel, preparing budgets or strategic plans that are later rejected, and wasted idle time during holiday periods when library use decreases. These and a number of other activities performed within a library may add no value to the patron-oriented objectives of the various departments. Activity-based accounting concentrates its efforts on reducing these costs first when cost curtailment is required. Under traditional accounting methods, the costs associated with these activities are part of the general overhead, and they are not separately reported, making it harder to control them or understand how they are interrelated. Consequently, it is common to see traditional cost control accomplished with 5 percent across-the-board expenditure reductions.

A first step in determining whether a departmental activity is adding value is to determine the mission objective for the department. The mission objective for the Circulation Department is "to maximize the availability of library materials to patrons" (*see* Figure 3-5). Once a department's primary objective is outlined, all the activities and tasks of the department should be written down, as is illustrated in Figure 4-4. This list of activities is an illustrative example of

Activity	Tasks
1. Copy machine maintenance	Adding paper and toner; making change and refunding money; making service calls; new machine selection
2. Search-holds	Handling search requests; reordering missing books and periodicals; recalling books
3. Circulation	Charging out books and periodicals; issuing library cards; answering questions; discharging books; recording the return of discharged materials; shelving in the stacks; checking for holds on returned materials
4. Fines and billings	Collecting cash; processing overdue receipts and notices; processing receipts and notices for damaged and lost books and periodicals; filing receipts and notices
5. Exit control	Processing magnetic protection strips for checkout
6. Stack maintenance	Shelving items used and left unshelved; processing new books and shelving them; shelving reading books; shifting materials on stacks
7. Exhibit preparation	Putting up and removing exhibits on bulletin boards, display cases, etc.; ensuring security of exhibits; handling exhibit promotion
8. Personnel services	Dealing with the appointment, tenure, promotion, and retainment of personnel; interviewing new candidates; serving on search committees; preparing required evaluation forms for personnel files
9. Administrative duties	Attending and conducting departmental meetings; preparing memos, workload statistics, board-requested information; attending committee meetings; planning; preparing work schedules; ordering and receiving supplies
10. Training	On-site reading, writing, and studying training materials; attending workshops and conferences; visiting other libraries to study new methods and techniques

FIGURE 4-4   Circulation Department activities list

the activities that could occur in a library's Circulation Department. The exact type of activities performed, however, would vary from library to library.

After the mission objective is described and all the activities and tasks outlined, the activities should be separated into those that do and those that do not assist in meeting the primary mission objective. For example, dealing with promotion and tenure tasks under personnel services activities does not directly contribute to the availability of library resources to patrons. Yet, in a university library, a great deal of time each year is devoted to promotion and tenure activities.

Once the value-added and nonvalue-added activities are separated, the costs associated with each activity need to be aggregated. Figure 4-5 presents an activity cost report for the Circulation Department using the concepts of value-added and nonvalue-added costs.

The benefit of separating nonvalue-added costs from value-added costs should be immediately obvious. The separation of these costs allows the department manager to concentrate on reducing nonvalue-added costs. This focus allows for a more surgical approach to cost cutting than the use of across-the-board budget cuts that are typical of traditional cost systems.

In addition, when activities are the focus of a cost report rather than object of expenditure reporting and overhead, identification of the specific factors causing cost incurrence is easier. These cost incurrers are called *cost drivers.* They are the activities that create the cost. In the traditional cost reports, it is difficult to isolate the specific activities that cause increases in cost. Under activity-based accounting, cost cutting can be achieved by reducing nonvalue-added activities that will leave patron services intact. For example, in Figure 4-5, the tasks associated with fine collections and billings do not have a direct impact on maximizing the availability of library materials to patrons under circulation's mission objective. If this activity could be transferred to the job functions of a university cashier or computerized, it would reduce costs and increase the time available for Circulation Department personnel to achieve their primary objective. Efforts should be made to reduce activities listed under the nonvalue-added column when cost curtailment becomes necessary.

Exercise 4-4

Nonvalue-Added and Value-Added Activities

Using the information provided in Exercise 4-2, identify those activities within the ILL Department that might be considered to be nonvalue-added activities.

Department **Circulation**

Mission Objective: To maximize the availability of library materials to patrons

Activity Cost Report
for the Month Ended March 31, 20xx

Activity	Cost Classifications			Monthly Actual Activity Cost	Monthly Estimated Activity Cost	Variance (U) or F*
	Value-Added Activity	Nonvalue-Added Activity	Nontraceable			
Copy machine maintenance	$ 100	$ 500	$ —	$ 600	$ 500	$ (100)
Search-holds	1,100	—	—	1,100	925	(175)
Circulation	7,000	—	—	7,000	6,200	(800)
Fines and billings	—	315	—	315	300	(15)
Exit control	—	85	—	85	68	(17)
Stack maintenance	150	1,000	—	1,150	1,100	(50)
Exhibit preparation	—	115	—	115	125	10
Personnel services	600	5,000	—	5,600	5,625	25
Administrative duties	1,400	700	—	2,100	1,900	(200)
Training	375	100	—	475	400	(75)
Nontraceable	—	—	1,200	1,200	1,200	—
Total	$10,725	$7,815	$1,200	$19,740	$18,343	$(1,397)

*(U) Unfavorable; F Favorable

FIGURE 4-5 Value-added and nonvalue-added activity cost report for the Circulation Department

The report in Figure 4-5 can be compared with Figure 4-2 as both reports are based on the same dollar amounts, but note the estimated and actual cost columns are reversed from one another in these figures. Although both illustrations use an activity-based accounting approach, the reporting improvement shown in Figure 4-5 gives the department manager a place to take immediate action in curtailing costs by reducing nonvalue-added activities where possible. In comparing Figure 4-2 to Figure 4-5, note that the technology costs of $3,700 are considered a value-added cost in Figure 4-5, and that these costs are proportioned among search-holds ($700) and circulation ($3,000) based on technology usage rates.[3] Referring back to Figure 3-3, one can see that it is even more difficult to determine the corrective action that should be taken based on the object of expenditure data reported there.

Finally, variances shown for activities in Figure 4-5 are not as important as whether an activity added primary service value to the department. For example, even though there was a favorable variance with exhibit preparation, the activity does not directly add primary services to patrons; therefore, even with a favorable variance, the costs incurred by these activities should be reduced if cost cutting and meeting the mission objective are primary goals. The tasks and costs of personnel services that are nonvalue added should be viewed in the same manner.

An activity cost report using value- and nonvalue-added classifications is illustrated for an entire library in Figure 4-6. These costs are not classified by objects of expenditure such as supplies and wages, for example. Instead, department activities are first analyzed; then the cost of these activities are aggregated and reported as value-added and nonvalue-added cost groupings for the library.

In the report, the variances are shown for each department, and the total cost for which a manager is responsible is divided into value-added and nonvalue-added cost groups. The method for allocating traceable costs has been agreed upon by department heads; they have accepted responsibility for the incurrence of these costs. Nontraceable costs, for which managers are not responsible, are the library's general overhead, which cannot be directly traced to a department. These costs are listed separately in the report. Nontraceable costs are allocated in the same manner that general overhead is allocated under traditional cost accounting, but now the dollar amount is much smaller.

If a director requires more detailed information about a department, the department's activity cost report may be reviewed. In such a case, a report like the one shown in Figure 4-5 is available for each department. This procedure provides the director with a form of management by exception as

Department: **Library Director**
Mission Objective: To maximize mission objectives of all departments

Activity Cost Report
for the Month Ended March 31, 20xx

Department	Value-Added Activity	Nonvalue-Added Activity	Nontraceable	Monthly Actual Dept. Cost	Monthly Estimated Dept. Cost	Variance (U) or F*
Service departments						
Technical Services	$21,250	$11,900	$3,200	$ 36,350	$ 35,800	$ (550)
Public Relations	7,750	1,350	1,700	10,800	11,000	200
Personnel	11,000	1,000	1,700	13,700	14,200	500
Business Office	19,700	4,000	4,000	27,700	26,600	1,100
Program departments						
Circulation	10,725	7,815	1,200	19,740	18,343	(1,397)
Children's Library	4,475	3,700	1,700	9,875	10,000	125
Special Collections	3,200	2,800	1,500	7,500	7,300	(200)
Extension Services	6,250	5,750	3,000	15,000	15,250	250
Reference	8,000	7,950	2,000	18,700	15,750	(2,950)
Total costs	$93,100	$46,265	$20,000	$159,365	$154,243	$(5,122)

*(U) Unfavorable; F Favorable

FIGURE 4-6 Value-added and nonvalue-added activity cost report for the library director

only those departments where corrective action may be required are reviewed in detail by the director. The report in Figure 4-6 allows the director to focus more on the activities adding or not adding value in achieving departmental mission objectives.

Activity Accounting Management

In the review of Figure 4-6, one question that arises is, Why is there a higher level of nonvalue-added costs in the program departments in comparison to the service departments? In the program departments, nonvalue-added costs are a higher percentage of total costs compared to those in the service departments. A number of reasons could exist for this difference. First, the mission objectives of the four program departments may not be correctly stated. If the true mission objective is not properly described, activities that should be considered value added are classified as nonvalue added. Perhaps program departments are required to perform a number of activities that are not directly related to their primary function. As a result, they are only able to devote slightly more than 50 percent of their activities and the corresponding costs to fulfilling their mission objective. This difference in the levels of nonvalue-added activities in the program and service departments becomes readily apparent in an activity cost report. In traditional cost reporting, this difference is difficult to detect. Of course, once these activities are classified in this manner, it becomes management's responsibility to correctly review each department.

One advantage of activity-based accounting is that it is closely related to activity measures that librarians normally use to evaluate performance. It relates accounting data to the activity measures commonly used in libraries. In this way, activity-based accounting makes accounting data more interpretable as it integrates accounting concepts with the concepts of professional librarianship to apply activity accounting management and ensure the library is efficiently using its resources.

Once activity-based accounting is adopted, it allows departments to review departmental activities for inefficiencies. For example, questions such as these can be asked: Can a new system be adopted that would curtail nonvalue-added activity costs? Can branches be networked together for better integration of value-added activities? Upper-level managers can then review department activities to determine if duplicated activities can be eliminated or dovetailed with other activities and tasks.

In terms of performance measures, the orientation under activity costing is significantly different than traditional cost accounting. The traditional cost center report contains controllable costs and possibly allocated overhead. Cost control is obtained by instituting across-the-board cuts.

Under activity-based accounting, when cost reductions are necessary, they are made from the viewpoint of reducing the activities that create the costs. This cost reduction program begins with reducing the cost of those activities generating nonvalue-added costs. In addition, this activity orientation looks more deeply into traceability patterns of costs in order to assign clear responsibility for overhead costs that in a traditional cost system would be put into a large overhead pool.

Unlike traditional accounting, activity-based accounting is more concerned with the effects of curtailed activities. For example, cutbacks in maintenance expenditures and activities that over time will leave crippled equipment and a deteriorated physical facility usually go unrecognized under traditional cost accounting. These cutbacks are easy to make when a large cut in overall budget appropriation is required. Under activity-based accounting, there is a higher possibility that these curtailed activities will be quickly detected because the activity costs for the Maintenance Department are separately disclosed.

The use of activity-based accounting is recommended because it fits well into the traditional performance measurement systems of libraries. Instead of running a parallel system for accounting data, the performance goals for a library can be incorporated into an activity-based accounting system. This creates an accounting system with a more commonsense orientation for those who are familiar with activity measures but not with accounting. In addition to this feature, activity-based accounting fits in well with the mission objectives of a library. Mission objectives are the long-range strategic objectives for a library, and although public service is the primary objective, slightly different objectives are found in different libraries: research, university, public, corporate, legal, and so forth. The mission objectives of a library help define departmental value-added and nonvalue-added costs and should be clearly outlined for each library and department before an activity-based accounting system is put into place.

SUMMARY

When a comparison is made between the traditional cost systems and activity-based systems, it should become apparent that activity accounting methods provide managers with more detailed information about library activities. Activity-based accounting is explained here as an alternative to the traditional cost system. Activity-based accounting is being adopted within the manufacturing environment by multiproduct firms with a need for advanced cost reporting. Certain aspects of activity cost reporting are adaptable to the nonprofit area, where it strongly supplements the professional librarian's already established orientation toward measuring performance with activity measures.

This chapter was directed toward helping the library manager use methods that ensure that the library's assets are not being wasted. Assets can be wasted because they are used inefficiently or because they are misappropriated. In both cases, it is the responsibility of each library manager to prevent this from happening and ensure that the maximum level of services is being provided to library patrons.

Notes

1. The technique for allocating overhead is based on the traditional cost system, but with activity-based costing, efforts are directed toward finding a more traceable relationship, not simply basing allocation of overhead on the direct labor hours or square footage within a department.

2. Depending on the life of the system, present values may be required to account for market value changes. As the asset in the example has a relatively short life, present values are not used in calculating current cost adjustments.

3. Estimated technology costs in Figure 4-2 are $3,700. Based on estimates, $3,000 was allocated to Circulation, making the balance $7,000 ($4,000 + $3,000). Search-holds received the remaining $700, increasing the balance to $1,100 ($400 + $700).

Bibliography

Cooper, R., and R. S. Kaplan. "Measure Costs Right: Make the Right Decisions." *Harvard Business Review* 66 (September-October 1988): 96–103.

Ellis-Newman, J., and P. Robinson. "The Cost of Library Services: Activity-Based Costing in an Australian Academic Library." *Journal of Academic Librarianship* 24 (September 1998): 373–79.

Mitchell, B. J., N. E. Tanis, and J. Jaffee. *Cost Analysis of Library Functions.* Greenwich, Conn.: JAI Press, 1978.

Wade, R., and V. Williamson. "Cataloguing Costed and Restructured at Curtin University of Technology." *Australian Academic and Research Libraries* 29 (December 1998): 177–89.

CHAPTER

5

Budgeting and Standard Cost Analysis

This chapter begins with an explanation of traditional budget reports and some of their format variations and explains standards related to time and the usage of materials in determining whether activities are being performed efficiently. This chapter also stresses how the system of accounting that is used affects the definition of a budget variance and, consequently, the managerial decision that is made. The discussion also focuses on the development of standard costs.

Initially, the term *budget* must be defined. A budget, usually prepared on an annual basis, is a plan for allocating resources to the mission objectives of a library. A budget is not concerned with determining the full cost of operations; it assumes that all budgeted dollars are controllable by the administrator receiving the allocation. The typical library budget is not concerned with efficient levels of operation. Its major purpose is to ensure that actual spending levels do not exceed appropriations. The budget can show the sources of funds. Although knowing fund sources is important, efforts in managerial decision making are directed at efficiently distributing and managing expenditures. In this chapter, the focus is on determining how to better understand and manage budget expenditures.

A budget sets up an expenditure plan based on the availability of projected resources, and once this plan is established, it has to be monitored for spending level compliance. Without a means to check expended resources and revenue projections against actual levels of expense and receipt of revenues, the budget is ineffective. Feedback on expenditure levels allows for compliance checking against budget plans through the determination of dollar variances from budget allocations. Variances may indicate the need to revise the budget projections or take other corrective actions.

The various ways expense variances are determined for managerial decision making are described in this chapter. There are several ways variances from the budget allocations can be computed. In each case, the dollar amount of the variance will be different. Because the purpose of reviewing variances is to take corrective actions, the different variance amounts will affect the corrective actions taken. Of course, the budget process is political, and the corrective actions taken are usually influenced by political considerations. Political considerations can vary from locality to locality; therefore, it is not the purpose of this chapter to discuss the political aspects of the budget process. Furthermore, it is not the purpose of this chapter to discuss the budget development process because there are already a number of books on this subject.

THE ACCOUNTING SYSTEMS: ACCRUAL, MODIFIED ACCRUAL, AND CASH

A variance from budget appropriations has different meanings, depending on the system of accounting that the library uses. Readers who are not familiar with the accrual, cash, and modified accrual systems of accounting should refer to appendix A. For a more extended discussion of the different systems of accounting, *see* chapter 3 in G. Stevenson Smith's *Accounting for Libraries and Other Not-for-Profit Organizations.*[1]

No matter which accounting system is used, a comparison can always be made between budgeted amounts and "actual" spending. But, the variance between these two amounts has a different meaning under the various accounting systems. Although board-approved spending limits can always be used as one comparison point in determining a variance, many times the method of accounting in use "hides" the actual cost of operations. The unavailability of cost information can be frustrating for a manager who is attempting to control costs. If cost information is not shown as a variance on the budget report, it is highly unlikely that such information would be available in the library's financial statements either. As a result, a manager may have to develop his or her own specially prepared, off-line reports to collect operational cost information.

Accrual Basis

Some libraries in preparing their financial statements may use the accrual system.[2] (Appendix A provides further information about accrual systems.) The accrual basis of accounting records expenses when they are incurred in providing services regardless of when these expenses are paid.[3] Revenue is recognized in the accounting records when it is earned. Contributions and support are recognized when they are available to be spent regardless of when the actual cash is received. When the accrual basis of accounting is used, the term *expense* is used. In other accounting systems, *expenditures* or *disbursements* may be used instead. These differences are significant because the actual costs of operations cannot be determined if the accrual system is not in use.

In considering these differences, expenses, expenditures, and disbursements need to be compared. Under an accrual system, expenses are cost incurrences that have no recognizable future benefit and therefore expire. For example, they become deductions on the income statement for the time period in which they were incurred in providing library services. Under a cash system, disbursements are recorded when cash is paid out. This is a checkbook system of accounting. Under a modified accrual system, expenditures generally include all cash disbursements found under a cash system, with some notable exceptions, making it slightly different than both the cash and the accrual systems. For example, inventory may be considered an expense at the time it is purchased (cash method) or when it is used (accrual method). Prepaid items, such as rent paid in advance, are not recognized as an asset. For these reasons, the recognition of expenditures does not show the full cost of operations during a period (*see* chapter 2 for a discussion of the difference between expenses and costs).

If a budget is developed in a true accrual accounting framework, the board-approved budget and spending during the year or period are based on the accrued expenses of operations. In this system, the approved budget is not the amount of *cash* expected to be spent on operations in the current year nor is it the estimated *expenditures;* it is the estimated accrued expenses of operations. In accrual accounting, some expenses may have been incurred but not yet paid because they are owed, a liability. They are still a budget expense for the period. The budget variance is determined by comparing the approved budget appropriations with accrued expenses—the incurred costs of the period, for example.

With accrual accounting, it is possible to use an encumbrance system. An encumbrance system can be used with whatever basis of accounting is in use in a library. *Encumbrances* are commitments of appropriations that occur when the library issues a purchase order. The encumbrance is recorded as a reduction in the appropriation at the time the purchase order is issued. When the purchased item is received, the encumbrance is eliminated from the records, and a liability is recognized until the obligation is paid. The purpose of an encumbrance is to show that legally appropriated funds have been committed to making a purchase, thus reducing the funding available for future spending.

If an encumbrance system is used with an accrual accounting system, the accrued expenses of operations are usually increased by the encumbrances outstanding at the end of the year and are then compared with the approved budget appropriation to determine variances. Budget appropriations may be thought of as incurred expenses plus outstanding year-end encumbrances. Because encumbrances represent a commitment of budgeted funds at the time a purchase order is issued, year-end encumbrances are commitments for goods or services out of the current year's budget. But encumbrances are not a cost of the current year's operations. True, they are used in reducing appropriations, but this is a legal question, not a managerial cost determination issue. In an encumbrance system, a variance is still determined, but it is not a cost variance when resources have only been committed but not expended with an encumbrance.

If a budget is developed in a nonaccrual system or with an encumbrance system, the cost of operations can only be determined after adjustments change these methods to the accrual basis. Several examples of these accounting adjustments to nonaccrual systems are illustrated in appendix A.

Modified Accrual

From an organizational viewpoint, most public libraries are part of a city or state, and as a result, the system of accounting used by the city or state is also the system used by the public library. Currently, the accepted accounting method prescribed by the Governmental Accounting Standards Board (GASB) for city and state government is modified accrual.[4] A number of differences exist between modified accrual and accrual accounting, most notably that the modified accrual system records expenditures rather than expenses.[5] This means that asset purchases are considered expenditures of the current fiscal year regardless of whether they are used in the current period. For example, under modified accrual, all supplies purchased in the current year can be considered budgetary expenditures. Under an accrual system, only the supplies actually *used* during the period are budgetary expenses. Therefore, the cost of supplies is likely to be misallocated between fiscal periods in a modified accrual system.

When budget variances are calculated in a modified accrual system, they are an expenditure/encumbrance variance because encumbrances are always used in modified accrual systems. These variances are the difference between the approved budget at the beginning of the period and the expenditures and any outstanding encumbrances at the end of the period. A number of accounting adjustments are needed to convert a modified accrual system to an accrual system and to determine the cost of operations.

Cash Method

Another method of accounting that city governments often use is the cash method, and as a result, it is used by that city's public library. This is not an accepted method of accounting for preparing a state and local government or library's financial reports, but in practice, it is widely used. If the approved budget is based on cash accounting, adjustments must be made to convert that system to the accrual basis in order to determine the cost of operations. The major purpose of the cash system is to record the total cash disbursements made each year. The cash method of budget formulation views each budget item as the amount of cash spent without concern about the expenses incurred. The budget variance is determined by comparing a forecasted cash budget with actual cash disbursements; this is a cash variance. For an example of some conversions needed to change the cash method to the accrual method, see appendix A.

Regardless of which accounting method is used, making comparisons between amounts budgeted and actual spending helps to determine legal compliance with spending guidelines. However, it is not possible to determine the cost of operations or cost variances unless an accrual basis of accounting is adopted. Therefore, budgetary variances determined on other than an accrual basis do not provide the manager with cost information. They simply show whether legal budget guidelines, however defined, were not exceeded. The actual cost of operations, however, is not known. This chapter assumes that accrual accounting is in use or, if it is not in use, that a conversion will be made to that system of accounting for preparing the reports described in this chapter. Without conversion, cost finding and cost variance analysis have little meaning.

BUDGET REPORTS

For a nonprofit organization, the major objective of a budget is to establish approved spending guidelines for the coming fiscal period. Of course, these guidelines may have to be changed if it becomes apparent that anticipated appropriations would not be received. To ensure that expenditure plans do not exceed preapproved budget guidelines, actual spending levels have to be monitored throughout the year. This comparison is usually performed on a monthly basis during the year. The purpose of the monthly report is to show the amount of funds that remain in each budget line during the year. However, a number of variations often occur in a monthly budgetary spending limit, so the main focus here will be on the annual budget report, where year-end cost variances are analyzed.

The difference between monthly and year-end cost variances should be noted at this point. The yearly budget variance is the difference between the *total* appropriation approved by the board for each budget item and the expenses (accrual), expenditures (modified accrual), or disbursements of cash shown for that budget item. When preparing a monthly budget variance, the expenses, expenditures, or disbursements can be compared with a portion of the yearly budget appropriation. There are a number of ways to subdivide the yearly appropriation. The simplest but least meaningful method is to divide the yearly budget amounts by twelve to arrive at a monthly figure. This is called a static budget. A more meaningful method is to base the monthly amounts on a volume figure, the number of library users, for example. Volume-based budgets are explained later in the chapter, when flexible budgets are described. The three methods of accounting can be combined with either a static or flexible budget to determine the total variance. Thus, the variance from one budgetary report to another can have several completely different meanings or no meaning depending on the combination of accounting and budget methods used.

Traditional Budget Reports: Legal Focus

A number of choices must be made in determining how an annual budget report should be prepared. For example, expense data could be aggregated by object of expense, activity, program, department, or even by mission objective. It is not necessary to choose just one of these methods because they can be used in combination with each other. With a computerized accounting system, transaction codes of at least fifteen digits can be used to identify expenses by any combination of these methods. A *transaction code* is a number by which transactions are entered into the computer for later report classification. The digits in a transaction code can be used to identify expenses by any combination of fund, grant, activity, budget line, or project.

The transaction codes make it easy to reclassify financial data for different reports. The data on financial statements need not, and should not, be prepared in the same manner as budget reports. Accrual-based financial statements show all *expenses* incurred in the current period but not encumbrances. Yet, encumbrances need to be shown on budget reports to reflect legal spending limits (i.e., actual spending plus encumbrances). Therefore, without transaction coding it would be very difficult to prepare reports for both external and internal reporting purposes.

The first two budget reports prepared in this chapter use a cost variance, based on actual expenses, and an expended variance that incorporates encumbrances. For libraries using this system, reconciliation is necessary if budget expenses and incurred financial statement expenses would be compared.

A budget report used to review annual budget variances is shown in Figure 5-1. This report has not been prepared for a specific responsibility center within a library, but it is still useful for a small public library with a manual reporting system. This budget report shows two different variances. Both variances are reported as the objects of expenditure. Column two, "Budget Expenses," lists the legal budget appropriation approved by the board. Column three, "Incurred Expenses," is the total of accrual-based expenses incurred by the library during the year. The cost variance, shown in column four, is the difference between the cost of operations and legally approved budget appropriation.

The second variance in column seven is the variance typically shown on most budget reports. In calculating this variance, the outstanding encumbrances at the end of the year, column five, are added to the incurred expenses, column three. This total is placed on column six as the "Total Expended." The difference between the amounts in column six and column two is called the "Total Expended Variance" in column seven. This variance shows the difference between the board-approved budget funding and the amount of incurred expenses and encumbrances. If more is spent and encumbered than was authorized, serious consequences for the director of the library can result.

Both variances provide different information for the manager. The *cost variance* is the difference between the legally approved budget appropriation and accrual-based expenses incurred during the year. These expenses are the same amounts that appear on the accrual-based financial statements. Unfortunately, the information on the financial statements is not usually provided in a format that is useful for managerial decision making. The *expended variance* shows the effect outstanding encumbrances have on the cost variance. Both variances have a place in managerial decision making. The cost variance provides information about the actual cost of operations that is not available from the expended variance. But, the expended variances show

Small Public Library Statement of Expenses and Encumbrances
Budget and Actual for the Year Ended June 30, 20xx

Budget Item (1)	Budget Expenses (2)	Incurred Expenses (3)	Cost Variance (U) or F* (4)	Total Cost Outstanding Encumbrances (5)	Total Expended (6)	Total Expended Variance (U) or F* (7)	Budget Percent Expended (%) (8)
Salaries	$130,000	$125,000	$5,000	$ —	$125,000	$ 5,000	96
Wages	26,000	30,000	(4,000)	—	30,000	(4,000)	115
FICA	10,000	10,250	(250)	—	10,250	(250)	103
Health	7,500	7,250	250	—	7,250	250	96
Retirement	14,000	13,500	500	—	13,500	500	96
Insurance	2,000	2,000	—	—	2,000	—	100
Building maintenance	6,500	6,000	500	750	6,750	(250)	104
Janitorial supplies	1,000	1,100	(100)	250	1,350	(350)	135
Utilities	9,000	11,000	(2,000)	—	11,000	(2,000)	122
Telephone	3,000	2,900	100	—	2,900	100	96
Postage	1,300	1,450	(150)	—	1,450	(150)	112
Photocopying	3,300	3,500	(200)	—	3,500	(200)	106
Audit fees	2,500	3,500	(1,000)	—	3,500	(1,000)	140
Petty cash expenses	300	300	—	—	300	—	100
Books	39,000	39,000	—	2,500	41,500	(2,500)	106
Periodicals	3,000	3,000	—	1,000	4,000	(1,000)	133
Equipment maintenance	2,000	1,500	500	—	1,500	500	75
Library supplies	4,000	3,800	200	500	4,300	(300)	108
Office supplies	2,100	1,900	200	500	2,400	(300)	114
Binding	700	750	(50)	—	750	(50)	107
Auto maintenance	500	600	(100)	750	1,350	(850)	270
Auto operations	800	700	100	—	700	100	88
Travel	500	—	500	—	—	500	0
Publicity	350	400	(50)	—	400	(50)	114
Totals	**$269,350**	**$269,400**	**$ (50)**	**$6,250**	**$275,650**	**$(6,300)**	**114**

*(U) Unfavorable; F Favorable

FIGURE 5-1   Annual budget report using line-item reporting

whether board-approved spending limits were exceeded. For example, a department head may attempt to encumber monies at the end of the year and overspend the budget in this manner. When the outstanding encumbrances are used to determine the expended variance, this tactic becomes apparent through a review of the budget report.

Column eight shows the percent of the budget appropriation expended during the year. The percent is determined by dividing column two into column six. If the percent in column eight is more than 100 percent, it shows that more expenses and encumbrances were incurred on that budget line than had been appropriated for spending.

This budget report prepared at the end of the year is useful for identifying variances by objects of expenditure, such as salaries, wages, and so forth. With a year-end budget report, it is too late to take corrective actions to reduce excessive spending levels that have already occurred. Of course, significant year-end variances on the budget report should always be investigated to determine their causes. Significant variances are defined by managerial judgment, but they include both significant favorable and unfavorable variances. It may be important to know the reason spending on a budget item fell below its appropriation. For example, in Figure 5-1, the reason there is a favorable variance of $5,000 in salaries should be investigated. A favorable variance may signal misallocated appropriations whereby excessive funds are provided in one area while underfunding a second area, for example.

Review of the budget items in Figure 5-1 shows that the incurred expenses for building maintenance did not exceed the budget appropriation until the outstanding encumbrances are taken into account. When the outstanding encumbrances are included, a favorable variance of $500 is changed into an unfavorable variance of $250. This trend is apparent in the column totals, and this overspending may have serious consequences for the library's director. The total cost variance is unfavorable by $50, but when outstanding encumbrances are considered, it is unfavorable by $6,250.

Problems can arise when a budget report such as the one shown in Figure 5-1 is used to analyze variances. This budget report only shows line items for the entire library, making it difficult to determine which department in the library is responsible for overspending. For example, the unfavorable wage variance of $4,000 in column four cannot be traced to departments. In a small library, it may be possible to isolate these variances in more detail without much difficulty, but the process becomes more complex as the library increases in size.

Figure 5-2 shows an example of a budget report that makes it easier to isolate budget variances by departments. Each of these departments can be

Small Public Library Statement of Expenses and Encumbrances
Budget and Actual for the Year Ended June 30, 20xx

Budget Item (1)	Budget Expenses (2)	Incurred Expenses (3)	Cost Variance (U) or F* (4)	Total Cost Outstanding Encumbrances (5)	Total Expended (6)	Total Expended Variance (U) or F* (7)	Budget Percent Expended (%) (8)
Children's Library							
Wages	$13,000	$12,500	$ 500	—	$12,500	$ 500	96
FICA	1,500	1,475	25	—	1,475	25	98
Books	4,000	3,900	100	$ 300	4,200	(200)	105
Periodicals	800	790	10	—	790	10	98
Library supplies	120	150	(30)	100	250	(130)	208
Office supplies	75	60	15	—	60	15	80
Totals	$19,495	$18,875	$ 620	$ 400	$19,275	$ 220	
Technical Services							
Salaries	$20,000	$20,000	—	—	$20,000	—	100
Wages	14,000	13,500	$ 500	—	13,500	500	96
FICA	3,000	2,950	50	—	2,950	50	98
Health	975	970	5	—	970	5	99
Retirement	1,200	1,175	25	—	1,175	25	98
Equip. maintenance	170	200	(30)	—	200	(30)	118
Library supplies	2,000	2,400	(400)	—	2,400	(400)	120
Office supplies	300	270	30	$ 30	300	0	100
Binding	300	350	(50)	—	350	(50)	117
Totals	$41,945	$41,815	$ 130	$ 30	$41,845	$ 100	
Maintenance							
Wages	$10,000	$15,000	$(5,000)	—	$15,000	$(5,000)	150
FICA	1,000	1,100	(100)	—	1,100	(100)	110
Janitorial supplies	1,000	1,100	(100)	$ 250	1,350	(350)	135
Bldg. maintenance	6,500	6,000	500	750	6,750	(250)	104
Totals	$18,500	$23,200	$(4,700)	$1,000	$24,200	$(5,700)	

*(U) Unfavorable; F Favorable

FIGURE 5-2 Budget report based on line items and departmental divisions

considered a responsibility center. Budget data are collected both by line item and by departments and are presented in an object-of-expenditure format by department. Although the information in Figure 5-2 is summarized for three departments, all library departments should be shown in this type of budget report. This is not a controllable cost report as was illustrated in chapter 3. Here, where all budget appropriations are shown, the major purpose is to illustrate the difference between both cost and expense/encumbrance variances and legally approved budget spending limits. Furthermore, because this is a budget report, no overhead is allocated to these three departments to determine the full-cost information shown in chapter 3.

As the budget report in Figure 5-1 is compared with the report in Figure 5-2, several differences are noted. One difference is the ease with which it is possible to determine specific responsibility for budget variances. For example, Figure 5-1 shows a $4,000 unfavorable variance in wages in the budget report, but without more investigation, it is impossible to determine which departments were responsible for the unfavorable variance. In the budget report in Figure 5-2, however, it is plain to see that the unfavorable variances of $5,000 in Maintenance and the favorable wage variance of $500 in both the Children's Library and the Technical Services Department were responsible for the overall unfavorable variance of $4,000.

This budget report immediately assigns departmental responsibility for variances. Once this determination is made, and if the variances are considered significant, they can be analyzed in more detail to determine their causes. At this point all variances shown in Figures 5-1 and 5-2 are *total* variances. Within each total variance, other more detailed variances can help to provide additional information about the cause of a total variance. For example, the unfavorable wage variance could occur because higher wages had to be paid—a spending variance—or because excessive labor hours were used on a library activity—an efficiency or time variance. Because the cause of a variance affects the prescription for correcting that variance, causes must be determined as accurately as possible. Later in the chapter, techniques for further analyzing the total variance will be discussed.

Target Budget Reports: A Managerial Focus

As stated, a budget's purpose is to compare actual spending levels to board-approved spending levels. Yet, when there is a strong working relationship between the library staff and the accounting staff, budget reports that are more directly oriented to meeting the needs of managerial decision making can be developed. One such report is the *target budget report*. A target budget report allows the library staff to evaluate more accurately the cost of library activities in a specific target area. Although it is not an activity accounting report, it identifies the costs of activities that are of special concern to library managers and makes the budget report useful for managerial decision making. These reports can reflect spending on grants, important policy initiatives, or other specifically identified library activities.

A target budget report is not prepared with a generalized accounting system. Therefore, this report needs to be developed in close cooperation with the accounting staff. The budget costs to be identified by library managers must be explained to accounting personnel who then properly precode transactions as they are entered into the computer system. Once cost data are coded, it is relatively easy to extract them from a database and prepare a report. The need for these reports always should be compared with the additional report preparation costs.

An example of a target budget report is shown in Figure 5-3. This budget report shows costs classified by three target activities. The activities shown and specifically described are "Selection/deselection," a collection development activity; "Processing"; and "Patron services." Although this budget report may appear similar to an activity cost report, it is not prepared for a specific responsibility center. It is based on a cost per labor hour rather than a cost per-unit activity, and no overhead has been allocated.

Only three activities are shown in Figure 5-3, but other activities, such as maintenance and repairs, could be included in this report. The incurred costs accumulated for the three activities in this budget report are based on the actual labor hours involved in performing the activity times the actual wage rate paid to the employee. It is not based on standard costs or the standard time allowed for performance. In column two, the budget dollars are assigned to each activity at the beginning of the period based on an estimate of the labor hours required for each activity times the wage rate. Figures in column two are compared with the actual incurred costs for each activity during the period, shown in column three, to determine the cost variances given in column four. This is a budget report based on labor hours budgeted and labor hours used to perform the highlighted activities. A cost variance, not an expended variance, is reported as an encumbrance system and is not used with salaries or wages.

For a report of this nature to be developed, the activities and job functions of library personnel have to be coded. This target report collects data about the costs of library activities based on the labor hours used to perform them. Therefore, labor hours expended on each activity must be carefully recorded and coded during the period.

Small Public Library
Statement of Expenses—Budget and Actual
for the Year Ended June 30, 20xx

Job Description (1)	Budget Expenses* (2)	Incurred Costs* (3)	Cost Variance (U) or F† (4)	Budget Percent Expenses (%) (5)
Selection/deselection				
Order requests	$1,000	$1,300	$(300)	130
Receiving new material	4,000	3,800	200	95
Weeding stacks	1,200	2,000	(800)	167
E-cataloging	700	500	200	71
Disposal of materials	400	500	(100)	125
Totals	$7,300	$8,100	$(800)	
Processing				
Overdues	$1,200	$1,100	$ 100	92
New books	3,000	2,800	200	93
Inventory records	1,500	1,500	—	100
Shelving	2,000	1,700	300	85
Shelf/e-shelf list	900	1,000	(100)	111
Shelf reading	800	900	(100)	113
Totals	$9,400	$9,000	$400	
Patron services				
Loans	$1,500	$1,750	$(250)	117
Searches	800	850	(50)	106
Desk services	3,000	3,000	—	100
Tours	1,500	1,600	(100)	107
Classes/workshops	2,000	1,500	500	75
Consultations	300	200	100	67
Totals	$9,100	$8,900	$ 200	

*Based on labor hours times wage rate; †(U) Unfavorable; F Favorable

Definition of Activities

Selection: Those activities related to the acquisition of books, periodicals, and so forth for the library: order processing, receiving, unpacking, distributing of new materials, returning defective materials, and processing cancellations

Deselection: Those activities involved in withdrawing circulating and noncirculating materials, weeding the collection, and disposing of withdrawn materials

Processing: Those activities involved in maintaining the status of the collection

Patron services: Those activities where there is direct contact with patrons

FIGURE 5-3   A target budget report for selected activities

When the cost variances are calculated, they indicate whether the budget has been overallocated to certain activities and underallocated elsewhere. The report is not directed at departmental costs or responsibility centers, but rather at activities that occur in a number of different departments at once.

In reviewing the costs of "Selection/deselection" in Figure 5-3, orders for new books, weeding, and disposal activities all show unfavorable variances. Receiving new materials and cataloging, however, were favorable. The high number of labor hours devoted to weeding and ordering activities could mean that library personnel made a special effort to order new books, and therefore the collection is being weeded in the current year to ensure enough available space for books in the subsequent year. As a result, next year's activities will probably be more concentrated in receiving new materials and cataloging and may require higher budget funding for the departments involved in these activities.

A target budget report provides a predetermined, specific perspective on cost reporting. These reports are directed at specific management problems and are not typically available from a generalized accounting system. They require extensive development and should not be prepared unless there is a special need for them, such as providing a means to determine if library policy is being carried out at the departmental level.

Target budget reports may be prepared to analyze short- or long-term periods. For example, if a five-year goal for the library is to increase the professional staff's computer skills as well as to support the development of PC resources within the library for public use, the first step in reaching this goal is a budget commitment. Assume that the library decides to commit 5 percent of its budget to this initiative over the next two years, with 2 percent spent over the remaining three years. This is an important goal for the library; therefore, annual target budget reports will be prepared for each library department over the five-year period of the initiative. The report will show, on a departmental level, the amount expended for computer resources. Of course, it will be necessary to specify carefully which specific activities qualify for inclusion in this program.

A target budget report of this nature is illustrated in Figure 5-4. In the Small Public Library, a policy decision has been reached to spend 5 percent of each operating department's budget on expanding the PC resources. The director of the library wants to measure the level of cooperation from department heads on this initiative. To prepare this report, all spending for computer resources has to be transaction coded during the year. For example, all computer-related purchase orders, travel to computer training sessions, and the cost of seminars have to be coded.

Small Public Library
Statement of Expenses—Budget and Actual
for the Year Ended June 30, 20xx

Budget Expended on Computer Resources (1)	Budget Expenses (2)	Amount Expended* (3)	Total Expended Variance (U) or F† (4)	Budget Percent Expenses (%) (5)
Circulation				
Books	$ 3,000	$ 3,100	$(100)	103
Periodicals	—	—	—	—
Equipment	5,900	6,400	(500)	108
Supplies	600	600	—	100
Staff training costs	2,500	2,000	500	80
Exhibits	—	—	—	—
Totals	$12,000	$12,100	$(100)	
Children's Library				
Books	$1,000	$1,100	$(100)	110
Periodicals	—	—	—	—
Equipment	2,500	2,100	400	84
Supplies	500	600	(100)	120
Staff training costs	500	700	(200)	140
Exhibits	500	300	200	60
Totals	$5,000	$4,800	$ 200	
Extension Department				
Books	—	—	—	—
Equipment	$2,700	$1,000	$1,700	37
Supplies	300	100	200	33
Exhibits	500	50	450	10
Totals	$3,500	$1,150	$2,350	

---

*This includes encumbrances outstanding; †(U) Unfavorable; F Favorable

FIGURE 5-4   A target budget used to evaluate a policy objective

Several program departments are shown in the first column. These program departments are responsibility centers, and the heads of each department are evaluated on their performance in this report. All costs shown are assumed to be controllable; noncontrollable costs have no place in measuring departmental performance. For each department, 5 percent of the department's budget is calculated. These amounts budgeted for computer resources, shown in column two, are $12,000, $5,000, and $3,500 for the Circulation Department, Children's Library, and the Extension Department, respectively. The exact manner of budgeting for PC resources, in column two, is left to the discretion of each department head. The third column gives the actual amount expended to achieve the computer initiative. The variances between columns two and three as well as the variance percentage based on the budget figures are shown. As a result of preparing this report, directors can determine if a policy objective is being achieved at the departmental level in the library.

The data in Figure 5-4 indicate that the Extension Department has not fully instituted the computer policy initiative and has underspent its budget on computer resources as required under the computer initiative. The reason for this department's lack of cooperation should be investigated. The two other departments appear to have given full cooperation in attempting to introduce computer resources into the library. The target report highlights a specific spending objective in the library and makes it easier to take corrective actions at the point where they are needed. Target budgets use the typical information on a budget report and recast it into a more useful managerial format. Yet, because target budgets are based on budget reporting, they do not have all the attributes of reports prepared using activity-based accounting.

The major purpose of a budget report is to provide feedback to an oversight board or director as to whether an approved budget is being followed. It is possible to adapt budget reports for more managerial-oriented uses. The budget reports in Figure 5-3 and Figure 5-4 are examples of these adaptations.

In all the budget reports presented up to this point, the variance between actual expenses and budget expenses may not always assist the library manager in understanding how well the organization is performing. The cost or expended variance is based on a comparison of board-approved spending limits with actual spending, but this comparison alone does not take into account the volume of patron services or the efficiency with which services are delivered. For example, if the yearly board-based appropriations are simply divided by twelve and used as monthly spending limits, no consideration is given to changes in patron usage patterns within a library. Changes in the volume of patrons using the library are an important consideration in budget analysis but are usually ignored when the board-approved appropriation at the beginning of the fiscal year is compared with total spending during the year.

Exercise 5-1

Working with Budget Reports

Alice Johnson is the head of acquisitions at the Abe Fuller Library. She recently received the following budget report for the year ending June 30, 20xx.

	Budget Expenses	Total Expended	Variances (U) F*
Salaries	$45,000	$45,000	$ 0
Wages	20,000	20,000	0
Supplies	7,000	8,000	(1,000)
Photocopying	1,200	1,500	(300)
Totals	$73,200	$74,500	$(1,300)

---

*(U) Unfavorable; F Favorable

Alice brought the report with her into the Business Office to discuss it with the library's bookkeeper the day after she received it. Her comments to the bookkeeper were as follows:

> *Our job is to order books, periodicals, and other materials for the library. We also cancel periodicals and other annual subscriptions that are no longer needed. When I look at the budget report, I can't tell how much ordering materials, accessioning, and cancel processing is costing. Is there any way to change the budget report to separately identify the costs of ordering, working with supplier invoices, accessioning materials, and cancellation processing?*

1. What problems do you see with the budget report as presented to Alice by the Business Office?

2. Using Figure 5-3 as an example, make some suggestions on the cost driver that makes the costs of ordering, supplier processing, accessioning, and cancellation processing increase.

3. Do you think the bookkeeper will be able to change the accounting system to allocate the expenditures for salary, wages, supplies, and photocopying to the costs of ordering, supplier processing, accessioning, and cancellation processing?

THE FLEXIBLE BUDGET: A MANAGERIAL TOOL

Library budgets are usually static budgets, meaning they do not change as the level of services or volume levels increase or decrease. A static budget does not take into account monthly or yearly changes in the volume of patron service provided. The static budget is set for only one level of services and spending— the projected level estimated at the beginning of the new budget year.

When variances from a static budget are computed, they may all show favorable cost variances and still not provide any indication of good performance. For example, if no one used the library, those costs that varied with the level of usage would be zero and, therefore, below budgeted appropriations, a favorable cost variance. In this case, no services were provided and no costs were incurred. Do these favorable variances mean a superior level of performance was achieved? The question cannot be answered by reviewing a static budget. One way to correct this situation is with a flexible budget. All budgets illustrated earlier could have been prepared as flexible budgets. The activity cost reports prepared in chapter 4 were flexible budgets based on the volume of activity.

A flexible budget shows how costs vary with changes in volume levels, such as volume of service, volume of use, and volume of activity. To prepare a flexible budget, the way costs respond to changes in volume must be known. Chapter 2 discussed the differences between fixed, variable, and mixed costs. Before preparing a flexible budget, it is important to analyze operations for costs that exhibit fixed, variable, or mixed patterns. A flexible budget is better than a static budget for managerial decision making because it realistically takes cost patterns and volume changes into account. Another important reason for using a flexible budget is that performance standards can be incorporated into its use. Standards for performance already should be an implicit consideration in any budget, but with the flexible budget, they can be explicitly incorporated.

Figure 5-5 shows the traditional budget variances calculated for the Library Instruction Division, a division and responsibility center in the Reference Department of a university library. All costs are reported, and no attempt is made to separate controllable and noncontrollable costs, as was done in chapter 3. This is the typical approach used in nonprofit budget reporting. The Library Instruction Division provides instruction to the freshman class regarding the use of the library's bibliographic resources and also provides tours of the library that show the students where to find library materials.

In Figure 5-5, budget variances show the difference between the board-approved budget, "Budget Expenses," and the actual costs of operations, "Incurred Expenses." The incurred expenses of operations exceed budget

	University Library		
	Reference Department—Library Instruction Division		
	Budget Report		
	Year Ended June 30, 20xx		
Budget Item	**Budget Expenses**	**Incurred Expenses**	**Total Cost Variance (Unfavorable)**
Salaries	$5,800	$6,000	$(200)
Supplies	1,000	1,150	(150)
Maintenance	1,400	1,500	(100)
Miscellaneous	200	250	(50)
Totals	$8,400	$8,900	$(500)

FIGURE 5-5 Using a budget report to identify variances

amounts by a total of $500. For this library, assume that it is possible to re-allocate budget dollars within departmental activities as long as the department's board-approved budget is not exceeded. Therefore, even though this division exceeded its portion of the budget, the Reference Department may not have exceeded its total budget appropriation.

All the variances in Figure 5-5 are unfavorable, indicating that this division is not performing up to budget expectations. However, other factors should be investigated before the division is criticized for the unfavorable variances.

Although the cost patterns for this division have not been previously analyzed, they will most likely point to the conclusion that instruction costs will vary with the number of lectures made. Therefore, if the university accepted a large freshman class, the number of lectures would increase along with the costs of this activity. This cause for cost incurrence is uncontrollable by the division manager. Yet, the analysis of variances, as presented in Figure 5-5, does not take this possibility into account. Also, the analysis does not consider whether the personnel providing the lectures are operating efficiently. In fact, in this analysis, the Library Instruction Division appears to be exhibiting poor performance. A flexible budget is needed to analyze these variances in more detail.

The Flexible Budget and Standards of Performance

A flexible budget is a managerial tool that should be used in the most efficient way possible. Therefore, preparing one for an entire library system may not be necessary or cost effective. But, it is a useful tool when prepared to show detailed analysis of specific library activities that are not responding to cost-control measures. It is most useful to library managers who are trying to control costs or evaluate efficiency. The flexible budget has little relationship to traditional board-approved budgets other than to use them as a possible starting point for analysis.

A first step in preparing the flexible budget is to identify the work activities within a department or subdivision of a department. These work activities should have already been a consideration in developing the board-approved budget. As an example, the work functions that are performed in three different responsibility centers in a library are illustrated in Figure 5-6. The three responsibility centers are the Technical Services Department and two functional areas within the Reference Department—Library Instruction and Database Search Services. The activities shown for these three centers may vary from one library to another, but they are typical of the functions performed.

Once the activities are identified, the standards of performance for these activities must be estimated. For example, a standard time allowed for cataloging or recataloging a book in the Technical Services Department can be

Technical Services Department
Requisition library materials
Receive new library materials
Process library materials for shelving
Catalog and recatalog
Maintain inventory awaiting cataloging

Reference Department
Division: Library Instruction
Prepare bibliographic lectures
Prepare general library tours
Deliver bibliographic lectures
Conduct general tours
Division: Database Search Services
Conduct searches
Review requests for new databases
Review adequacy of old databases
Complete paperwork on patron billing
Check invoices from database companies
Select equipment and search aids
Maintain statistics on searches

FIGURE 5-6   Work activities in three library responsibility centers

set. Standards should be measured as *reasonably attainable* standards instead of *ideal* standards. Reasonably attainable standards allow for certain normal inefficiencies, whereas ideal standards assume every task will be performed at 100 percent efficiency all the time. Ideal standards assume that no allowances for breakdowns of equipment or idle time will be made. Attainable standards take into account the actual level of professional skill of the library's staff.

Standards can be established for the cost of an item, the time required to finish a task, or the quantity of materials to be used in completing the job. Standard costs are predetermined costs per completed unit. They are forecasted based on estimates of inflation and quantity discounts, for example. They provide a standard against which actual costs per unit can be compared. The standard time allowed to complete a task is the time it should take to complete the actual number of successfully completed units. For example, if five books are processed and the standard time is ten minutes per book, the entire process should take fifty minutes. If the actual time to process the five books was fifty-seven minutes, cost can be attached to the seven-minute unfavorable variance. The standard amount of materials to complete a job can also be specified in terms of cards, sheets of paper, amount of tape, computer time, and so forth, and variances can be determined between the actual amount used and the standard.

The activities to be performed in the Library Instruction Division are identified in Figure 5-6 and analyzed in detail in Figure 5-7. The activities performed are preparing lectures and tours, delivering lectures, and conducting

University Library
Reference Department—Library Instruction Division
Year Ended June 30, 20xx

Project Activities	Standard Number of Times	Annual Time Required per Task	Labor Hours Expected to Be Used at Standard Time (Hours)
Prepare bibliographic lectures	1	13 hours	13
Prepare general tours	3	4 hours	12
Deliver bibliographic lectures	54	50 minutes	45
Conduct general tours	50	36 minutes	30
Total projected time required to perform activities:			100

FIGURE 5-7 Annual projected task work sheet

tours. The number of times these activities will be performed during the year is estimated, as is the standard time it takes to perform them. The standard can be estimated from an average of previous years' times adjusted to good performance levels, and the average time required to perform these activities can serve as an attainable standard time for performance.

The annual labor hours expected to be used during the year are computed by multiplying the number of times the activity is performed times the standard time required to perform the activity. In other words, the amount of time estimated to conduct a library tour is thirty-six minutes; this time allotment is an attainable standard. During the year, it is estimated that fifty tours for incoming freshmen will be necessary. Therefore, the total time allocated to this activity is 30 hours. Once the labor hours are computed for each activity, the total standard time projected to perform all division activities is 100 hours. This is an attainable performance standard for the activities to be conducted by the division during the year.

The next step in preparing the flexible budget for the Library Instruction Division is to analyze the budgeted expenses in Figure 5-5 and separate the variable and fixed costs. For this illustration, it is assumed that the board-approved budget expenses of $8,400 are the total costs that are acceptable for the expected performance. Only variable and fixed costs are recognized; mixed costs are separated into their fixed and variable components. For example, both salary and maintenance costs can be separated into fixed and variable portions. The salary costs that are fixed are supervisory costs. Supplies and miscellaneous costs are entirely variable.

The separation of the budget expenses of $8,400 into fixed and variable costs is shown in Figure 5-8. The variable costs are shown in the top left section of the report, and the fixed costs are shown in the bottom left portion. The variable costs are assumed to be controllable by the division manager. The fixed costs are overhead costs of the division. They are not allocated to this division as uncontrollable overhead from another department, but they are the overhead costs of running the Library Instruction Division and still not directly controllable by the division manager. Although variances are computed for the fixed costs, the manager should not be held accountable for any unfavorable results.

Once the variable and fixed costs are separated from one another, it is possible to calculate a standard rate per unit. Here, the per-unit measure will be based on labor hours. Labor hours are used because the division relies entirely on personnel to provide its services. If the job functions in the division do not use a high percentage of labor, it is acceptable to use another activity to determine per-unit cost. The rate for each labor hour is calculated for each

University Library
Reference Department—Library Instruction Division
Year Ended June 30, 20xx

Total Variable and Fixed Costs

Variable costs

Salaries	$4,800	
Supplies & miscellaneous	1,200	
Classroom maintenance	750	
Total variable costs		$6,750

Fixed costs

Supervision	$1,000	
Classroom maintenance	650	
Total fixed costs		$1,650
Total budgeted costs		$8,400

Per-Unit Calculation of Variable and Fixed Costs
(Costs Divided by Projected Labor Hours)

Variable costs

Salaries	$4,800/100	=	$48.00
Supplies & miscellaneous	$1,200/100	=	12.00
Classroom maintenance	$750/100	=	7.50
Total variable costs per labor hour			$67.50

Fixed costs

Supervision	$1,000/100	=	$10.00
Classroom maintenance	$650/100	=	6.50
Total fixed costs per labor hour			$16.50

FIGURE 5-8 Analysis of variable and fixed costs in the Library Instruction Division

budget line by dividing the appropriation for that budget line by the 100 total estimated labor hours budgeted to perform the division's services. Good performance in time (100 hours) is matched with good performance in appropriated budget dollars. This process is illustrated on the right side of Figure 5-8. Although total fixed costs do not change over the period, this calculation for fixed costs will show that as the volume of services performed increases, the fixed cost per unit decreases. Therefore, the fixed cost per unit is understood to vary if the standard labor hours to complete division activities change. The total variable costs are computed to be $67.50 per labor hour and total fixed costs are $16.50 per labor hour. These are the standard costs per labor hour to operate the Library Instruction Division.

Exercise 5-2

Analyzing Cost Patterns within a Library Department

The director of the Landover Free Library wants to find a way to determine how to assign the costs of information technology (IT) to the various library departments. The first step in this process is to analyze the cost patterns within the library's IT Department; the next step is to find a cost driver for assigning those costs to the other departments in the library based on their usage of IT services.

The IT Department is responsible for Web page development and maintenance as well as maintenance of all library PCs, the databases used by library personnel and patrons, and all electronic communications, such as e-mail. The following information about the IT Department has been collected.

	Fixed	*Variable*
Salary for full-time personnel	$54,000	—
Wages for part-time personnel	—	$24,000
Computer maintenance costs		5,000
Equipment/software purchases	12,000	—
Supplies	—	6,000
Totals	$66,000	$35,000

Annually, 20,000 labor hours are worked by full-time IT personnel, and 4,000 labor hours are worked by part-time employees. The computer hours logged each year that directly relate to library activities are 126,000 hours. A consultant has indicated that these IT activities would have been expected to use 15,000 direct labor hours and 110,000 hours of computer time.

1. Determine the cost driver that should be used to allocate IT costs to other library departments.
2. What number of hours represents good performance in completing annual IT activities? Why?
3. Using Figure 5-8 as a guide, determine the hourly rate that should be used to charge the other library departments for the services provided by the IT Department.
4. What might be a problem with the solution shown in the appendix for question 3?

Once the standard per-unit labor hour cost for each budget line is calculated, the standard time it should have taken to complete the activities that actually took place in the Library Instruction Division must be determined. In Figure 5-9, the actual level of services provided during the year is shown; the number of lectures and tours conducted is higher than the number originally estimated at the beginning of the period. One lecture was prepared, and preparation for general tours was reduced to two times. Therefore, the actual services provided, determined at the end of the budget year, are different from the level of services that had been estimated at the beginning of the year. It would be very unusual for the estimated level of services projected at the beginning of a year to be equal to the actual service level.

In Figure 5-9, the total amount of time in standard labor hours required to perform each activity is determined. This calculation is based on the standard time allowed for each of the activities as originally established in the budget and the number of times the activity was performed. The total standard amount of time allowed to perform the actual activities is 110.6 labor hours. The task reports prepared by library personnel show that only 105 actual labor hours were used in providing the division's services.

Once the total standard time allowed for the services is determined, a flexible budget can be constructed by multiplying the standard labor hours times the previously determined standard rate. This calculation is made in the bottom part of Figure 5-9, and the flexible budget dollars are shown there for each variable and fixed cost.

In Figure 5-10, the flexible budget dollars are compared with the incurred expenses, as reported in Figure 5-5, to find cost variances. The flexible budget shows the standard cost of activities at 110.6 labor hours. This

University Library
Reference Department—Library Instruction Division
Year Ended June 30, 20xx

Project Activities	Number of Times	Standard Time Required per Task	Annual Labor Hours Expected at Standard Time (Standard Hours)
Prepare bibliographic lectures	1	13 hours	13.0
Prepare general tours	2	4 hours	8.0
Deliver bibliographic lectures	60	50 minutes	50.0
Conduct general tours	66	36 minutes	39.6
Total standard time required to perform activities			110.6*

*105 actual labor hours were used to complete work activities

Flexible Budget Costs Based on Standard Hours and Standard Costs per Labor Hour

	Standard Costs		Standard Hours		Flexible Budget Dollars (at Standard)
Variable costs					
Salaries	$48.00	×	110.6	=	$5,308.80
Supplies and miscellaneous	12.00	×	110.6	=	1,327.20
Classroom maintenance	7.50	×	110.6	=	829.50
Fixed costs					
Supervision	$10.00	×	110.6	=	$1,106.00
Maintenance	6.50	×	110.6	=	718.90

FIGURE 5-9 Annual task work sheet—standard hours

University Library
Reference Department—Library Instruction Division
Flexible Budget Report
Year Ended June 30, 20xx

Budget Item	Flexible Budget Dollars (at Std. Hrs.)	Incurred Expenses (Actual Hrs.)	Total Cost Variance (Unfavorable)
Variable costs			
Salaries	$5,308.80	$5,000.00	$308.80
Supplies and miscellaneous	1,327.20	1,400.00	(72.80)
Classroom maintenance	829.50	800.00	29.50
Fixed costs			
Supervision	$1,106.00	$1,000.00	$106.00
Maintenance	718.90	700.00	18.90
Totals	$9,290.40	$8,900.00*	$390.40

*Note that the total here is the same as that shown in Figure 5-5 except that the incurred expenses have been separated into variable and fixed costs

FIGURE 5-10 Determining variances using the flexible budget report

period is the standard time it should have taken to complete the tasks assigned to the Library Instruction Division.

There is a significant difference between the variances shown here and the variances calculated in Figure 5-5. All the variances in Figure 5-5 are unfavorable. In Figure 5-10, however, there is only one unfavorable variance. The level of services provided during the year explains this difference in the direction of the variances. In Figure 5-5, the comparison between budgeted amounts and actual dollars does not take into account the increase in the level of services. Therefore, all variances are unfavorable. When the budget comparison takes into account the increased level of actual services and the standard labor hours required to provide those services, it is apparent that the lectures and tours were provided at a cost lower than standard costs. The actual time used by the staff was 105 labor hours, and the standard time required was 110.6; therefore, the staff provided this level of service more efficiently than the standard time established for providing the service. This is reflected in the favorable variances. The staff should be commended rather than criticized for their cost performance.[6]

Another aspect of performance relates to how well the instruction was provided or whether quality instruction was provided. A number of nonfinancial measures must be considered when evaluating projects, performance, or programs in a nonprofit context. It is possible to have good cost performance, represented by the variances computed here or by the variances on the budgeted figures, and at the same time provide poor-quality services. Financial and nonfinancial information should be combined to see how well operations are being performed.

Exercise 5-3

Nonfinancial Performance Measures

In Figures 5-8 and 5-9, the university library's Reference Department's financial performance was analyzed using standard costs and budget reports. Financial performance is one measure used in evaluating departmental performance, but nonfinancial performance measures are also important.

Describe several nonfinancial measures that the Reference Department might also consider in evaluating patron satisfaction with department services, employee contributions to departmental goals, and the department's general success in meeting its internal policy goals.

From a managerial point of view, determining if services are being provided efficiently is more important than whether the legal budget is being exceeded. Unfavorable variances on the report in Figure 5-10 detect whether library resources are being used inefficiently or wasted. The long-term effect of operating the library inefficiently, assuming limited funding, is likely to be a reduction in services. Yet, the board-approved budget cannot be exceeded. If the legal budget is exceeded, it may mean the director of the library will possibly be fired. In Figures 5-5 and 5-10, the total variances shown are $500 unfavorable and $390.40 favorable, respectively. The first variance is a legal budget variance, and the second variance is an efficiency variance. For different reasons, it is important to calculate both of them. Although the illustrations here are for the entire fiscal year, computing variance calculations during the budget year is important so that corrective actions can be taken before the end of the year.

The budget variance that is determined under either of these methods allows the manager to determine where corrections need to be made. For example, if the Reference Department's total appropriation is exceeded, the costs in the Reference Department have to be reviewed.

Although the flexible budget variances provide assistance in evaluating efficiency, it would be helpful to have detailed information as to the specific causes of the total favorable variance of $390.40. The total flexible budget variance is composed of the price of assets used, the inefficient or efficient use of those assets, and the total labor hours used in providing services. Determining how these three factors interacted and contributed to the total variance is difficult but important. It may be that prices and usage of materials were unfavorable, but the time factor was so favorable that it overcame the unfavorable effect of prices and usage. This mixture of detailed variances in a total variance should be calculated because it changes the managerial actions required to make corrections.

THE DETAILED VARIANCES: SPENDING, USAGE, AND TIME

To separate the total flexible budget variance into its component parts, additional analysis is required. The trade-off between the costs of this additional effort should be compared with anticipated benefits before any calculations are made. This analysis may be useful in one area of the library where costs have been difficult to control, but these calculations are not useful for analyzing costs throughout the organization.

The flexible budget variance can be divided into spending, usage, and time variances. These three new variances will assist the manager in trying to control costs. The spending variance is the difference between the actual costs incurred and the total budgeted costs incurred at the actual level of services (Library Instruction Division labor hours of 105). There is both a variable and a fixed portion to the budget dollars incurred at actual labor hours. The variable portion of the budgeted dollars is based on standard costs at the actual volume level. The fixed portion of this variance is based on the total fixed cost in the budget of $1,650. The spending variance is caused by changes in prices.

Fixed-cost variances are isolated with the usage variance. A usage variance relates the fixed costs of using the library facilities more or less intensely than originally estimated when the budget was formulated. This may or may not be controllable by a manager. The usage variance should be calculated to determine how efficiently fixed costs are being used, but the manager in charge of the division should only be held accountable for controllable costs. The usage variance measures how much more service fixed costs provided under or over what was originally estimated. In this example, the facilities are used more (105 labor hours) than originally anticipated (100 labor hours);

therefore, facilities have been used more efficiently. The last variance, the time variance, is the standard amount of time (110.6 labor hours) it should have taken to perform an activity compared with the actual amount of time (105 labor hours) it took to complete the activity.

Figure 5-11 shows how these variances are calculated for the Library Instruction Division in the Reference Department. On the left side of the schematic are the total actual costs of $8,900 and on the right side are the total flexible budget costs at standard of $9,290.40. The difference between these two amounts is the *total* favorable variance of $390.40 previously calculated in Figure 5-10. Although the total variance is useful, it is important to be able to separate the total variance into its component parts.

One portion of the total variance is a spending variance. The schematic in Figure 5-11 shows a $162.50 unfavorable spending variance. This is the difference between the actual dollars, $8,900, and the budgeted dollars of $8,737.50. The latter amount is computed by adding the fixed budgeted amount ($1,650 in Figure 5-8) and variable costs computed by multiplying the standard variable cost per labor hour ($67.50) times the actual labor hours used to provide the services (105 hours). The variance is caused by increases in the price of services. Hence, it is called a spending variance. The reason for the increase could be related to a change in a variable cost, such

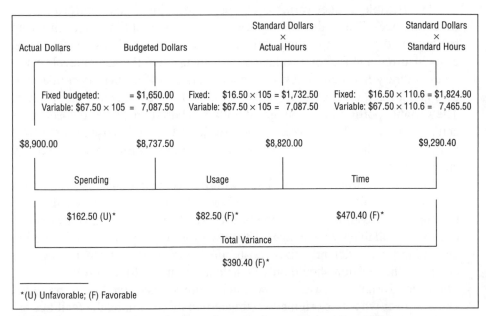

FIGURE 5-11 Dividing the total variance into spending, usage, and time variances

as an increase in the cost of supplies. Another reason for this unfavorable variance might be related to the fixed rate paid to a professor who lectures for the library. An unfavorable spending variance could have been created by an increase in the amount paid for the professor's services.

There is an $82.50 favorable usage variance in Figure 5-11. This variance is based entirely on the usage level of facilities. If facilities are used below their budgeted capacity of 100 hours, they are being underutilized, which is an inefficient use of capital assets. The usage variance is the difference between $8,737.50 and $8,820. As shown, both these figures include the same variable cost of $7,087.50; therefore, only the difference in the fixed costs causes this variance. The facilities, represented by fixed costs, were used more extensively than estimated in the budget, and as a result, fixed costs are spread out over more labor hours. In this example, five additional labor hours (5 × $16.50 = $82.50) account for this increased usage of fixed costs and the favorable variance. The five additional labor hours are the difference between the original estimate of 100 labor hours and the 105 labor hours that were actually used. A higher level of usage spread the fixed costs over more labor hours, resulting in lower fixed costs per labor hour and a favorable variance of $82.50.

In Figure 5-11, there is a favorable time variance of $470.40. The time variance is the difference between $8,820 and $9,290.40. The latter figure is the total standard cost in flexible budget (*see* Figure 5-10). It is calculated by multiplying the standard fixed ($16.50) and variable ($67.50) rates per labor hour times the 110.6 labor hours of standard time required to complete the tasks. Because the staff completed all the activities in 105 hours instead of 110.6 hours, they performed more efficiently than standard, and the time variance is favorable.

The three variances—two favorable and one unfavorable—are equal to the total favorable variance of $390.40. This is the same total variance that was computed between actual dollar expenses and the flexible budget dollars in Figure 5-10. But, these three detailed variances provide more information about the variables that cause the total variance. From this analysis, the conclusion is that the fixed costs provided more service than originally estimated at standard, and the staff performed above established standards. These two factors are responsible for the overall favorable variance. The analysis also shows that prices are increasing, represented by the unfavorable spending variance, and may be a trend that should be watched in the future.

Plans for handling additional price increases should be developed. If the price rises are caused by supply price increases, it may be possible to switch to a different vendor. If the increased cost of hiring outside professionals to conduct the lectures is the reason for the cost increase, then it may be possible to use library personnel to conduct the lectures. These steps may help to reduce this $162.50 unfavorable spending variance.

Detailed variance analysis is suggested as a way to analyze the total budget variances in order to institute specific corrective actions. It allows the manager to focus on the specific reasons for the total variance. Analysis of variances at this detailed level could be carried to each line item shown (salaries, supplies, maintenance, and supervision) rather than just the totals. Such a detailed analysis for each line item would immediately show whether the unfavorable spending variance was caused by increases in the price of supplies or caused by the increased charges from hiring outside professionals to teach portions of the lecture sessions.

Exercise 5-4

Analyzing Spending, Usage, and Time Variances

Books for a new historical collection are being cataloged and shelved at the Desota Public Library. The librarian-manager in charge of the project is responsible for closely monitoring the actual costs in cataloging and shelving the collection. Full- and part-time employees are being used to complete the project.

The librarian-manager determined that actual labor dollars expended on the project up to the current date were $8,300. Employees worked a total of 250 hours on the project. Fixed salary costs assigned to the project were $4,600, and variable labor costs were charged at a standard hourly rate of $17.

1. Determine the amount of the spending variance and whether it is favorable or unfavorable.

2. Suggest a reason for the occurrence of the spending variance.

3. Assume that fixed costs could be charged at a standard rate per hour of $23, and good performance for completing the work up to this point would have required 175 hours. Now, determine the usage and time variances on the project as well as whether they are favorable or unfavorable.

4. Can you explain the usage variance?

5. What would recommend the actions that the librarian-manager should take in completing the project once these variances are determined?

Once the reasons for the variances are determined, changes can be made. Of course, in the political environment in which the budget is constructed, some cost changes may not be able to be instituted. For example, it may be politically astute to hire a specific outside professional to conduct the lecture sessions. This person may be invaluable in helping the library have its budget approved. Therefore, even though the hiring of a professional may be the reason there is an unfavorable spending variance, a correction of the variance may be politically harmful to the library's overall programs.

SUMMARY

Chapters 4 and 5 show that the best reporting systems for managerial decision making are activity-based responsibility cost centers that use both accrual accounting and standard costs. The activity-based system focuses managerial efforts on controlling activities that are the cost creators. Cost-control responsibility is assigned to one manager in the cost-center structure. Cost control is further improved when standards of efficient performance are used and compared with actual costs. Finally, the only basis of accounting that reports the *costs* of operations during an accounting period is the accrual system.

This chapter reviewed the area of budget variance cost analysis. A library's operating manager who wants to analyze variances from approved budget amounts should recognize that variances can differ depending on how the accounting data are collected. The accounting systems define the variances. Knowing the accounting method under which the budget was prepared will help to ensure that the cost of a budget item is recorded appropriately.

The reporting format of budget documents does impact on the decision-making process. The format in which data are presented affects the corrective actions taken to control costs. The budget reports shown in the chapter illustrate the potential for differences in the managerial decisions that can be chosen.

The chapter has shown that not all variances are the same. There is a significant difference between a cost variance based on a flexible budget report and a variance that is calculated using a static budget and based on board-approved spending levels. The analysis of variances shows how to separate a total variance into its component parts so that the specific reason for the variance can be identified and corrected.

The information presented in this chapter has been directed at reporting historical data. These reports are developed after the fiscal period is over and are used as instruments of feedback to evaluate managerial performance.

Performance evaluation is directed at providing feedback based on what has occurred and how well managers have succeeded in achieving goals. The basic nature of managerial performance evaluation requires that it be developed from a historical perspective. Other techniques allow a manager to make decisions based on cost forecasts. These techniques are the subject of chapter 6.

Notes

1. G. S. Smith, *Accounting for Libraries and Other Not-for-Profit Organizations* (Chicago: American Library Association, 1999).

2. Governmental not-for-profit organizations use accrual and modified accrual accounting methods for preparing financial reports. Currently, GASB Statement No. 34 is being implemented by governmental organizations of which state and local libraries are a component unit. Thus, the method of accounting for all such organizations is in flux until 2003, when these standards are to be implemented.

3. Accrual accounting is sometimes used by libraries that are a unit of state or local government. In some of the accounting funds used by these governmental organizations, accrual accounting is followed. In addition, any library that is part of the business sector would use accrual accounting.

4. The significant difference in accrual accounting systems compared to other accounting systems is the timing difference for recognizing many expense and revenue items.

5. Modified accrual is being changed by Statement No. 34 so that there is less of a difference between modified accrual and accrual methods of accounting for governmental revenues and expenditures (expenses).

6. Flexible budgets at actual levels of production (105 labor hours) can be prepared and compared with the incurred expenses to determine variances. The variance calculated in this manner shows the variance from actual labor hours but is not an efficiency variance because it is not known whether the actual hours are reflective of efficient performance. Without the introduction of standard labor hours (110.6 labor hours), there can be no measure of efficiency. Unless additional monies can be appropriated, exceeding the legal budget levels during the year will result in immediate curtailments in programs in an attempt to make up for excessive spending.

Bibliography

Governmental Accounting Standards Board. Statement No. 34, *Basic Financial Statements— and Management's Discussion and Analysis—for State and Local Governments.* Norwalk, Conn.: GASB, 1999.

Wilson, E. R., S. C. Kattelus, and L. E. Hay. *Accounting for Governmental and Nonprofit Entities.* Boston: McGraw-Hill/Irwin, 2001.

CHAPTER

6

Life Cycle
Costing

The previous three chapters discussed concepts and methods that can be used to exercise managerial control over wide areas of the organization. The next three chapters provide a review of techniques that are related to solving very specific managerial problems rather than organization-wide ones. Chapter 6 discusses the first of these techniques.

A managerial technique that allows a library manager to evaluate purchase decisions between similar assets effectively is called *life cycle costing* (LCC). LCC is defined as the accumulation of all costs related to an asset, project, service, or management policy over its entire life from start to completion or abandonment. In some organizations, no long-term purchase decisions can be completed without an LCC analysis showing the best and next-best purchase choices and reasons for a final selection. LCC analysis goes beyond the initial purchase price of an asset or the initial cost of providing a new service. With LCC, the annual operating costs of an asset in addition to the asset's initial purchase price need to be known. Operating costs include the costs of support, maintenance and repair, personnel training, debugging systems, and equipment overhauling or upgrading costs. Depending on the asset, the after-purchase costs can be equal to 100 times the initial cost of the asset. If decisions are made to acquire assets based solely on a comparison of purchase prices and amounts available in the budget, the decision is being made without considering the effect of total costs.

Before describing how to use LCC, several aspects of the technique should be emphasized. First, it is a technique that requires the use of present value analysis. Appendix B contains a discussion of how present value analysis is used in evaluating long-term cash flows. In acquiring an asset with a life longer than one year, present value analysis is a consideration in the acquisition decision.

A second point about LCC is that it is not a way to determine profit or net income. In fact, financial reports used in determining net income are based on a completely different system than the one used with LCC. Under financial accounting, the accrual concepts are used. With LCC, cash flow is the primary concern. Because the accrual method of accounting is the only method that determines the cost of operations (*see* chapter 5), the term *cost* in LCC may be thought to be a misnomer. But, as the time period for analysis is the entire life of the asset, there is no difference in the total cost under the cash or accrual methods.

With LCC, the salaries of personnel involved in the planning and design of a new system are assigned to the life cycle costs of the new asset. These personnel costs are especially important when there is a great deal of planning and design commitment required, such as in planning for the construction of a new building. With simpler purchases that have fewer options and lower time commitments, these costs may be ignored because they are likely to be insignificant.

The organization's cost commitment to an asset grows after a purchase decision is made. This growth occurs because of the annual operating costs. Operating costs can be significantly different among assets that are designed to provide the same level and type of service. For example, a company analyzing the purchase choices between several computer models may determine that a savings in energy costs per machine per year would occur if a more expensive but faster-working model were purchased. The faster-working computer uses less electricity because it completes its tasks more quickly. In this case, LCC significantly affected the purchase decision. The operating costs of an asset are preset in the planning and design stage of equipment selection or service planning. This preset cost is determined by the performance criteria for speed and other options that are selected.

With LCC, tracing the annual operating costs to the new asset acquired is necessary. With a generalized accounting system, however, it is difficult to collect data of this nature. Unless special reports are prepared to collect operating costs by asset, LCC cannot be used effectively. In the typical accounting system, the costs of supplies used in a new asset, for example, are combined with the costs of all annual supply expenses; therefore, determining the operating costs of the new equipment is difficult. Without specialized reporting procedures, information cannot be collected. Specific transaction codes are needed to prepare specialized accounting reports.

LCC is useful in many asset acquisition decisions, but not all. LCC uses present value analysis and, therefore, is not useful for analyzing the purchase choices among very short-lived—less than one year—assets. (*See* appendix B for a discussion of present values.) Although the cost of materials and supplies is important as it relates to the operating costs of a long-lived asset, the purchase choice for a one-year source of supplies is not analyzed under LCC.[1] Yet, if a long-term vendor contract for materials and supplies is to be signed, LCC can be used in evaluating the vendor selection process.

LCC also loses its practical utility as the life of an asset reaches and extends beyond five years. The estimates in LCC may become more tenuous and subject to serious estimation error. The application of LCC to cost estimates made fifteen to thirty years into the future becomes more and more uncertain. These estimates can be made, but many times they turn into crystal-ball gazing, and the financial predictions based on them never materialize.[2] Thus, LCC analysis is most useful for analyzing assets with an estimated life of more than one year and less than five years. Both LCC and present value analysis can, and are, used to evaluate projects that extend beyond a five-year period, but the practical, not theoretical, limitations quickly become apparent. The projections can become more and more biased by managerial interpretations and the uncertainty of changes in future costs.

This chapter is divided into two sections. The first part introduces and discusses the concepts that must be considered in using LCC management in a nonprofit organization. It outlines the costs that must be predicted and provides insights into how to predict these costs. The second part of the chapter contains two cases in which LCC techniques are applied.

COST DESIGN CONSIDERATIONS

Costs are designed and preset in an asset purchase decision by the performance or service requirements established for an asset. For example, the stress levels in a building designed to be a library are higher than those of similar-sized office buildings. The design requirements for increased structural support in a library increase the building's cost. This cost increase was preset in the *planning stages* of the new building. If a new photocopying machine is to be purchased and the primary performance criterion for selection is the fastest speed for making copies, then that particular requirement will be the *cost driver*—cause of cost incurrence—that forces up the purchase price of a machine. The increase in the purchase price was built into the design or planning stage by the performance requirement for copy speed. The criteria for selection are the cost drivers in a new asset; they can affect both the initial purchase price as well as future operating costs.

Clearly not all costs can be accurately predicted. But within a five-year time frame, cost estimation can be performed with reasonable accuracy, and it is important to make an attempt to predict these costs because they can be substantial. Furthermore, the annual operating costs of new assets have the capacity to consume larger and larger portions of future budget appropriations. When no annual forecasted operating cost prediction is made, the organization approaches its future in a hit-or-miss fashion.

Design Stage Costs

Design stage costs are those costs arising prior to deciding whether to purchase a new asset or prior to beginning the construction of a new building. With most important asset purchases, a selection committee is formed to recommend the best asset to purchase. Thus, design stage costs can begin very modestly with the salary and wages of committee members who have been charged with selecting a new library asset. These costs are likely to be significant when the construction of a new building or the selection of a major computer system is being undertaken; with small equipment purchases, however, they are probably not significant enough to include in the cost analysis.

The design stage costs for a building include building committee members' salaries equal to the time they spend on committee work, the architecture fees for the design and redesign of the building, the legal fees necessary for zoning approval, and possible charges for environmental impact studies. The total of all these costs is significant and should be included in the LCC analysis.

Figure 6-1 depicts the points where design stage cash outflows may occur in the new equipment selection process. The total of these initial costs, shown as Stage A, slowly increases as more time is spent by an asset selection committee in making the final purchase choice and as other design stage costs are incurred.

Purchase Price and Installation Costs

In Figure 6-1, purchase price and installation costs are represented by Stage B costs. The large cost increase represents the price paid for the asset plus the

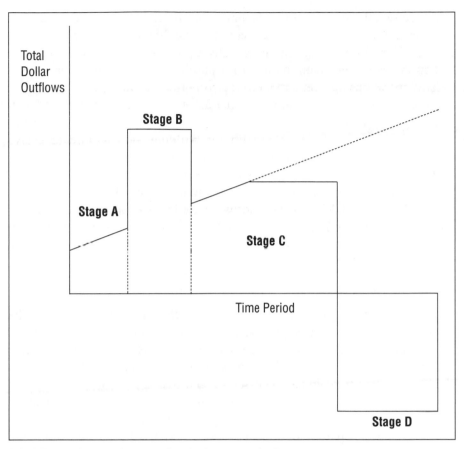

FIGURE 6-1 Stages of cash outflow in the asset selection process

installation costs of putting the asset into successful operation. For equipment, the purchase price is the actual cash purchase price paid after any discounts or amounts received for the trade-in of an old asset. The cash needed to purchase the equipment is assumed to have been appropriated in the budget. Therefore, the purchase is not paid for with periodic installment payments. If installment payments are used to purchase the asset, the analysis can incorporate, without difficulty, periodic payments as well as interest on the payments.

The installation costs are costs incurred to put the new asset into successful operation. Installation costs include freight charges paid by the library, the cost of removing old equipment, debugging the new asset so that it will successfully operate within the library's current systems, and the cost of training employees. If it is necessary for the library to incur additional charges for rewiring or repositioning walls, these costs are also part of the installation costs. Depending on the asset purchased, the culmination of successful operations may require a protracted period of time.

Installation costs vary among similar assets because of the physical surroundings in which the new asset is being installed. For example, the installation of new systems in an old library building may require extensive rewiring, but such costs would be minimal in a more recently constructed building. Installation costs may vary because of the manner in which an asset is acquired. Therefore, if software is designed in-house, all the salary costs of the employees who developed the software are included as part of the installation costs of the software. In contrast, the cost of software purchased from a vendor may be only its purchase price.

Annual Operating Costs

The annual operating costs of an asset are significant when viewed over the life of that asset. These annual costs have trade-offs in the design stage, but by the purchase date they have been built into the asset by the performance requirements set for the asset. Examples of these costs are (1) the labor costs used to operate and maintain the asset, (2) the cost of materials and supplies used in operations, and (3) the costs of energy, insurance payments, and retraining costs incurred as the system is updated to take advantage of technological changes. A portion of annual operating expenses is the cost of repairs and maintenance including charges for labor, new parts, cleaning, and periodic preventive maintenance checkups. Some of these charges may be built into the cost of the asset or purchased as a separate maintenance or warranty package. Yet, they, too, are part of the annual operating costs of the asset.

Depreciation expense is not considered to be an operating cost under LCC. LCC is concerned with the actual cash spent over the life of an asset, and depreciation is the allocation of the purchase price of the asset to the time periods during which the asset is used. Therefore, if depreciation expense were counted, the analysis would include a noncash payment that had already been considered in the initial purchase price of the asset.

Figure 6-1 depicts these costs. In Stage C, the costs initially rise rapidly; then they stabilize. This cost curve is the sought-after cost pattern. Unfortunately, the Stage C cost pattern may appear as the dotted line, also shown in Figure 6-1. This operating cost pattern represents continually escalating costs. An example of how this could occur would be the situation where a library had purchased computer equipment from a manufacturer who later went out of business. Under these conditions, as the equipment becomes older and more difficult to service, its annual operating costs could continually rise.

Miscellaneous Costs

Other miscellaneous costs may be a consideration under LCC. The significance of these costs will vary depending on the asset under analysis. An example of these charges is the cost of removing and replacing the asset, such as a worn-out furnace, especially if it requires structural renovation or the use of special equipment to remove the old asset.[3]

Another cost consideration is the cost of downtime. If an unreliable system is purchased, there is a cost associated with the time that system is in need of repair. For example, if a database is not working or not working properly, there is a cost to the library. The cost arises from the loss of patron goodwill and possibly the loss of actual dollars that would have been collected in performing a database search. It is assumed that there are other ways for patrons to make the literature search, and as a result, the lost dollars are never recovered. But, more importantly, significant downtime on a system reduces patron use, and with insufficient patron usage, it is difficult to justify the decision to purchase the system.

A Note on Cost Reductions

LCC is concerned with determining the total cost of the purchased asset over its entire life. In that process, LCC analysis incorporates any cost reductions that may occur over the life of the asset. There are several reasons why cash inflows may occur. For example, if it is estimated that an asset can be sold for salvage at the end of its useful life, the estimated salvage value receivable can affect the purchase decision. Salvage values are only estimates that will change if the asset's useful life is over- or underestimated or if premature obsolescence of the asset occurs. But, the salvage value reduces the cost of the asset and provides the library with a positive cash inflow at the end of the asset's life. Because it is not a cost, it is shown below the cost line in Figure 6-1, and it is labeled Stage D. Another source of cash inflows may occur if the asset generates chargeable service revenues. Revenue inflows are not illustrated.

The illustrated cost flow is representative of equipment or computer systems. In contrast, if the new asset had been a building, it would change Stage B costs in the illustration. With the purchase of a building, there would not be a single large outflow of cash when the building was completed and purchased. But, rather, the building contractor would be paid installment payments as construction was completed. This would result in a step-by-step increase in costs rather than a single large increase.

PROJECTING LIFE CYCLE COSTS

Typical costs encountered in the life cycle of a new asset have been discussed. This section is devoted to identifying and projecting annual operating costs. A number of methods can be used to identify the annual operating costs of a new asset. Several methods are presented here.

As stated, the initial cost of most assets is relatively easy to determine. In general this is true, but with new construction it may be more difficult. If a request for proposals (RFP) for constructing a building is issued, the initial cost of the building will be readily determined as contractors submit their proposals. Of course, prior to receiving a contractor's bid, it is more difficult to estimate the construction costs of a new building. But there are sources of information about building costs available to assist managers in projecting these cost estimates. For example, construction cost indexes provided by the *Engineering News-Record,* <http://www.enr.com>, are useful for predicting construction costs. Other books provide the data for making new construction cost estimates, such as the Dodge cost series from Marshall & Swift (i.e., *National Building Cost Manual*) and the Means cost series from R. S. Means Consultants (i.e., *Building Construction Cost Data*), <http://www. cmdg.com/products>.

In calculating annual operating costs, it is useful to maintain cost records on the assets that are currently used in the library. With this information, it may be possible to make projections of the operating costs of a new asset. Even if cost records are not maintained within the library, cost data may be available from other libraries that are already using the new asset. Cost records are an invaluable source of information for making LCC projections. Vendor information also may be obtained and used to provide annual LCC estimates. Vendor information may have to be used with caution, however.

It is also possible to use analytical techniques to determine the various elements of operating costs. Three methods of cost projection that can be used are analogy, parametric, and engineering estimations. The method used depends on the cost behavior being analyzed as well as the stage of asset selection. For example, as the project moves from a conceptual stage to its actual selection, the cost data and performance criteria for the asset becomes more clearly defined. As a result, the cost projection technique is likely to change.

In the analogy method, an old asset that is similar to the new one being se-lected is chosen for analysis. The old asset should be in use in the library or a similar-sized library. Once the annual operating costs of the old system are col-lected, they are adjusted to account for dissimilarities in operating the old and new assets. The adjustment is illustrated for the cost of material as follows:

$$
\begin{aligned}
\text{Old system materials cost} \ &= \ \$450 \text{ per month} \\
\text{New system materials cost} \ &= \ \$450 \times 1.10 \\
&= \ \$495
\end{aligned}
$$

The analogy indicates that the cost of materials in the new system is ex-pected to be 10 percent higher than in the old system. The increase may be because of the use of more costly material, a higher level of operational use, or a combination of the two factors. In analogy estimating, a straightforward percentage adjustment is made to the historical cost of materials used in an older system.

Analogy estimation is especially useful in the early stages of the asset se-lection process when the least amount of cost information is available about the new asset. It is a useful technique because it can be simply applied, but it is subject to the limitation that the results are strongly influenced by the opin-ion of the individual making the estimate. As a result, estimates may vary a great deal.

Another cost projection technique is the parametric method. This method uses a mathematical equation called a parametric equation that relates an asset's performance characteristics to its costs. A linear relationship is as-sumed to exist between the operating costs and the performance character-istics of an asset. A linear cost equation is formulated by analyzing the relationship between the past changes in costs and performance. The esti-mated energy cost of new heating equipment can serve as an illustration of this technique.

There is a linear relationship between the total cost of electricity used by new heating equipment and the amount of power consumed per hour (the British thermal unit [Btu] rating), the number of hours the equipment is op-erated per year, and the cost of electricity per watt-hour. This relationship lends itself to the following formulation.

Total cost of power consumption = Btu rating × annual operating hours × cost of power per watt-hour

With this equation, the cost of energy consumption by equipment per-forming similar functions (i.e., heating) can be evaluated. It may become ap-parent that a higher purchase price is justified because an asset performs its tasks more efficiently, which results in lower total energy costs.

The equation formulates a linear relationship between power consumption and cost. It also assumes that factors in the equation will not influence one another; therefore, the Btu rating will not change if the cost per watt changes, nor will usage. It should be noted that if the cost of power per watt varied as more power was consumed—a varying charge per watt—the relationship is considered nonlinear.[4]

The third method of projecting annual operating costs is the engineering method. This method is more exact than the other methods, but it cannot be used until all cost details about the choices are known. When the cost occurrence patterns are precisely known, they are added as they occur. The problem with this method is that the required information becomes available only after it is too late to influence the design and planning activities, when the largest percentage of the costs is preset. Therefore, the engineering method is not useful for LCC analysis, which is mainly concerned with cost projections.

Throughout cost estimation, a persistent factor is the effect of inflation on cost projections. Two assumptions about inflation are that (1) inflation will exist in the future, and (2) inflation is very difficult to predict. In LCC, future costs are not likely to be affected in the same way by inflationary increases. Some costs may see constant inflation rates from year to year, and others will see inflation rates that will change radically on a yearly basis. Therefore, the inflation effect depends on the cost under consideration. In general, two methods have been suggested for controlling the effects of inflation when LCC is used.

The first method for incorporating the effects of inflation into LCC uses time value of money concepts (*see* appendix B), and it adjusts the present value discount factors for the escalating effects of inflation. The present value table factors change as the interest rate is adjusted for the assumed future inflation level. This method is easiest to use when a constant rate of inflation in the future is assumed.

The second method to adjust LCC for inflation is to use constant dollars. This method attempts to eliminate the time period effect of inflation by using dollars that have the same value. For example, the future inflated dollars are deflated so that they have the same capacity to purchase assets as current dollars. Those costs that have a projected increase in the future are deflated to current dollars using a general inflation price index. This method involves a projection of costs that can increase at different inflation rates as well as projections about the general level of inflation in the future.

By projecting future costs and inflation, the effects of inflation are taken out of the cost data. This process normalizes all cost data to a base year, which is the point in time that the asset is purchased. An advantage of this method is that it is not necessary to assume that inflation is increasing at a constant rate over the asset's life cycle. A disadvantage is the added complexity in the analysis based on inflation projections that are rarely accurate.

There is disagreement over how to incorporate inflation into the LCC analysis. Because the nonprofit environment involves politics, some inflation projections may be skewed to put a more favorable light on a proposed project.

It can be argued that there is no need to adjust for inflation in evaluating future cash flows. This argument states that if future cash flows, such as wage increases, are adjusted for inflation, the discount rate also needs to be adjusted to reflect a higher cost of funds; therefore, these effects neutralize themselves. Because they tend to neutralize each other, there is no reason to incorporate them into the analysis in the first place.

In the examples shown here, inflation will not be incorporated into LCC analysis because the additional complexity of the analysis is not justified based on the inaccurate inflation predictions that are available. Additional emphasis on inflation can only detract from the primary and already difficult objective of cost estimating without a commensurate benefit to better analysis.

If a decision is made to accept LCC as a technique, then managerial performance evaluators based on LCC should also be used. LCC has a long-term orientation, and any managerial performance evaluation based on LCC must also adopt a long-term orientation. Performance evaluation based on one-year criteria does not fit the LCC model. The primary objective of LCC performance evaluation is to determine how well asset life cycle costs are being controlled. It is one thing to predict costs and base asset selections on these predictions, but after the purchase date, costs must be monitored and efforts taken to keep them in line with projections. When cost projections have been predicted with a high level of uncertainty, variances from projected levels may be acceptable depending on the initial uncertainty in the original estimations. The level of uncertainty would correspond closely with the type of asset purchased. For example, a higher level of cost certainty would exist in projecting the costs of a new photocopying machine than in estimating the costs of constructing a new building. All these considerations must also take into account organizational objectives beyond those related to financial objectives.[5]

DEVELOPING LIFE CYCLE MANAGEMENT IN THE LIBRARY

Traditional asset selection methods review the purchase price of a new asset and compare it with the amount appropriated in the budget for asset acquisitions. If the purchase price is less than the appropriation, the asset is considered for purchase. Little consideration is usually given to the annual operating costs of the asset. The result can be a library with an extremely high cost of operations. With LCC, the potential exists for the efficient management of costs over an asset's entire life. This is called life cycle management and goes further than just the selection of assets. It includes the long-term evaluation of the asset performance and its costs. Life cycle management focuses on costs incurred before the asset is acquired as well as the requirements for asset performance that set the pattern for cost incurrence after the purchase. Traditional purchasing policies focus on costs before the purchase, primarily the purchase price, but have little concern with cost incurrence over the entire life of the asset.

LCC is a library management technique that can serve effectively as a benchmark for asset cost performance after the purchase decision has been made as well as being used in the initial asset selection process. The acceptance of LCC as a managerial tool requires the full support of top-level management. It requires the utilization of LCC reports in the asset selection process and an understanding of both the benefits and limitations of this analysis. The use of LCC does not mean that the asset with the lowest costs must always be purchased, but it does mean that the reasons for selecting an alternative with higher costs should be clearly justified. This section of the chapter is concerned with illustrating two examples of previously discussed LCC techniques for selecting library assets.

Exercise 6-1

Calculating the Cost of Lightbulbs

The business manager at the Bright Library is considering replacing all the remaining incandescent lights in the library with fluorescent bulbs. The following life cycle information has been collected on both types of lighting.

	Incandescent	*Fluorescent*
Life in hours	760	10,000
Purchase price	$1.00	$15.00
Cost to replace*	$4.75	$3.00
Cost per kWh‡	$0.10	$0.10
Light wattage usage	60 watts per hour	15 watts per hour

---

*Replacement costs include the ordering costs, the cost of custodians replacing the bulbs, and inventory carrying costs of storage and damage.
‡Kilowatt-hour

Using the 10,000-hour life cycle of the fluorescent bulb, determine which bulb is more costly and by how much. Do not take present values into account.

Photocopying Machines

The first step in selecting assets with LCC is to design a report that incorporates LCC methods. Figure 6-2 shows such a report—the *asset selection form*. Depending on the library's asset selection policy, a report of life cycle costs may be required for every asset considered for purchase. In Figure 6-2, the asset selection form is used to evaluate the purchase alternatives between two new photocopying machines. Several machines were considered for use in the library, and LCC analysis for two of these machines is presented.

In the asset selection form, costs are separated into three classifications: purchase price, installation costs, and annual operating costs. The total life cycle costs are equal to these three costs reduced by the salvage value—estimated disposal value—received for the asset at the end of its useful life.[6] Once the total life cycle costs are computed, the annual average cost of operating the machine over its estimated five-year life is shown along with its cost per unit of output. The output in this case is number of photocopies made on an annual basis, but this output measure varies with the asset.

The initial purchase price difference between the two machines in this example is $200. Model B is cheaper and has the ability to produce more copies per month. Under traditional purchase methods, the photocopy machine to purchase is Model B. Many purchase decisions in nonprofit organizations are made with only this information. The decision is based on the purchase price and a performance criterion such as the number of annual copies or copy speed characteristics. If the equipment appropriation in the budget is $4,000, Model B can be purchased, and a net budget surplus of $150 becomes available for other uses.

Yet, when using LCC, the least-cost asset is Model A. The costs that account for this difference in the total life cycle costs need to be reviewed. In terms of installation costs, Model B is slightly more expensive because of higher freight costs, but not significantly. The annual operating costs represent the biggest difference between the two assets. The cost estimates on the asset selection form for material and supplies and energy usage are based on parametric equations. The equation used to calculate the cost of materials and supplies follows:

Cost of materials and supplies = cost per copy × number of copies per year

Asset	Model A	Model B	
Number of copies per year	180,000	480,000	
Purchase price	$4,050.00	$3,850.00	(A)
Installation costs			
Relocation costs	—	—	
Freight charges	200.00	225.00	
Rewiring	35.00	35.00	
Total installation costs	$235.00	$260.00	(B)
Annual operating costs			
Training	—	—	
Material and supplies	$3,600.00	$4,800.00	
Model A .02 per unit			
Model B .01 per unit			
Energy	869.44	1,029.60	
Maintenance & repairs	457.00	637.00	
Staff/student salary	750.00	875.00	
In-house technical servicing salary	1,200.00	1,700.00	
Total annual operating costs	$6,876.44	$9,041.60	
Estimated life (five years)	×5	×5	
Total life cycle operating costs	$34,382.20	$45,208.00	(C)
Less estimated salvage value	($375.00)	(200.00)	(D)
Total life cycle cost (A) + (B) + (C) − (D)	$38,292.20	$49,118.00	
Annual average cost (based on five-year life)	$7,658.44	$9,823.60	
Cost per unit (based on number of copies per year)	.0425	.0205	

Asset Recommended for Purchase and Justification:

_____

Energy cost = Btu rating × total annual operating hours × cost per watt hour
Model A = 38 × 2080 × .011
Model B = 45 × 2080 × .011

FIGURE 6-2   Asset selection form for two photocopying machines

The cost per copy, based on vendor-supplied data, is $0.02 for Model A and $0.01 per copy for Model B (*see* "Materials and supplies"). The maximum number of copies per year is shown at the top of the asset selection form at 180,000 and 480,000 copies for Models A and B, respectively.[7] The present photocopy configuration existing within the library will allow for a choice between these two machines.

As the cost of energy usage is becoming more important, a parametric equation is also used to calculate the cost of energy usage for the two machines. The equation is the same as previously illustrated (Btu rating × total annual operating hours × cost per watt-hour). In this illustration, the Btu ratings, obtainable from the vendor, for Models A and B are 38 and 45, respectively. In addition to determining energy usage in this manner, the efficiency of the units can be determined from the energy guide information, which is required by federal law to be attached to electrical equipment.[8] The asset selection form shows that Model A has a more efficient energy rating and thus a lower energy cost.

In regard to maintenance and repairs, Model B will incur more maintenance costs than Model A. This estimate is based on the cost of five-year warranties that can be separately purchased with the photocopier and from cost data provided from another similar-sized library that is already using Model B.

The staff time that is needed to service the machines is estimated based on the size of the copy trays and the complexity of the paper path in the machines. The larger the trays and the less complex the paper path, the less staff time and corresponding salary are assignable to a machine. Here, too, Model B is more costly. Often when new technology or equipment is introduced into an organization, there may be a tendency to contain costs by not training personnel to use the new asset. It must be realized that an intangible cost attached to inefficient staff performance arises from inadequate training.

The technician's salary is allocated to the machines based on past experience with photocopying machines and with the use of an analogy equation as well as service information provided about Model B's performance from another library that already uses Model B. At this stage in the selection form, the annual operating costs are multiplied by five to determine the annual life cycle operating costs over the five-year lives of the two models.[9]

After this calculation is completed, the salvage values are deducted to arrive at the total life cycle costs of the two assets. As shown in Figure 6-2, Model B is estimated to have a lower salvage value or trade-in value at the end of its life expectancy.

Once these calculations are completed, the results of LCC show that Model B has the higher total life cycle costs. The cost difference between the models is $10,825.80. On an average annual basis, this is $2,165.16. Also, this analysis shows that the differences in the models' purchase prices are less significant than other considerations in purchase choice. The difference in the copy cost per page favors Model B at $0.0205 per copy, compared to Model A at $0.0425 per copy. This difference is caused by the large number of annual copies that can be made by Model B. The importance of a larger number of annual copies available from a photocopier depends on the particular needs of a library. If Model A's number of annual copies is at an acceptable level, then Model A is the best choice by both performance requirements and LCC criteria.

Under LCC analysis, the asset with the lowest operating cost is Model A, but Model B provides the lowest cost per copy. Therefore, a question still remains about which is the best asset to purchase: the model with the lowest operating cost or the one with the lowest cost per copy. Space is provided at the bottom of the asset selection form in Figure 6-2 for the manager's purchase choice to be made. Here, the manager can override the LCC choice. The portion of the asset selection form entitled "Asset Recommended for Purchase and Justification" allows the manager to make a recommendation for the asset of his or her choice. Here, the manager would state any quality or performance considerations he or she believes override selecting the asset with the lowest life cycle costs. In the present illustration, if the manager believes that a high number of copies is more important than lower overall costs, Model B should be recommended. In making that recommendation, the manager should recognize that the number of copies is a cost driver. On the other hand, if the manager believes that lowest overall cost is the most important criterion and the number of annual copies from Model A is acceptable, then Model A should be the recommended choice. LCC analysis is an important tool in managerial decision making, but as with any tool, it should be used in conjunction with managerial judgment. The purpose of LCC is to outline more clearly the effect of the choices available to the manager, not to supplant the manager's decision-making authority.

Present Values and LCC Analysis

The costs shown in Figure 6-2 are not all incurred in the year the asset is purchased. The purchase price, freight, and rewiring costs are incurred in the year the asset is purchased, but the annual operating costs are incurred uniformly over the five-year life of the asset. Therefore, there is a timing difference in these cash outflows. When timing differences exist, another factor needs to be incorporated into the analysis—the time value of money. (For a complete discussion of present values, net present values, and the time value of money, *see* appendix B.) Briefly, present value concepts assume that there is a time value to money and that $1 received today is worth more than if it is received tomorrow or one month from today because money received today can be invested and interest can be earned on that investment. When LCC analysis incorporates time-value concepts, funds received in more distant time periods need to be equated with currently received funds. The process that equates these funds is called *discounting*. When using time-value concepts in asset acquisitions, it is still acceptable to use an asset selection form as illustrated in Figure 6-2. But this form represents only the preliminary step of at least four steps in the asset selection process.

Figure 6-3 begins the process of incorporating both LCC and present value analysis by sequencing the cash outflows by year. It shows the cash outflows and inflows from the two photocopying machines over their estimated five-year lives. The cash flow data are taken from Figure 6-2 and extended over a five-year time frame. The purchase price and installation costs are the same as shown in Figure 6-2, and they, along with the operating cash expenses for Year 1, are $11,161 and $13,152 for Models A and B, respectively. The operating costs are assumed to occur uniformly over the five-year life of the assets. As stated earlier, inflationary changes are ignored. The salvage value obtained from disposing of the equipment is shown as a cash inflow at the end of the assets' lives. As the salvage received is a cash inflow, it is deducted from the cash outflows in Year 5.

It is easy to incorporate other changes in the pattern of inflows and outflows. For example, if a scheduled cash outflow occurs in Year 3 for a periodic overhaul of the equipment, this outflow can easily be incorporated into the schedule. If the lives of the two machines are not both five years, this also can easily be incorporated into the schedule.

The total cash outflows over the five years for the two photocopying machines are shown at the bottom of Figure 6-3, in Part 2. The cash outflows for Model A are less than Model B for each of the five years. In making a comparison among possible machine purchases, the purchase price of one asset may be higher, but the estimated lower operating costs of that asset may make it the least-cost alternative.

In Figure 6-4, the present values of the cash outflows for Models A and B are calculated. In this illustration, the discount rate is assumed to be 10 percent. (*See* appendix B for an explanation of the methods that can be followed in selecting a discount rate.) Using the 10 percent discount rate, a five-year time period, and the present value factors from Table 1 in appendix B,

PART 1: Annual Cash Outflows

	Year				
	1	*2*	*3*	*4*	*5*
Model A					
Purchase price	$ 4,050	—	—	—	—
Installation cost	235	—	—	—	—
Operating costs	6,876	$6,876	$6,876	$6,876	$6,876
Salvage value	—	—	—	—	(375)
Annual cash outflow	$11,161	$6,876	$6,876	$6,876	$6,501
Model B					
Purchase price	$ 3,850	—	—	—	—
Installation cost	260	—	—	—	—
Operating costs	9,042	$9,042	$9,042	$9,042	$9,042
Salvage value	—	—	—	—	(200)
Annual cash outflow	$13,152	$9,042	$9,042	$9,042	$8,842

PART 2: Total Cash Outflow

Year	Model A	Model B
1	$11,161	$13,152
2	6,876	9,042
3	6,876	9,042
4	6,876	9,042
5	6,501	8,842
Total cash outflow	$38,290*	$49,120*

*The slight difference from results in Figure 6-2 is caused by rounding

FIGURE 6-3   Annual and total cash flow schedule by model

entitled "Present Value of a Lump Sum," the total present value for each model is computed.

In making this calculation, the table factors are multiplied by the cash outflow for the corresponding year, resulting in the present value of the cash outflow. After this step, the present values for the five-year period are added to determine the total present value for each model. Notice that the cash out-flow in the last year is lower because of the receipt of cash from the asset's salvage value.

Model A is the better purchase choice because it has the lowest present value. The total difference between the present value of Model A and Model

B is $8,158.73. When present values were not a consideration, the total difference between the two copiers was $10,825.80, favoring Model A. The decrease in the difference in value between the models is caused by discounting the cash outflows, but in both illustrations, with or without present values, the lowest-cost solution is Model A. Although the results in both Figures 6-2 and 6-4 suggest that Model A should be purchased, these results do not always correspond with one another.

The illustrations have concentrated on cash *outflows* in making an asset choice. Although keeping cash outflows to a minimum while providing a full level of services is a major concern for most nonprofit organizations, some assets purchased by a library may provide an opportunity for earning revenues. This is true with a photocopying machine. If the copy machine is used by both library personnel and patrons, patron usage will provide a source of revenue through the cash paid for copies made. When there are both cash outflows and inflows incorporated with time value of money concepts, the technique used to analyze the cash flows is called the *net present value method* rather than present value analysis.

Figure 6-5 shows how cash revenues and cash outflows are netted against one another. In the illustration, the copies made by patrons are sold for $0.05 each, and 50 percent of the total annual copy capacity of each machine will be used by paying patrons. In this case, Model B has a higher annual revenue because it can produce a greater number of copies annually than Model A.

For years one through five, the annual revenues from copy sales are deducted from the annual costs as previously computed. Once the cash inflow is deducted, the two models show quite different results. Model B begins to show net cash inflows in year two, but Model A continues to show net cash

	Model A			Model B		
Year	Cash Outflow	Table Factor (10%)	Present Value	Cash Outflow	Table Factor (10%)	Present Value
1	$11,161	× .909 =	$10,145.35	$13,152	× .909 =	$11,955.17
2	6,876	× .826 =	5,679.58	9,042	× .826 =	7,468.69
3	6,876	× .751 =	5,163.88	9,042	× .751 =	6,790.54
4	6,876	× .683 =	4,696.31	9,042	× .683 =	6,175.69
5	6,501	× .621 =	4,037.12	8,842	× .621 =	5,490.88
Total present values			$29,722.24			$37,880.97

FIGURE 6-4 Present values of cash outflows for five-year period

		Model A				Model B	
Year	Cash Outflow	Cash Inflow Revenues	Net Amount (Out) In		Cash Outflow	Cash Inflow Revenues	Net Amount (Out) In
1	$11,161	– $4,500*	= $ (6,661)		$13,152	– $12,000†	= $ (1,152)
2	6,876	– 4,500	= (2,376)		9,042	– 12,000	= 2,958
3	6,876	– 4,500	= (2,376)		9,042	– 12,000	= 2,958
4	6,876	– 4,500	= (2,376)		9,042	– 12,000	= 2,958
5	6,501	– 4,500	= (2,001)		8,842	– 12,000	= 3,158
Net cash outflow			$(15,790)		Net cash inflow		$10,880

*Model A's photocopying revenues: 180,000 × .50 × .05 = $4,500
† Model B's photocopying revenues: 480,000 × .50 × .05 = $12,000

FIGURE 6-5 Determining the net cash outflow or inflow based on photocopying revenues

outflows over the entire time period. Once the net cash flows are determined for the two models, the next step is to equate the net cash inflows and outflows from the different time periods by using the table factors for 10 percent from Table 1 in appendix B. This calculation is made in Figure 6-6.

The net cash inflows and outflows for each year are multiplied by the present value table factor for that year. The sum of these amounts is called the net present value for Models A and B. This total is now called the net present value rather than the present value because both cash outflows and inflows are part of the calculation. The net present values show a $12,667.24 net cash *outflow* for Model A and a net cash *inflow* of $7,599.03 for Model B. This significant cost difference between the two models is equal to $20,266.27

		Model A			Model B	
Year	Cash (Outflow) or Inflow	Table Factor (10%)	Present Value	Cash (Outflow) or Inflow	Table Factor (10%)	Present Value
1	$(6,661)	× .909	= $ (6,054.85)	$(1,152)	× .909 =	$(1,047.17)
2	(2,376)	× .826	= (1,962.58)	2,958	× .826 =	2,443.31
3	(2,376)	× .751	= (1,784.38)	2,958	× .751 =	2,221.46
4	(2,376)	× .683	= (1,622.81)	2,958	× .683 =	2,020.31
5	(2,001)	× .621	= (1,242.62)	3,158	× .621 =	1,961.12
Net present value			$(12,667.24)			$ 7,599.03

FIGURE 6-6 Determining the net present values based on photocopying revenues

over the five-year life of the assets. The results of these calculations indicate that Model B is now the best purchase choice for the library. This change is caused by the cash inflows generated from copy revenues and Model B's ability to produce a higher volume of copies. Of course, this assumes that all copies estimated to be sold to patrons are actually sold. Most library assets do not provide the opportunity to generate revenues; therefore, LCC analysis usually emphasizes cost outflows.

Exercise 6-2

A Heating System Replacement

The steam heating system at Hot Springs Community Library, a small library in West Virginia, was very inefficient and expensive to operate. The library director wanted to determine if it would be more economical to purchase a new gas heating system. Information was collected about the old system, and a vendor provided cost information about the new system that was being considered for purchase. The new system would require ductwork in the ceiling and attic of the library building. The following information was collected about the costs of the two systems.

	Current System	*New Furnace*
Purchase price	None; already in place	$30,000
Expected life	10 years	15 years
Annual electricity use @ .10 per kWh	160,000 kWh	50,000 kWh
Annual gas use	none	$7,000
Salvage value	none	$2,000
Annual maintenance cost	$800	$1,000
Installation	none	$4,000

1. Determine the life cycle costs of the two assets over the ten years of the remaining life of the old asset. Use present value analysis and assume a 9 percent interest rate.

2. How would the life cycle analysis change if the library expected to move to a new building eight years from the current date?

Integrated Library Computer System

As a second example, assume a library is evaluating several integrated library computer systems it is considering for purchase. This example is slightly different from the previous illustration because there are no revenues, but there is a cash savings that reduces the total cash outflow from the purchase. The analysis concentrates on the cost aspects of this purchase. This system is reviewed for a medium-sized university library consisting of 450,000 circulations and titles and 25,000 patrons. It will provide for database management, cataloging, acquisitions, serials control, authority record management, public access control, and circulation control. It will include central site hardware, ninety terminals, and supporting hardware for management reports with database inquiry and OCLC/OPAC interface. There will be no telecommunication equipment in this package. Assume that integrated library management packages for medium-sized university libraries vary in price from $575,000 to $800,000.

Multiple factors need to be evaluated when a system of this nature is being purchased by a library. The competitive bid process, the level of service by the vendor, the ability of the system to meet the library's need, and the cost of upgrades are examples of some of the considerations. In Figure 6-7, the focus is on the cost incurrence over the estimated five-year life cycle of the system. At the end of this life cycle, the system will be technologically obsolete. This cost evaluation does not mean that other nonfinancial factors are not important, but the main concern in this illustration is on cost aspects of the investment.

The cost data from two vendors of integrated library management systems are analyzed using an asset selection form in Figure 6-7. The one-time initial costs are shown in the upper part of the form and annual operating costs in the lower section. Initial costs include charges for hardware at the central site, terminals, software, license fee, file preparation cost, and developmental charges. For Vendor A, file preparation costs are based on a charge of $0.1556 per title in the library (450,000 titles). Vendor B is not charging a separate fee for file preparation charges. Both vendors will merge current holdings into the new bibliographic database. Developmental costs include the temporary assignment to the library of two programmers from the university's computer services division to help the library debug and adapt the new system, along with the library's internal computer staff costs. The developmental costs also include the cost of staff time devoted to selecting the vendor and design alternatives for the library. More committee time will probably be involved with Vendor B because more options and configurations are available from this vendor. Another cost under developmental charges is the construction costs required to rewire and update the library's electrical system so that the integrated management system can be installed. The amount for rewiring shown in the asset selection form is based on preliminary estimates from electrical contractors.

	Vendor A	Vendor B	
Initial costs			
Central site hardware	$ 280,000	$ 330,000	
Terminals and support costs	140,000	100,000	
Software cost	200,000	106,000	
License fee (one-time charge)	150,000	175,000	
File preparation cost (cost per title:	70,000	—	
$.1556 × 450,000)			
Developmental and implementation charges			
Assignment to library of two programmers			
from central administration	50,000	50,000	
Other computer staff	18,000	18,000	
Staff allocated time to selection committee	19,000	23,000	
Construction cost (rewiring)	112,000	95,000	
Total purchase price and installation cost	$1,039,000	$ 897,000	(A)
Annual operating costs			
Central site hardware maintenance	$ 18,000	$ 40,000	
Terminal maintenance	18,000	22,000	
Software maintenance	24,000	7,000	
Additional training	10,000	15,000	
Annual upgrades	50,000	70,000	
Annual license fee	20,000	10,000	
Material and supplies	18,000	30,000	
Increase in staff idle time between computer			
cycles (est.)	2,800	700	
Total annual operating costs	$ 160,800	$ 194,700	
Estimated life	× 5	× 5	
Life cycle costs without telephone charges	$ 804,000	$ 973,500	
Telephone support charges			
Vendor A (after first year 6,000 × 4)	24,000	—	
Vendor B (after second year 5,000 × 3)	—	15,000	
Total life cycle operating costs	$ 828,000	$ 988,500	(B)
Less estimated salvage value	$ (17,000)	$ (14,000)	(C)
Total life cycle costs (A)+(B)−(C)	$1,850,000	$1,871,500	
Annual average cost (based on five-year life)	$ 371,200	$ 376,300	
Cost per title (450,000) per year	.825	.836	

Asset Recommended for Purchase and Justification:

FIGURE 6-7   Asset selection form for a computerized integrated library management system

Under developmental costs, there are $18,000 and $50,000 charges for other computer staff and programmer assignment, respectively. These charges are the same in both vendor's cost estimates. If a charge is the same for both alternatives, it does not affect a cost-based choice between the assets. In this example, the $18,000 and $50,000 charges were included in the analysis to show the library's total cost commitment, but these costs have no effect on the final asset selected. Only costs that differ—differential costs—influence the selection process. This concept will be discussed in more detail in chapter 7.

The lower portion of the illustration shows the annual operating costs that will be incurred to properly maintain the system: charges for hardware and software maintenance, training, annual upgrades in the system, and an annual license fee. The estimated cost of materials and supplies differs widely between the two systems. Another cost factor is the increase in staff idle time as a result of cycle time between computer jobs. *Cycle time* can be defined as the unproductive time between different activities.[10] This changes from a manual system, where personnel can put one job down and immediately continue work on a second job. With a computerized system, preparation time is required prior to data entry; waiting time for access and from downtime on the system also occurs. The system provided by Vendor A has a higher cycle time component. Also, included in this section are telephone support charges. These vary slightly between vendors. Vendor A provides free telephone support for the first year; Vendor B provides this support for the first two years.

Finally, as in the photocopying machine example presented earlier, the cost of energy use is a factor in the annual operating costs. Here, however, the energy use between the systems would have to be calculated separately for each electrical component in the system. For example, electrical cost for the central computer hardware, terminals, and printers would have to be calculated for both systems. This complication was not included in the illustration.

The total of the life cycle costs shows a purchase decision favoring Vendor A by $21,500—the difference in total life cycle costs. This difference is significant, but a purchase decision made at this point does not take into account the time value of money. The annual average cost and the cost per title are calculated at the bottom of the asset selection form. It is always useful to develop a per-unit activity measure for the assets being evaluated.

When the time value of money is taken into consideration, cash outflows are sequenced to the proper year of the five-year period. In Figure 6-8, which can be included as part of an asset selection report, the cash inflows and outflows for the integrated management system are shown for Vendors A and B based on the cost data in Figure 6-7. The total cash outflows for Vendors A and B are shown at the bottom of Figure 6-8. Model A has a higher initial cash outlay, but its cost of operations is less, resulting in the smallest total cash outflow.

Once the yearly cash outflows are determined for the five-year period, they are multiplied by the present value discount factors of 10 percent from Table 1 in appendix B. The results are shown in Figure 6-9. This step is used to calculate the present value of the yearly cash outflows for Vendors A and B and totaled for each vendor. The total present value over the five-year period

---

PART 1: Annual Cash Flow

	Year				
	1	*2*	*3*	*4*	*5*
Vendor A					
Total purchase and installation cost	$1,039,000	—	—	—	—
Operating costs	160,800*	$166,800	$166,800	$166,800	$166,800
Salvage value—an inflow	—	—	—	—	(17,000)
Annual cash outflow	$1,199,800	$166,800	$166,800	$166,800	$149,800
Vendor B					
Total purchase and installation cost	$ 897,000	—	—	—	—
Operating costs	194,700	$194,700	$199,700	$199,700	$199,700
Salvage value—an inflow	—	—	—	—	(14,000)
Annual cash outflow	$1,091,700	$194,700	$199,700	$199,700	$185,700

*Adjustment for telephone charges: Vendor A, $6,000 less in year one; Vendor B, $5,000 less in years one and two

PART 2: Total Cash Outflow

Year	Vendor A	Vendor B
1	$1,199,800	$1,091,700
2	166,800	194,700
3	166,800	199,700
4	166,800	199,700
5	149,800	185,700
Total cash outflow	$1,850,000	$1,871,500

FIGURE 6-8   Annual and total cash flow schedule by vendor

	Vendor A			Vendor B		
Year	**Cash Outflow**	**Table Factor (10%)**	**Present Value**	**Cash Outflow**	**Table Factor (10%)**	**Present Value**
1	$1,199,800	× .909 =	$1,090,618	$1,091,700	× .909 =	$ 992,355
2	166,800	× .826 =	137,777	194,700	× .826 =	160,822
3	166,800	× .751 =	125,267	199,700	× .751 =	149,975
4	166,800	× .683 =	113,924	199,700	× .683 =	136,395
5	149,800	× .621 =	93,026	185,700	× .621 =	115,320
Total present value			$1,560,612			$1,554,867

FIGURE 6-9   Present values of cash outflows for five-year period

for Vendors A and B are $1,560,612 and $1,554,867, respectively—a difference of $5,745 in favor of Vendor B. The difference in this case is not significant when compared with the price of the systems. Therefore, the selection decision could be based on other criteria—service levels, reputation of the vendors, and so forth.

At this point, it is necessary to ascertain whether there are any other cost considerations affecting the two systems. In evaluating the photocopying machines earlier, it was determined that if photocopies were sold to the public, it would change the purchase choice between the machines. Although there are no revenues that can be generated from these two integrated library systems, salary cost reductions may affect the decision.

One additional facet of this analysis relates to the savings in salary and fringe benefits that may occur from a reduction in the clerical staff needed to process an increasing volume of circulated items in the future. In other words, without the integrated system, additional clerical staff would be necessary to handle the increase in items circulated in the library. With the new system, future clerical staff hirings could be curtailed. In Figure 6-10, without the integrated system from Vendor A, it would be necessary to hire additional staff whose salaries would total $40,000.[11] Vendor B's system is slightly more labor intensive. For that reason, the salary savings are only $30,000 annually.

The present value of the cost outflows is recalculated, taking into consideration the estimated salary savings from limiting the future expansion of clerical positions in the library. The salary and fringe benefit savings are deducted from the cash outflows calculated in Figure 6-9. After this, the present value table factors for a discount rate of 10 percent are multiplied times the remainder. The net present values for Vendor A and B differ from those pres-

	Vendor A			Vendor B		
Year	Cash Outflow Less Salary Savings	Table Factor (10%)	Present Value	Cash Outflow Less Salary Savings	Table Factor (10%)	Present Value
1	[$1,199,800 – $40,000] × .909 =		$1,054,258	[$1,091,700 – $30,000] × .909 =		$ 965,085
2	[$166,800 – $40,000] × .826 =		104,737	[$194,700 – $30,000] × .826 =		136,042
3	[$166,800 – $40,000] × .751 =		95,227	[$199,700 – $30,000] × .751 =		127,445
4	[$166,800 – $40,000] × .683 =		86,604	[$199,700 – $30,000] × .683 =		115,905
5	[$149,800 – $40,000] × .621 =		68,186	[$185,700 – $30,000] × .621 =		96,690
	Total present value		$1,409,012			$1,441,167

FIGURE 6-10   Determining the net present values of cash outflows with projected salary savings

ent values previously calculated in Figure 6-9. The total net present values for Vendor A and B are $1,409,012 and $1,441,167, respectively, a difference of $32,155 in favor of Vendor A's system. A difference of $32,155 is significant enough to influence the choice between the two systems, and the decision under LCC analysis would be to purchase Vendor A's system.

Again, note that a number of other performance criteria and quality of service considerations are not being taken into account in the analysis. The illustration concentrates only on the differences between the cost factors.

Exercise 6-3

Starting a Revenue Venture

Joe Java, the director of the Heartland Library, is trying to determine whether the library should devote a section of its floor space to a revenue-generating coffee bar. The coffee bar would be called the Book Nook. Patrons could sit at tables and in comfortable chairs while they sipped coffee, ate bakery products, and read books or decided which book to check out of the library.

The board has approved the idea and provided the initial monies to purchase equipment, but the board insists that the operation must not use up any budget dollars for its operating expenses and it must generate enough money to replace its equipment. Joe has decided to use present value analysis to determine the feasibility of opening up a coffee bar. He has received estimates of $10,000 for an espresso machine that will produce all the lattes and espressos required. In addition, the library will hire a part-time employee to work in the coffee bar at an annual salary of $15,000. The library will purchase chairs and tables for $1,500 and the necessary tableware and silverware for $200.

A time period of seven years has been selected to evaluate the project because at the end of seven years, the equipment will need to be replaced. Using a time period of seven years and a discount rate of 5 percent, Joe wants to determine whether the coffee bar will earn a positive net present value or cash profit. It is estimated that fifty cups of coffee will be sold each day for $2 each, and the library will net $1.50 on each cup sold. Although bakery products will be sold, these products will be sold to break even. The library expects to earn revenues on its coffee sales only.

1. Determine whether the coffee bar will earn a profit over the seven-year period. If it will earn a cash profit, how much will be earned?

2. If you determined in number 1 that the coffee bar will make a cash profit, calculate the minimum number of cups of coffee that can be sold each day for the coffee bar to break even over the seven years.

Limitations of LCC Analysis

The limitations to present value or net present value analysis should be mentioned. The major limitation of this technique is the short-term time frame in which it can practically, not theoretically, be applied. This occurs for three reasons. The first reason is the assumption that the discount rate used at the beginning of the project will remain unchanged over the period of the analysis. Obviously, as the time period for the analysis becomes longer, this assumption becomes more inaccurate. Essentially, this is a problem in selecting the correct discount rate. Interest rates do change, sometimes dramatically, from projected rates, and as the time period of analysis is extended, reliable results are more difficult to obtain.

A second reason for the short-term nature of the technique is that any cash outflow estimates are likely to change significantly from actual amounts as the projection is extended further into the future. Again, this is an estimation problem. As a result, managers may place more faith in short-term projections.

A third reason present value methods are more closely tied to short-term periods is because many times high discount rates are chosen to evaluate projects with the hope that this practice will eliminate less desirable purchase choices. As a result of choosing a high discount rate, assets with a long period of cash flows are automatically viewed less favorably than those with shorter periods of cash flows. The selection of a single discount rate to be used throughout the organization helps to eliminate this problem.

A number of managerial estimates must be made in evaluating the purchase decision for long-term assets. Some estimates may be purposely biased by managers to provide a more favorable result in the asset acquisition trade-offs. This type of behavior was discussed in chapter 1 under the managerial model of agency theory. A large portion of the hard data required for making cost projections is based on managerial estimates, and if the agency theory behavioral model is accepted, these estimates need to be scrutinized both before and after the investment is made to ensure that realistic estimates are provided.

Finally, nonquantifiable factors, such as the quality of vendor services and political realities within the library, are likely to be just as important as financial information in the asset selection process. These nonquantifiable factors are not considered in present value analysis; therefore, this is another limitation of the method.

LCC PERFORMANCE EVALUATION

Managerial performance should be viewed from a wider perspective than just financial results. A financial perspective is important, but to gain a complete evaluation, financial performance cannot be viewed alone. For example, successful financial performance does not automatically translate into satisfactory patron service or employee development. For this reason, LCC performance evaluation needs to go beyond a singular financial outcome. Here, the financial perspective is reviewed, and then LCC effects on patron satisfaction and employee performance will be considered.

PART 1: Financial Evaluation

LCC analysis is a useful technique for asset selection. By itself, it provides managers with a structured way of analyzing asset choices. But, to use LCC management within a library environment, LCC must be taken one step further, to the postpurchase stage. LCC management incorporates long-term cost control over assets. Therefore, the selection of assets with the use of LCC analysis techniques is only the first step in asset cost control. Follow-up procedures must be in place to ensure that the cost estimates of annual operating costs were made with reasonable accuracy. If significant deviations are occurring on per-unit output measures or total costs, the reasons for those cost increases need to be determined. Follow-up cost information needs to be accumulated on a long-term basis, with the shortest reporting period equal to one year. The cost data need to be accumulated in a way that shows the cumulative costs incurred. This information then needs to be compared with the data that were initially estimated in the original LCC analysis. If costs are out of control, the library manager needs to provide information and reasons that costs are increasing more rapidly than had been projected by the initial LCC analysis. Depending on the difference between initial life cycle costs and the current level of cost incurrence, it may be necessary to make future, multi-year cost projections based on current cost data to estimate how rapidly costs will continue to increase over the remaining life of the asset. If these cost levels are unacceptable and it appears they cannot be controlled, it may be necessary to consider the abandonment of the asset prior to the end of its useful life as a last resort to curtail accelerating or uncontrollable costs.

Figure 6-11 illustrates a cost report that can be prepared on a yearly basis to determine how accurately an asset's costs are following LCC projections. The asset in Figure 6-11 is the photocopying machine, Model B. Here the data are developed after the machine has been in use for three years. It should be noted that the costs shown are the actual costs, unadjusted for the time value of money. Only total costs and not present values are a consideration.

There are three basic aspects to the report in Figure 6-11. Part 1 deals with three-year cumulative cost comparisons. Part 2 records several asset activity measures, such as the average and annual number of copies made, cost data per copy, and the percentage of time the machine is not properly working. Part 3 shows the revenues collected from the copies made by patrons, estimated to be one-half of the copies made. Therefore, the revenues represent one-half the copies made. Part 3 is unique to this asset; most library assets do not provide a source of revenues.

The headings across the top of Part 1 of the report show costs accumulated for the current year (column two), compared with the yearly cost estimates under LCC analysis (column one), and the variance between these two costs (column three). The headings also show the actual average costs for the three years the photocopying machine has been in service (column four), including the current year. The actual average costs are compared with the annual projected costs (column one) in determining the three-year average variances (column five).

Significant variances in the report need to be analyzed in more detail. The manager who developed and approved the original LCC estimates will need to explain these deviations. By analyzing significant variances, the operating cost of an asset can be better controlled. Aspects of a manager's performance evaluation should be related to this report. If the reasons for cost

PART 1: Operating Costs

Annual Operating Costs	1 Annual LCC Projected Costs	2 Cash Operating Costs for Year 3	3 Cash Cost Variance F or (U)*	4 Three-Year Average Annual Operating Costs	5 Three-Year Average Variance F or (J)*
Material and supplies	$4,800.00	$5,500.00	$(700.00)	$ 7,000.00	$(2,200.00)
Energy	1,029.60	1,200.00	(170.40)	1,600.00	(570.40)
Maintenance and repairs	637.00	650.00	(13.00)	725.00	(88.00)
Staff/student salary	875.00	900.00	(25.00)	1,000.00	(125.00)
In-house technician	1,700.00	1,200.00	500.00	1,800.00	(100.00)
Total annual operating costs	$9,041.60	$9,450.00	$(408.40)	$12,125.00	$(3,083.40)
Average purchase/installation cost	$ 822.00	$ 822.00		$ 822.00	

* (U) Unfavorable; F Favorable

PART 2: Activity Measures

	1	2		4	
Number of copies	480,000	500,000		560,000	
Cost per copy	.020	.020		.023	
Downtime percent†	3%	4%		3%	

†Downtime percent = hours of downtime/total machine hours available (2,080)

PART 3: Revenues Earned

	1	2	3	4	5
Total cash received	$12,000	$15,000	$3,000	$11,000	$(1,000)

FIGURE 6-11 Year 3 annual performance evaluation of LCC projections for photocopying machine (Model B) annual operating costs and revenues shown on an annual asset cost report

overruns are not reasonable, this should be reflected negatively on a manager's performance evaluation.

In reviewing this report, it is immediately apparent that over the three years the average use of materials and supplies has been excessive. Under the original LCC analysis, $4,800 was predicted (*see* column one), but the actual amount used over the three-year period averaged $7,000 (column four). Certain indications may provide a reason for this discrepancy from the projected amount. In the current year, the cost per copy is equal to the projection made at $0.02 per copy (shown in Part 2), but over the three-year period the average cost per copy, shown in column four, is $0.023 per copy. Furthermore, when the number of copies based on the average revenue collected of $11,000 is computed $\{[(\$11,000 \times 3 \text{ years})/\$0.05] \times 2 = 1,320,000 \text{ copies}\}$ and compared with the total number of copies based on the three-year average of 560,000 per year $(560,000 \times 3 = 1,680,000 \text{ copies})$, the difference is 360,000 copies.

There are two possible explanations for this wide difference. First, the managerial projection that half the annual copies made would be purchased by paying patrons is incorrect as fewer copies were purchased. The second explanation is that the difference arose because someone was able to gain unauthorized access to the machine. The $7,000 average annual expenditure on materials and supplies indicates that 700,000 annual copies ($7,000/.01) or 2,100,000 copies over the three-year period should have been made based on LCC projections of materials and supplies cost of $0.01 for this machine. This additional evidence shows that photocopies may have been made without proper authorization during the first two years the machine was in use.

The discrepancy needs to be investigated. If the copy discrepancy can be traced to increases in the cost of supplies, then the manager in charge of the machine need only provide information to show that attempts are being made to provide good-quality materials at reasonable prices. Additionally, original LCC estimates should be checked to ensure that bias was not purposefully introduced into the estimates.

If the discrepancy is traceable to unauthorized use, the situation is more serious, and the manager in charge of the photocopying machine needs to be held accountable for the lack of control in this area of responsibility. In addition, new controls need to be instituted to prevent continued unauthorized access to the machine.

Part 2 of the report includes information about asset activity measures. One is the number of copies produced by the photocopying machine on both an annual basis and as an average. Although the vendor indicated that the copy capacity of the machine was 480,000 copies annually, the actual number produced has been higher than that in each year. The second activity measure is the downtime or the time the machine has not been working. This is deemed as the time the problem was recognized to the time it was repaired by the vendor. The total amount of downtime is recorded for each year and divided by the total time the photocopy machine should be available for use during the year, in this case 2,080 hours. Downtime is equal to 3 to 4 percent of the total available time. This downtime percentage is not significantly different than originally projected in column one at 3 percent, and in light of the number of copies made above the original estimate of 480,000, it appears acceptable. But, it is a measure that should be recorded to provide an indication of the machine's reliability and whether repairs are performed on a timely basis by the vendor.

Activity measures will vary with the specific asset under consideration. For example, downtime measures could include the mean time to repair the system after a breakdown, the percent of time the machine is down compared with the total time that it should be in use during a specific period, or the time lapse between the date the service call was placed and the time it took to satisfactorily repair the equipment. Downtime might be a significant contributor to the increase in per-unit cost of a system. This occurs as output declines causing the total costs, which remain relatively constant, to be spread over fewer units, thus automatically increasing per-unit cost.

Another activity measure that may contribute to cost increases is waiting time. Staff time and salary costs may be wasted because of the significant waiting time required to use a new system. This cost increase may be traced to several causes. For example, a computer system may have significant waiting time if the system is internally slow or if there is limited access because of a lack of terminal stations. Waiting time can be caused by a system not working at peak efficiency because of breakdowns or it may be caused by scheduling difficulties. Waiting time cost may have been unintentionally designed into the system if attempts were made to save money by not purchasing sufficient terminals or selecting software with minimum capabilities, and as a result, turnaround time is slow. Although it may be apparent that the system is not working properly as the number of complaints increase, without the collection of activity data, the exact problem may be difficult to identify.

Other activity measures can be related to the amount of preparation time required to access a system. This may be dependent on machine requirements for job input, or it can be related to the amount of staff time required to service a machine. For example, supplies required by a photocopying machine may be inconveniently stored so that it adds to the staff time and salary costs of servicing the machine.

These are some examples of some additional activity measures besides those shown in Figure 6-11. Activity measures are used to provide clues as to the reasons the annual operating costs of an asset are higher than anticipated in the original LCC projection. Of course, inflation does impact the annual cost of operations, but its effect should not automatically be assumed to be the lone cause of cost increases.

The third section of the annual asset cost report shows the revenues that have been collected from the sale of photocopies to the public. This information should be traced to this asset; it has been shown as an important factor in the purchase decision. In Figure 6-11, third-year revenues are above those projected; in the first two years, revenues were below projections. This could be related to the assumed unauthorized use of the photocopying machine, which was stopped in the third year.

One difficulty with preparing the annual asset cost report is that the cost information in the accounting records may not be readily available in the format needed. Much of the cost information in the accounting records is aggregated by expense categories. Although this is useful for preparing financial statements, it is not useful in analyzing the cost of important asset systems in a library or in implementing LCC management techniques. Cost increases are part of the effort to reclassify accounting information. If reporting costs can be controlled and the reclassified information used effectively, then the additional costs of reclassification can be justified. If the annual cost information is not going to be used by managers, for whatever reason, then it should not be accumulated. In those cases, LCC analysis may still be used, but the cost-control system is incomplete without LCC management as well as LCC analysis for asset acquisition.

LCC management is concerned with comparing the projected costs with the actual costs incurred and reviewing activity measures that can cause those costs to increase. LCC management is long-term management, and this is seen in Figure 6-11 as activity information is provided not just for the current year, but also for the entire period that the asset has been in use.

PART 2: Nonfinancial Measures

Wider performance dimensions than just financial are important in evaluating managerial-instituted changes. Many times these other measures are referred to as nonfinancial measures because the data needed for their development are found outside the regular financial records maintained within the organization.

The approach used here is based on the balanced scorecard (BSC) approach developed by R. S. Kaplan and D. P Norton.[12] The BSC views four areas of evaluation—financial, patron, employee, and organization process measures—as being integrated with one another. Here, LCC performance evaluation will be expanded beyond financial measures to include nonfinancial measures as related to patron services and employee functions. Organizational process measures will be reserved for a later chapter.

Under BSC, employee measures have been described as those growth and learning goals that result in the development of a well-prepared and highly motivated workforce. Patron measures are directed at determining how satisfied users of library services are with those services. All measures must fit within overall library mission objectives. In Figure 6-12, a matrix of financial, employee/staff, and patron measures are illustrated. The library's mission statement is "to provide effective performance to patrons."

In Figure 6-12, measures are divided into short-term (i.e., tactical) measures and long-term (i.e., strategic) measures. Yet, all evaluative measures are united under the library's mission of effective performance to patrons, and all measures need to be directed toward helping each other achieve that goal. For example, additional staff training would be expected to increase patron satisfaction in their use of the new technology and help avoid variances from projected LCC cost projections.

Mission Statement: To Provide Effective Performance to Patrons

	Financial	Employee/Staff	Patrons
Short-Term		Number of training seminars provided	Satisfaction survey as related to specific technology-related questions
		Number of staff voluntarily attending training seminars	Trends in the type and number of complaints, before and after introduction of new technology
Long-Term	Variances from projected LCC costs	Number of new LCC reports filed/compared with those approved for purchase	Support at library board meetings as those meetings relate to new technology proposals

FIGURE 6-12 Integrating financial performance measures with nonfinancial performance measures

As LCC is a long-term approach, the variance measure shown in Figure 6-12 is considered to be a long-term measure. Variances from LCC cost projections are shown as the only financial measure. The importance of this measure was explained in Part 1. Under employee/staff measures, the evaluation is based on training employees to use the new integrated library system. Suggested measures to evaluate training levels could be the number of seminars provided, the number of staff voluntarily attending training seminars, and the number of new LCC reports filed. These measures are divided into long-term and short-term measures in the matrix. A long-term measure is the number of new LCC reports. It is assumed that as the staff become more familiar with LCC, they would file more requests using LCC. The training seminars on the integrated library computer system, previously described, would be necessary to have a well-motivated and well-versed workforce in understanding this technology.

Nonfinancial measures of patron satisfaction are related to survey questionnaire results as associated with the new technology purchase, the type and the number of written complaints before and after the introduction of the technology, and patron support at library board meetings related to technology agendas as compared with other nontechnology-oriented board meetings. It can be seen that the term *measures* also needs to be interpreted in a broad nonfinancial perspective as some of these measures are subjective and cannot be reduced to numerical counts.

It can be seen that financial measures by themselves cannot be used to determine how well the organization is meeting its mission objective. Having LCC cost variances that are favorable does not mean that employee learning is adequate, nor does it mean that patrons are satisfied with the service that is being provided.

Exercise 6-4

Nonfinancial Performance Measures

The Central Meza Library has recently set up a series of ten new PCs with Internet access in a room that had previously been used for library board meetings. This room was the only available space in the building. The board had concurred with the change. The installed cost of the PCs was $15,000.

Make a recommendation as to several nonfinancial performance measures that could be coordinated with one another to meet the library's mission of providing "the best" service to its patrons. Explain how the measures are coordinated with one another.

SUMMARY

In using these LCC techniques to project future costs, an understanding of the interrelationship of the costs and the elements that cause costs to increase should develop. The selection of assets using LCC techniques does not use the traditional selection method of matching the budget appropriation with the cost of a new asset to determine which asset to purchase. LCC requires consideration of factors that are usually given little emphasis under traditional asset selection methods. LCC management goes beyond the selection choice as it requires follow-up procedures to be in place to determine if the projected benefits from the assets are eventually received and how accurately costs were predicted. Furthermore, the effective use of LCC requires that follow-up procedures be related to management performance evaluation.

Notes

1. If a single one-year source of supplies becomes a series of short-term contracts over a long-term period, then this supply source should be evaluated using LCC.

2. When there is a great deal of uncertainty in the level of cash flows arising from the installation of an asset, there may be a value attached to delaying the decision to make a purchase until the forecasted cash flow streams become more certain. A derivative of net present value called real options analysis is used to evaluate the present value of an asset in such cases. *See* Martha Amram and Nalin Kulatilaka, *Real Options: Managing Strategic Investment in an Uncertain World* (Boston: Harvard Business School Press, 1999).

3. For example, asbestos removal costs can be extremely expensive and should be considered to be part of the cost of the new asset because these costs would not be incurred if the old asset were not being replaced.

4. Estimating costs with parametric equations can become very complex. It is possible to use regression analysis in parametric estimation of operating costs. An equation of this nature is based on historical data and used to predict cost levels for a new asset. Such an equation would be as follows:

$$\text{Total cost} = A + B(x) + C(y) + D(z) + \text{systemic error (I)}$$

In this equation, x, y, and z are elements that represent factors computed through the mathematics of regression analysis. The elements B, C, and D represent real data, such as the Btu rating, that influence the total cost. The element A represents a constant computed with regression analysis.

5. Although LCC is largely related to financial objectives, the entire library must have long-term goals that go beyond only financial objectives. For example, the level of patron satisfaction and employee learning and growth goals are other important long-term goals.

6. In Figure 6-2, the total life cycle costs are shown as (A) + (B) + (C) − (D). This total is the summation of the purchase price (A), installation costs (B), and annual operation costs (C) reduced by the salvage value (D).

7. Model A: $3,600 = ($0.02 × 180,000); Model B: $4,800 = ($0.01 × 480,000).

8. Energy guide information is attached to many consumer products, such as air conditioners. This information provides estimates of the annual energy cost of operating such equipment. Cost data are provided based on hours of yearly use translated into kilowatt-hours (kWh). The vendor of any type of electrical equipment should provide the same type of information to a potential purchaser.

9. It is assumed that these costs are constant over the five-year period, but they may not remain constant. For example, if an asset such as a bookmobile is scheduled for an overhaul in Year 4 of its five-year life, this expenditure must be incorporated into the asset selection form as a one-time addition and not multiplied by five.

10. This idle time, or downtime, is also known as setup time required for the next job.

11. Note that changes for inflation are not incorporated into the salary figures.

12. *See* R. S. Kaplan and D. P. Norton, "The Balanced Scorecard: Measures That Drive Performance," *Harvard Business Review* (January-February 1992): 71-79; and Kaplan and Norton, *The Balanced Scorecard: Translating Strategy into Action* (Boston: Harvard Business School Press, 1996).

Bibliography

Anthony, R. N., and D. W. Young. *Management Control in Nonprofit Organizations.* Homewood, Ill.: Irwin, 1988.

Brown, R. J., and R. R. Yanuck. *Introduction to Life Cycle Costing.* Englewood Cliffs, N.J.: Prentice-Hall, 1985.

Dillon, B. S. *Life-Cycle Costing: Techniques, Models, and Applications.* Newark, N.J.: Gordon & Breach Science Publishers, 1989.

CHAPTER

7

Selected Managerial
Decision-Making Techniques

Both chapters 6 and 7 explain techniques for solving very specific managerial problems rather than discussing the organization-wide control issues covered in chapters 3 and 4. A number of for-profit managerial techniques can be adapted to the special environment of the nonprofit organization and used to help make operating decisions. In this chapter, four methods are selected for detailed analysis: break-even analysis combined with high-low methods, differential cost analysis, probability forecasting, and learning-curve applications.

These managerial techniques are used to make decisions about the use of scarce library resources. This process consists of two parts. Managers first use analytical techniques as their justification for using the organization's resources to achieve a predetermined objective. Afterward, managerial performance is evaluated by comparing forecasted plans and actual results to determine if stated objectives were actually achieved. Chapter 7 is directed at the first part of this two-step process. The second part of the process—performance evaluation—is discussed in chapter 9.

BREAK-EVEN ANALYSIS

The first managerial technique for making operating decisions that will be explained and illustrated is break-even analysis. *Break-even analysis* utilizes projections of costs, revenues, contributions, and appropriations to determine the level of operations where total costs are equal to total revenues (contributions and appropriations). The point of intersection between total cost and total revenue is called the break-even point because there is no profit. The accrual accounting method is the basis for break-even analysis. Operations conducted below the break-even point result in losses or reduction in nonprofit resources; operations above the break-even point represent a profit or inflow of resources. When nonprofit operations are established to provide the highest level of service without impairing the underlying resources of the organization, then that point is the break-even point.

This analysis can be used for a number of different purposes in the library environment. For example, if a new self-sustaining service is going to be provided by the library, break-even analysis can be used to determine the number of patrons required to use the service at the break-even point—the point where costs are equal to users' fees. As will be explained, break-even analysis can be used to help library management determine the least painful places for budget reductions.

If a public library is selling library T-shirts, book bags, or posters, break-even analysis is used to determine how many units have to be sold before profits are received. This analysis determines if the project is feasible because it may not be possible to sell the required number of items to earn a profit.

The determination of the break-even point is a relatively simple calculation. Two versions of the equation used to calculate the break-even point in units follow:

1. Break-even point $= \dfrac{\text{Fixed cost dollars}}{\underset{\text{(Per unit)}}{\text{Selling price}} - \underset{\text{(Per unit)}}{\text{Variable cost}}}$

2. Break-even point $= \dfrac{\text{Fixed cost dollars}}{\text{Contribution margin per unit}}$

The denominator in equation 2 is the contribution margin. The contribution margin is defined as the difference between the per-unit selling price of an item and its variable cost per unit, and that relationship is shown in the denominator in equation 1. To calculate the break-even point, costs must be separated into fixed and variable costs. The fixed costs represent the numerator of the equation, and the variable costs are used in calculating the contribution margin.[1]

In a simple illustration of this technique, assume a library is considering selling book bags to patrons. The fixed cost of the book bags is their purchased cost from the supplier, which in this case is $12. A total of 300 bags will be purchased, none of which can be returned to the supplier. The library intends to sell them for $15 each. The question to ask is, How many bags will the library have to sell to break even?

The computation of the break-even point requires that the contribution margin be determined. The contribution margin is equal to the difference between the selling price and the variable costs. As there are no variable costs, the contribution margin is equal to the selling price of $15. The break-even point is determined as follows:

$$\text{Break-even point in units } = \frac{\text{Total fixed costs } (\$12 \times 300)}{\text{Contribution margin } (\$15)} = 240 \text{ bags}$$

This means that the library will have to sell 240 book bags before it starts receiving any profits above the original cost for the book bags of $3,600 ($12 × 300). If the library should sell all 300 book bags, it will earn a profit of $900 ($15 received for a book bag × 60 book bags sold above the break-even point of 240 (or $3 × 300). If the library does not believe that 240 book bags can be sold, it should reduce the order. In this example, the break-even point is equal to 80 percent of the number of book bags they order (12/15 = 80 percent).

This calculation provides a quick, easy method to determine when a simple sales project can result in a net inflow of cash to the library. Remember that this is a projection into the future based on managerial estimates, and these estimates are often incorrect. Figure 7-1 shows a graphic illustration of the break-even point.

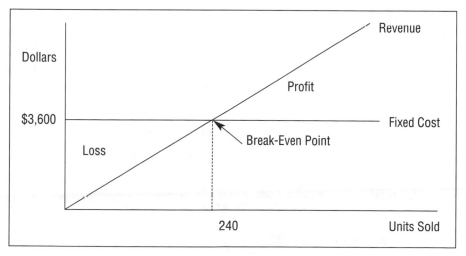

FIGURE 7-1   Break-even chart with fixed costs only

Several characteristics of break-even analysis are shown here. The break-even point is shown in both dollars and units. The horizontal line on the graph represents the fixed costs of $3,600, and the break-even point occurs along this line where it is intersected by revenues. There are no variable costs in this illustration; therefore, the major point of concern relates to the number of book bags sold at the break-even point. This is 240 bags, and it is illustrated with a dotted line from the horizontal axis to the break-even point. The profit and loss areas are shown above and below the break-even point, respectively. This simple break-even chart changes significantly when variable costs are included in the analysis.

To incorporate variable costs into this illustration, assume that the book bags will be personalized with the patron's name when the bag is purchased. The artist, Mr. Z., who will do the personalization requires a fixed payment of $300, and his contract requires that a rate of $0.50 per letter must be paid by the *library* to him. The library wants to maintain a break-even point of 240 bags as previously determined. If the average name has a total of ten letters, the break-even point of 240 book bags will require a total of 2,400 letters. What should the library charge patrons per letter on the book bags?

The selling price and the cost of the bags purchased remain the same, so the break-even point is still 240 bags or 2,400 letters. In this illustration, a price that patrons are charged per letter must be determined at an already specified break-even point. The easiest method for solving this problem is to place all the information given into the break-even equation, shown in Figure 7-2. As we are looking for the selling price, equation 1 is used as in Figure 7-2.

In the equation, the unknown selling price and the variable cost of $0.50 for each letter are in the denominator. The fixed cost of $300 is the numerator. When the equation is solved for the unknown selling price, it is equal to $0.625. This is the minimum price the library should charge for each letter placed on a personalized bag. The average patron's name of ten letters can be placed on the bag for a minimum charge of $6.25 ($0.625 × 10).

$$\text{Break-even point (2,400 letters)} = \frac{\text{Fixed cost dollars (\$300)}}{\text{Unknown selling price (X)} - \text{Variable cost (\$0.50)}}$$

$$2{,}400 \text{ letters} = \frac{\$300}{\text{Unknown selling price (X)} - \$0.50}$$

$$\text{Unknown selling price (x)} = \$0.625$$

FIGURE 7-2 Calculating the price per letter at the break-even point

Figure 7-3 shows the break-even analysis *for the letters only,* in the graphic break-even format. This graph is similar to the one shown in Figure 7-1; however, it also includes a variable cost based on lettering costs. The fixed cost is the fixed payment of $300 required to be paid to Mr. Z. The break-even point is shown in the number of letters (2,400) and dollars ($1,500 = $0.625 × 2,400) charged patrons at the break-even point. This graph is different than the one shown in Figure 7-1 because the variable costs are included as a triangle (ABC) above fixed costs. The areas of profit and loss are shown above and below, respectively, the break-even point on the graph.

The illustrations in Figures 7-1 and 7-3 are examples of how break-even analysis can be used to evaluate decisions in small moneymaking projects such as the sale of book bags, T-shirts, and posters, for example. Break-even analysis can be easily applied to a number of other uses in a library environment. But before those applications are shown, some of the limitations of break-even analysis should be considered.

Break-Even Limitations

There are a number of limitations to break-even analysis. The first limitation is related to distinguishing between fixed and variable costs. In calculating a break-even point, it is necessary to separate fixed costs from variable costs. Doing so may be difficult for several reasons. First, some costs may be a mixture of both fixed and variable costs. To place all costs into a fixed or variable category for break-even analysis, somewhat arbitrary rules are adopted, and unless this is remembered, incorrect decisions may be made.[2]

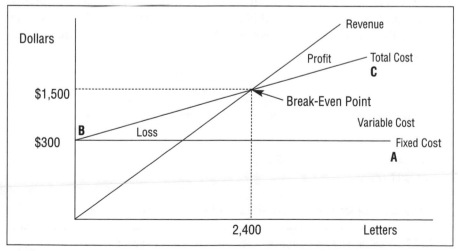

FIGURE 7-3   Break-even chart with variable and fixed costs for personalized letters

Another limitation is related to the concept of fixed costs and the time period under analysis. In a very short time period, costs will maintain their fixed/variable characteristics. But fixed costs may not remain constant over the long-term.

As an example of this difficulty, consider a break-even decision for database searching. Assume that the Reference Department in the library currently accesses only one database and has isolated the costs related to its database search functions: $350 per year for depreciation of equipment (terminal, furniture, etc.), a $150 fee for a maintenance agreement, a $100 charge for phone service to the database, and $1,200 for yearly training updates. There is a $15 per hour charge for the staff person conducting the search, a $30 hourly charge by the vendor, and a $5 communication charge per hour. The library wants to determine the break-even charge per search, assuming that 500 searches will be conducted per year. The average search takes a half hour. Using the break-even equation, these costs can be separated into fixed and variable components.

The fixed costs are depreciation ($350), maintenance charges ($150), phone service ($100), and training ($1,200). The per-hour charges are variable costs. The break-even equation incorporates these costs to solve for the unknown charge per search as shown in Figure 7-4.

In solving the equation, the result is a break-even charge of $28.60 per search when 500 searches are made. This is the average charge for searches. In reviewing the equation relationships, it appears that the best way to reduce the average cost per search would be to increase the number of searches performed each year. This conclusion is reached because the total fixed costs are assumed to be constant, and variable costs will remain constant per unit. If all fixed costs remain constant, this conclusion is true. Using the break-even equation, the average cost per search will be lowered to $26.80 if the number

$$\text{Break-even searches (500)} = \frac{\text{Fixed costs (\$1,800)}}{\text{Cost charged per search (x)} - \text{Variable costs (\$25)}^*}$$

$$\text{Cost charged per search (x)} = \$28.60$$

*The hourly rate for searches is $50 per hour ($15 + $30 + $5) or $25 per half hour

FIGURE 7-4   Calculating the charge per search at the break-even point

of searches is doubled to 1,000. Assume that the library decides to promote this service and increase the number of searches as a convenience to its patrons and to lower its search costs. The analysis assumes that fixed costs remain constant. But, will they stay constant?

To perform 1,000 searches, the number of databases is increased to serve a wider variety of search requests. When this occurs, the service costs increase. With an expansion in databases, additional staff training would increase the training costs. Even if the number of database searches were not increased, training costs would increase in order to qualify more staff to perform the increased number of searches. If the number of searches is doubled, it is reflected in the higher usage of equipment. Charges for usage, such as depreciation, should be recalculated to reflect this change. All these costs are fixed costs, and they are fixed costs in the short run. But, the time horizon for many managerial decisions extends beyond the short time period found in break-even analysis. In this example, the increase in fixed costs causes the average cost per search to remain higher than anticipated. Therefore, decisions based on a short-term managerial tool may result in mistakes.

In addition to the time period effect, two other limitations of break-even analysis should be mentioned: the linearity assumption and the effect of the relevant range on operating decisions based on break-even analysis. The linearity assumption states that the changing relationship between volume and costs is linear—a straight line. Some costs do not follow the linearity assumption, such as costs that step up in constant increments. An example of a step cost is the fixed cost of hiring a staff supervisor. This fixed salary cost steps up with each new supervisor hired; it is not linear. (*See* Figure 2-4 for an illustration of the step function in costs.) Also, not all costs maintain the same linear relationship with volume over the entire volume range under analysis. As has been illustrated, the fixed costs changed as the volume of database searches increased. Additionally, variable costs may not increase at the same constant dollar amount per unit over the entire range of the break-even chart. Some costs may have a curvilinear relationship to volume. Therefore, care needs to be exercised so that the linearity assumption will not mislead decision makers.

A final limitation of break-even analysis is related to the relevant range. It states that the cost behavior is assumed not to change within a given high- and low-volume range; therefore, managerial analysis should be limited to the relevant range in break-even analysis. In the break-even charts shown in Figures 7-1 and 7-3, the cost and revenue lines are drawn so that they go from zero to very high volume levels. But, costs may not behave in the fashion illustrated over this entire range, especially if the organization has never operated in the high or low end of this volume range before. Therefore, costs and revenues are likely to behave as shown in the break-even chart only within the *relevant range*. This range exists within the volume levels at which the organization has had prior operating experience.

Exercise 7-1

Break-Even Analysis

Breakers Point Library is going to sell coffee cups with the library logo on it. The cups cost the library $2 each, and the library wants to set them for $5 each. The library hopes to raise enough money to purchase two new PCs for the library. The cost of both PCs is estimated at $3,600.

1. How many coffee cups will the library have to sell?
2. If the library wants to double the number of PCs that it purchases while not selling any more cups than were determined in number 1, what selling price should the library charge?

IDENTIFYING COST BEHAVIOR FOR BREAK-EVEN ANALYSIS

There are several ways to estimate the way that costs behave and the relationship between fixed and variable costs in break-even analysis. Two such methods are the high-low method and regression analysis. Although linear regression analysis is theoretically the more accurate method, its real-world accuracy depends on how well the equation parameters are picked, especially with multiple regression. In many cases, the high-low method may provide results similar to those obtained in regression analysis. For our purpose, the high-low method will be illustrated.

Both the high-low method and linear regression provide an equation for the linear cost line in the break-even chart. The formula for the cost line follows:

$$Y = a + bx$$

Where: Y = total cost
a = fixed cost
bx = variable cost; representing the two variables such as hours times the variable cost per hour (b)

Again, it is important to separate fixed costs from variable costs. The high-low method provides a more systemic way to make that separation. As an illustration of how to use the high-low method, assume that the following data series represents the total costs and operating hours for a small gift shop in a library with a Web e-store.

	Days of the week						
	M	*T*	*W*	*Th*	*F*	*S*	*S*
Operating hours	6	6	6	6	6	3	3
Total operating costs*	$135	$155[†]	$130	$140	$147	$90[†]	$90[†]

---

*Operating costs include salaries, materials used to wrap gifts, packaging for carryout gifts, and mailing gifts from online sales, but it does not include the purchase cost of items sold.
[†]High and low points in the data sequence

The data points that are selected from the schedule are the highest and lowest points for total operating costs that fairly represent the data. In this case, they are where the total operating costs are $155 and $90, respectively. The number of operating hours and the operating cost data from these two points are used to compute the equation for the total cost line. The total cost line appeared in the break-even chart in Figure 7-3.

The calculations used to compute the equation for a linear cost line follow with steps 1, 2, and 3:

STEP 1: In step 1, the variable component in the total cost of operations is determined.

$$\text{Variable cost per hour (b)} = \frac{\text{Difference between costs for the high and low points}}{\text{Difference in the value of the cost driver (hours) for the high and low points}}$$

$$\text{Variable cost per hour (b)} = \frac{\$155 - \$90 \text{ difference in high and low costs}}{6 - 3 \text{ difference in high and low hours}}$$

$$\text{Variable cost per hour (b)} = 65/3 = \$22 \text{ (rounded)}$$

The $22 represents the variable cost per cost driver, in this case hours (x), in the total cost equation. Now, it is necessary to determine the fixed cost in the total cost of $155 and $90. The fixed component should be the same amount regardless of the total cost of operations.

STEP 2: In step 2, the fixed component in the total cost of operations is determined. The calculation can be made either using the high or low numbers.

Both are illustrated. Using the equation, a = Y − (bx), with the high point results in:

$$a = \$155 - (\$22 \times 6) = 23 \text{ fixed cost (rounded)}$$

Using the equation, a = Y − (bx), with the low point results in:

$$a = \$90 - (\$22 \times 3) = 24 \text{ fixed cost (rounded)}$$

There is a rounding difference, but the fixed cost in the operating costs of the gift shop is in the $23 to $24 range, or about $23.50.

STEP 3: The final step is the equation used to estimate the total cost of operating the gift shop at any hourly level within the relevant range.

$$Y = \$23.50 + \$22 \text{ (hours)}$$

These relationships are illustrated in Figure 7-5. The $23.50 in fixed costs is represented by a straight line, and the variable costs are shown as increasing as the number of hours of operation increases. Figure 7-5 is a chart similar to the break-even chart but without a revenue line. In this chart, the total cost is separated into its fixed and variable components. Here, the process of separating variable and fixed costs is completed in a more systematic manner than trying to use judgmental analysis to separate them.

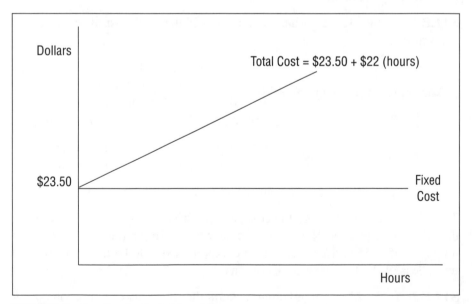

FIGURE 7-5   Equation for the total cost line

The total cost equation also allows for the prediction of how cost will behave if the number of hours should change from those shown in the original data. For example, if the gift shop is open eight hours rather than six, the estimated total cost of operations would be approximately $200, as follows:

$$Y = \$23.50 + (22 \times 8)$$
$$= \$23.50 + \$176.00$$
$$= \$199.50 \text{ or about } \$200$$

The total cost equation determines how cost can behave in the future assuming these cost relationships do not change and within the outline limitations for break-even analysis.

Exercise 7-2

High-Low Analysis

The Green Mountain Library is trying to analyze its database access charges. The library is concerned that these costs have been continually rising over the last few years driven by an increase in demand from patrons that has expanded the number of databases available for searches. The following data have been collected over the last few years, beginning when database searches were first provided to patrons. Using the data provided:

1. Create a straight-line equation for the total cost equation.

2. Determine and explain the cost relationships in the equation and why they exist in this fashion.

3. Use the equation to predict costs if there is a 10 percent increase in the number of searches in the coming year.

Year	Cost	Patron Demand (as Recorded by the Number of Searches)
1	$1,000	5,500
2	3,000	10,000
3	4,000	15,000
4	7,000	25,000
5	7,500	35,000

BREAK-EVEN ANALYSIS AND APPROPRIATIONS

In nonprofit organizations, break-even analysis can occur when there are no revenues. Instead of revenues, the nonprofit organization receives appropriations. The next examples of break-even analysis incorporate budget appropriations into the analysis. When a budget appropriation is incorporated into break-even analysis, it means that fixed costs are reduced by the amount of the appropriation. Essentially, the budget appropriation is deducted from the total fixed costs, and the remainder is used as the numerator of the break-even equation. Once the effect of the appropriation is taken into account, break-even calculations are performed as previously illustrated.

For example, assume that a public library is starting a shut-in service. The cost components of this service will include an assignment of staff time, a public relations campaign to advertise the service, training costs of staff, additional supplies, additional use of telephones, and new equipment such as fax machines, audiovisual equipment, and a van. The costs can be separated into yearly fixed costs of $13,500 and variable costs of $7.50 per shut-in. Assume that the library has received a state grant of $10,000. Because the grant does not cover the fixed cost of providing the service, the library has decided they will charge a small fee for the service. The volume cost driver is related to the number of patrons using the service, which is estimated at 1,000 shut-ins using the service in the first year. The library would like to know the fee they should charge.

The first step in making this calculation is to subtract the grant of $10,000 from the fixed costs of operating the program, $13,500. The net fixed costs of $3,500 and the variable cost per shut-in are placed into the break-even equation in Figure 7-6 to determine the fee to charge.

In this case, the fee charged is above the per-unit variable cost. The break-even chart would be similar to the ones shown in Figures 7-1 and 7-3

$$\text{Break-even (1,000 shut-ins)} = \frac{\text{Remaining fixed costs (\$3,500)}}{\text{Fee (X)} - \text{Variable cost (\$7.50)}}$$

$$\text{Shut-ins 1,000} = \frac{\$3,500}{X - \$7.50}$$

$$\text{Fee (X)} = \$11 \text{ Yearly fee}$$

FIGURE 7-6   Break-even analysis with an appropriation

with the exception of a $10,000 appropriation line across the bottom of the chart *below* the fixed cost line.

If the assumptions are changed so the grant specifies that a maximum of $5 can be charged per shut-in by a library accepting the grant, this grant will provide an appropriation of $2,500 above the library's fixed costs of $13,500, or $16,000. Under these conditions, it is assumed that the number of shut-ins wanting the service will expand to 1,200. What financial situation will the library be facing if the library accepts the grant? Again, the break-even equation can help in making this determination by determining the break-even point.

$$\text{Break-even (X)} = \frac{\$2,500 \text{ grant proceeds above fixed costs}}{\$5.00 - \$7.50}$$

$$= 1,000 \text{ shut-ins}$$

The break-even point for this service is 1,000 shut-ins. If 1,200 shut-ins will use this service, should the library accept the grant? The break-even chart in Figure 7-7 is used to help make the determination.

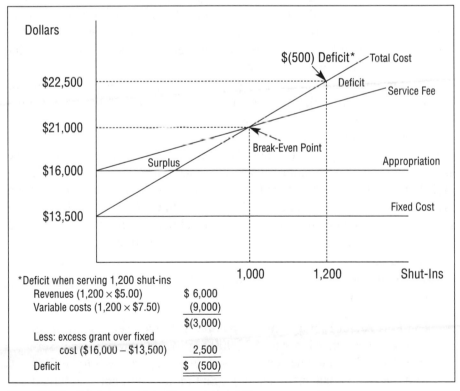

FIGURE 7-7 Break-even point with an appropriation

As the library provides service above the break-even point, it goes into a larger and larger deficit. At the bottom of Figure 7-7, the computation is shown for 1,200 shut-ins enrolled in the program. At that level, a deficit of $500 will occur. The deficit increases as the volume of shut-ins increases. This trend is shown in the break-even chart where the loss at levels above 1,200 shut-ins continues to increase.

On the other hand, as the level of service decreases below the break-even point the library receives a surplus from the shut-in program. This is a reversal of the typical break-even analysis shown for a for-profit organization. A computation can be made to show that if only 800 shut-ins use the service, the library receives a surplus of $500. These calculations result in a number of interesting choices for management to make, such as how intensively to promote the program, whether the library will be able to handle the widening deficit if the program expands to more shut-ins, or if budgetary curtailment is mandated. In this example of break-even analysis, the library is better off financially to curtail this program as well as other programs with the cost relationships exhibited here. Curtailment of the shut-in program in a budget reduction is more beneficial, or retains more resources, for the library than using across-the-board percentage cuts in the budget. As shown in Figure 7-7, decreasing the number of shut-ins serviced below the break-even point increases the surplus from this program.

For a program that charges no fee and has no appropriation, the deficit or loss begins as soon as the program starts. The example in Figure 7-7 illustrates that a surplus can occur below the break-even point, instead of a loss, when the fee charged for program services is less than the program's variable costs, and the appropriation is more than the fixed costs of the program. The shut-in program is an example of a service that is receiving an appropriation and charges a fee that is less than its variable costs. As a result, this program is simply delaying the initial onset of the inevitable deficit. The point of these illustrations is that no standard assumptions about cost relationships should be accepted until all cost behaviors are examined and understood.

Exercise 7-3

Ethics and Grants

The Port Angel Library director has recently received a grant from the county commissioner for $25,000 to provide library literacy services to the low-income community. A grant report needs to be filed with the county, but any remaining grant monies will not be returned to the county, and the library can decide on spending priorities.

The cost of hiring trained tutors and providing these services is estimated to run about $100 per client for 250 people. It is also estimated that once the program is made available, the demand for the program will attract at least twice as many clients, or 500 people. The director is faced with several issues.

- Should she limit the number enrolled in the program to 250 people? Such a program is expected to provide basic literacy training.
- Should she expand the program to all who request the services and consequently reduce the library's ability to provide other services as well as reduce the basic operating resources of the library? Such a program is expected to provide basic literacy training.
- Should she restrict the services to less than 250 people and provide a more advanced literacy training program for these participants by using some of the grant monies to purchase needed equipment and other items that can be used in the literacy program but also in other library activities?

Facing these choices, what would you advise the library director as the best choice for the county library? Can break-even analysis help her make a decision?

DIFFERENTIAL COST ANALYSIS

The next analytical technique explained in this chapter is differential cost analysis (DCA). Incremental cost analysis, a subtopic within DCA, deals with cost increases caused by alternative courses of action. Differential costs are all costs that may increase or decrease because of alternative courses of action taken. Like break-even analysis, DCA uses projected cost information for making decisions. Unlike break-even analysis, DCA is concerned with only the costs that change when the library manager is faced with making a choice between two alternatives.

With life cycle costing (LCC), in chapter 6, the cash costs of new assets were compared with each other to determine which one had the lowest cost over its life. DCA is similar to LCC in that it is concerned with the cash costs of operating assets over their lives. But, it is different from LCC analysis because DCA is only concerned with the cost differences between two alternatives, not their total costs. As a result, DCA can be a shortcut to arrive at similar decisions to those made under LCC. DCA can be used in conjunction with LCC analysis. Once the least-cost asset is chosen with LCC, the costs of operating that new asset can then be compared with the costs of operating the old asset to be replaced in order to determine if replacement is a cost-effective decision. When the latter comparison is made using DCA, the costs that differ are the only ones taken into consideration.

Another difference between LCC analysis and DCA is that present values are often not incorporated into DCA because many differential cost decisions are related to short-term time periods. If DCA decision analysis does extend into longer time periods, present value factors need to be incorporated into the calculations.

In using DCA, only the cash costs that differ between the alternatives are considered. The accounting method used to accrue expenses to the various fiscal periods should not affect the outcome of a decision when this method is used. Differential costs are the costs that will change because of selecting one decision alternative over another. Examples of DCA use in a library are listed below.

- Whether to develop a new asset within the library or purchase it from an outside vendor
- Whether to replace equipment
- Amount and mixture of resources allocated to various projects

In analyzing the costs that change between alternatives, exercise caution again in studying cost patterns; variable costs are not the only costs that can change between alternatives. For example, a decision may result in the elimination of a fixed cost, such as the fixed salary of an administrator if that administrator's position is eliminated. Therefore, no assumptions should be made about the changeability of variable and fixed costs until the decision alternatives are fully understood.

Remember, the data collected in studying decision alternatives are not "hard" data. The data are based on projections from managers and vendors. These data may be biased in one direction or another because of behavioral influences. This bias may be extremely difficult to detect because the manager directly in charge of a department or a program, for example, is assumed to have the best information about the proposed alternatives. Many estimates provided by that manager may be difficult to verify. For this reason, it is difficult for others outside the department to determine if unbiased data are being provided or whether the data provided have been biased to make the manager look better or to elicit more resources for the department. The degree of bias introduced into these estimates is difficult to isolate because evaluative information is received only after the action has been implemented. In many organizations, evaluative information is never collected for making comparisons with original estimates.

Two examples of DCA are presented here. The first one, illustrated in Figure 7-8, deals with a choice between developing a software program within the library with the employees of the library who have programming skills or purchasing the software from a vendor. The second example deals with the decision to replace an aging asset, and the cost information for it is presented in Figure 7-9.

In Figure 7-8, the cash cost of developing customized software is compared with the cash cost of purchasing it, and the difference, which is the cost saving or loss from purchase, is shown in the last column, "Difference." The costs of developing the software are listed under the heading "Computer resources." These costs include the costs of computer time, supplies, and the use of other assets that would not otherwise have been used if the software had not been developed within the library.

The cost of salaries and wages assigned to the software development team is based on the actual time incurred, and these costs are included as direct labor. Labor costs are related to the activities—such as writing and debugging programs—that are required to complete the system and get it up and running in the library.

It may be argued that direct labor costs are not differential costs because they would be incurred by the library anyway. In other words, the individuals who developed the software would have been performing other tasks within

Item	Developmental Costs	Purchase Cost	Difference
Computer resources	$ 40,000	—	$ 40,000
Direct labor	80,000	—	80,000
Allocated overhead	—	—	—
Purchase price	—	$200,000	(200,000)
Debugging costs	—	15,000	(15,000)
	$120,000	$215,000	$(95,000)

This illustration assumes that any software maintenance costs are insignificant.

FIGURE 7-8   Analyzing the decision to purchase software from a vendor or develop it within the library with library resources

the library before they were assigned to developing the software. If the personnel assigned to the software project are taken away from these other library tasks and not replaced, the library still incurs the same labor costs. If this is so, these labor costs are not differential costs, nor are they part of the costs of developing the software. On the other hand, if these labor costs are related to hiring additional workers to replace staff assigned to the computer project, then these costs are differential costs of the project. Labor and resource costs must be carefully analyzed to determine if they are true differential costs. In the illustration, it is assumed that the labor costs are differential costs.

The cash developmental costs of the software have to be compared with the cash cost of purchasing the software, which is equal to the purchase price and the costs of getting the software up and running on the library's computer equipment. The start-up costs of labor time and training are classified as "debugging" costs. The vendor's developmental costs for the system are unknown. The library is only aware of the vendor's selling price for the software.

The differential cost is $95,000, meaning the library would save $95,000 if it developed the software with its own resources and personnel, assuming all estimates of the cost of internal development are accurate. Therefore, DCA indicates that the best choice for the library is to develop customized software within the library with the use of library personnel.

The item titled "Allocated overhead" is shown with no balance in the developmental cost column. This is to emphasize that the actual cash out-of-pocket costs related to the alternatives are the costs that need to be compared with each other. Any currently incurred library overhead costs that are allocated to software development will still remain within the library whether or not it is allocated; therefore, allocated overhead is not a differential cost related

Cash Item	Old Furnace	New Furnace	Difference
Operating cost outlay*	$400,000	$275,000	$125,000
Old equipment depreciation	—	—	—
Disposal value of old	—	(2,000)	2,000
Cost of new furnace	—	35,000	(35,000)
Disposal value of new	—	(3,500)	3,500
	$400,000	$304,500	$ 95,500

*Assumes a ten-year period for the old furnace and a twenty-year period for the new furnace

FIGURE 7-9 Analyzing the decision to replace a furnace

to the project and should not be a consideration in this decision process. Of course, any future incurrence of overhead that would be different because of the developing or purchasing of software should be included in the analysis.

Figure 7-9 provides another example of differential cost analysis to determine whether an old furnace should be replaced. The illustration represents the cash flows arising from the decision to trade in an old furnace for a new one. The cash cost of operating the new furnace over its estimated twenty-year life and the cash cost of operating the old furnace over its remaining estimated life of ten years is shown in the first row of Figure 7-9. These are historic ten- and twenty-year estimates about operating costs, which assume that these costs will not change—that fuel costs will remain constant, for example. Today, with rolling blackouts of electricity in some areas, this may not be an accurate assumption.

These operating costs include fuel and maintenance and repair costs but not depreciation. To emphasize that depreciation is not part of this calculation, the second item in the first column is listed as depreciation and left without a dollar balance. Depreciation is considered a sunk cost and does not affect the decision to purchase or not to purchase a new asset in a nonprofit organization. The third item in the first column is the current disposal value of the old asset. This is the amount of cash that will be received for the old furnace if it is disposed of now. This $2,000 is deducted from the cash outlays for the new furnace, reducing the net amount of cash paid out. It is assumed that ten years from now the old furnace will have a disposal value of zero. The fourth item is the cost of the new furnace, and the last item is the estimated salvage value that will be received for the new furnace at the end of its twenty-year useful life. This amount is also deducted because it is a reduction of the total cash outlays for the new furnace.

The "Difference" column shows that purchasing the new asset will save $95,500. This column records the differential or incremental costs between the costs associated with purchasing or not purchasing the new asset. It should be noted that the useful lives of the two assets are different and longer than one year. In such a case, the time value of money may affect the decision. Many illustrations overlook the difference in assets' lives by assuming that the old asset will have the same remaining useful life as that of the new asset, which tends to equalize the cash flows. The assumption of equal lives for new and old assets is an oversimplification. It is uncommon in actual practice to find a new asset with the same remaining life as the older asset it is replacing. Therefore, present values are an additional factor that can be added to the analysis.[3] (*See* appendix B for a discussion of present value analysis.)

Another difficulty with DCA in actual practice is the quality of the data. Data may be incorrect or purposely biased. A technique called sensitivity analysis can help to overcome the problem of biased data. *Sensitivity analysis* is a method that allows variations in the data or allows assumptions about the data relationships to be incorporated into the analysis to determine how the final solution is affected by these changes. For example, if the fixed costs in a break-even calculation are biased low, it is possible to recalculate the equation with higher fixed costs to show how "sensitive" the break-even point is to the biased data. This indicates how sensitive the final solution is to possible errors in the data. Sensitivity analysis can incorporate a number of additional what-if scenarios into the data and is a useful technique if the quality of the data is suspect or if a number of different scenarios have an equal chance of occurrence. Sensitivity analysis introduces outcomes that may occur if the original expectations are not fulfilled, for whatever reason.

For example, in Figure 7-9 the operating cost of the new furnace is $275,000, but if this cost is biased because of a favorable estimate provided by a vendor, the analysis should be recalculated. Additional what-if calculations could be related to changes in the estimated useful lives of the furnaces. Numerous what-if calculations can be added to the analysis to help overcome some of the difficulties caused by biased or incorrect data, and several illustrations are provided in the next section. In addition, after-the-fact performance analysis can help determine if there is a tendency for results to be biased.

Exercise 7-4

Differential Cost-Decision Analysis

The director at the Freeburg County Library is considering replacing its two custodians, Lou and Fred, with a janitorial service offered by Clean-All, a local janitorial supply company in the metro area. Clean-All has offered the service at a cost of $5 per square foot to the library. The library has 10,000 square feet in its building. The internal cost of janitorial services follows:

Salaries and benefits	$40,000
Allocated overhead	10,000
Janitorial supplies used	2,200
Maintenance of janitorial equipment	1,000

In addition, the library would be required to pay severance pay to the two custodians equal to $10,000. The reduction of the janitorial staff would result in the opening of a small bookshop in the library area that formerly housed the custodians. It is estimated that the revenues from the bookshop would net about $12,000 annually.

1. Should the outside service be used and the two custodians fired?
2. What other factors might be considered in this decision?

USING PROBABILITIES AND SENSITIVITY ANALYSIS IN COST ESTIMATING

As most managerial operating decisions are made with some uncertainty, the use of probabilities is another tool helpful in controlling that uncertainty and allowing for the explicit evaluation of the events that may occur. The three main probability classifications are called subjective, empirical, and a priori. Only the first two of these probabilities are important for real-world managerial decision making. Those two, subjective and empirical, are illustrated here with the use of sensitivity analysis to estimate the probable occurrence of outcomes.

If the chance of an event occurring is estimated by an individual manager, it is called a *subjective* probability. An event should be considered one of several effects that can influence an outcome and its probability of occurrence. If one event occurs, it means another alternative event cannot occur; these series of events are the only alternatives that can take place.

A second probability classification that can be used in managerial decision making is an empirical probability. *Empirical* probabilities are calculated through a sampling or count of activities. The probability is then calculated based on the frequency of the past occurrence of these counted activities.

Because most managerial decisions are made with some uncertainty as to their outcome, there is a need to make the chance of an event's occurrence an explicit consideration in decision making. If there is only one event or outcome that can result from a different combination or use of resources, then there is no uncertainty in that decision. For example, if invested monies earn a 10 percent return regardless of how or where they are invested, there is no uncertainty about a future outcome, which is the dollar return.

But, if a number of different and mutually exclusive outcomes can occur from different combinations or uses of resources, then uncertainty exists. Where certainty exists, a library can stock and offer for sale 100 library T-shirts to their patrons for $6 each, and the library knows that all 100 will be sold.

Where there is uncertainty, a number of different combinations of T-shirts may be purchased and sold. With uncertainty, stocking 100 T-shirts may not result in the sale of all of them. The most successful decision maker is able to select the best combination of resources (T-shirts) and actions (prices) to obtain the highest profit.

An illustration of decision making in the face of uncertainty is found in Figure 7-10. In this example, subjective probabilities are used in conjunction with a fund-raising project proposed by the library to determine the number of T-shirts to purchase for resale. The demand for the T-shirts is shown as occurring in increments of twenty. The probabilities for selling these T-shirts are subjective probabilities as estimated by the manager in charge of the sale. Essentially, this probability is based on managerial judgment. A subjective probability distribution must be 100 percent because these probabilities indicate all alternatives are taken into account in the demand and probability schedule. The schedule shows that there is a 15 percent chance of selling forty T-shirts. Remember that for each T-shirt sold a profit of $2 is received ($6 selling price – $4 cost). However, no T-shirt can be returned; for each T-shirt left unsold a loss of $4 is incurred—the T-shirt's cost to the library. This analysis is not being used to determine the break-even point, but the expected profit from stocking different levels of T-shirts for sale in the face of different levels of sales.

The expected profit to be received from purchasing 20 to 100 T-shirts is determined in Figure 7-10. The subjective probabilities are shown for selling 20 to 100 T-shirts. These probabilities are determined in the same manner a bettor at a horse race determines the odds of a horse winning the race—a judgmental decision.

If the library stocks 40 T-shirts, for example, the first possible outcome is that the library may only be able to sell 20 T-shirts. In that case, there will be a loss of $4 on each of the 20 unsold T-shirts and a profit of $2 on each of the 20 that are sold. As shown, there is a 5 percent probability of this outcome. Therefore, if 40 T-shirts are purchased and 20 are sold, there is an expected loss of $4 [(– 20 × $4).05] on the 20 unsold T-shirts and an expected profit of $2 [(20 × $2).05] on the 20 shirts sold. The net loss {–[40(.05)]} is shown under the outcome for "Number Sold: 20" with 40 T-shirts purchased. The net expected loss is $2 when 40 T-shirts are stocked and only 20 are sold. If the library stocks 40 and sells 40, 60, 80, or 100 there are expected profits of $12, $16, $40, and $8, respectively. These expected profits are the results of the multiplication of each of the profit/probability combinations under each sold column. The most probable outcome from stocking 40 T-shirts is an expected profit of $74 (– 2 + 12 + 16 + 40 + 8) as shown in the "Expected

Case: The public library has decided to sell T-shirts as a fund-raising project. A decision needs to be made on the number of T-shirts to order from a vendor who requires orders be made in multiples of 20. The T-shirts will sell for $6, and they cost the library $4 each. The estimated demand for the first 100 T-shirts is shown below.

Demand	Probability of Selling
20	5%
40	15%
60	20%
80	50%
100	10%
	100%

This shows that in the judgment of the manager in charge of the sale, there is a 5% chance of selling 20 T-shirts and a separate 10% chance of selling 100 T-shirts. The expected profit from each demand level is calculated as follows:

Number Purchased	20		40		60		80		100	Expected Profit
20	[20(2)(.05)]	+	[40(.15)]	+	[40(.20)]	+	[40(.50)]	+	[40(.10)]	= $40
40	[40(.05)]	−	[40×2(.15)]	+	[80(.20)]	+	[80(.50)]	+	[80(.10)]	= 74
60	[120(.05)]	+	[0(.15)]	+	[60×2(.20)]	+	[120(.50)]	+	[120(.10)]	= 90
80	[200(.05)]	−	[80(.15)]	+	[40(.20)]	+	[80×2(.50)]	+	[160(.10)]	= 82
100	[280(.05)]	−	[160(.15)]	−	[40(.20)]	+	[80(.50)]	+	[100×2(.10)]	= 14

Number Sold

FIGURE 7-10 Illustrative example of the application of subjective probabilities in decision making

Profit" column. The best use of library resources is to purchase 60 T-shirts. With 60 T-shirts, the highest expected profit of $90 is likely to be earned as shown under the "Expected Profit" column. Of course, there is another decision alternative that is not shown, which is not to have a T-shirt sale.

In reviewing Figure 7-10, stocking sixty T-shirts results in the highest expected benefit—profit—with the given demand and probability schedules. This method of using subjective probabilities is useful in explicitly formulating the possibilities of earning the highest expected profit from library activities such as selling T-shirts, posters, and book bags. Probability analysis is a useful technique for making managerial decisions because almost all decisions face some level of uncertainty. The determination of the demand schedule has incorporated sensitivity analysis into the probability calculations as various scenarios were established for the different levels of T-shirt purchases.

As stated, subjective probabilities are one probability distribution that can be used to aid decision making in libraries. Another useful probability technique occurs when empirical probabilities are incorporated into the decision-making process. Empirical probabilities are developed from activity samples. Based on the frequency with which these activities occur, relative frequencies can be established for their expected occurrence in the future. A characteristic of empirical probabilities is that the probability distribution will vary with each sample taken of the activity. If the probabilities did not differ with each sample they would be called a priori probabilities. Illustrative of the latter is the probability of heads on a coin toss or the probability of "snake eyes" on dice.

The following example will show how empirical probabilities can be used in making library operating decisions. The Rexus Library is considering changing its hours of operation on Saturday. The library currently opens at 9:00 in the morning but wants to open at 10:30 instead. The library wants to determine the expected number of patrons who use the library early Saturday morning and would be inconvenienced by opening at 10:30 instead of 9:00.

To determine how many patrons will be inconvenienced, a count is made of the number of patrons entering the library on Saturday each half hour from 9:00 to 10:30 over a ten-week period. These activity counts are then turned into the empirical probabilities shown in Figure 7-11.

An illustration is provided in Figure 7-11 to show how empirical probabilities can be calculated. Assume that another library is analyzing the same problem as the Rexus Library—later opening hours. During a ten-week period, the number of patrons entering this library for a preselected half-hour time period was counted.

For this library, the numbers of patrons arriving in this half-hour period ranged from zero to four, and these results are shown in the left-hand column

Patrons Arriving	Empirical Number of Weeks with This Many Arrivals	Probability of Patron Usage		
0	2	2/10	=	0.20
1	2	2/10	=	0.20
2	1	1/10	=	0.10
3	3	3/10	=	0.30
4	2	2/10	=	0.20
	10 weeks			1.00

FIGURE 7-11   The calculation of empirical probabilities

of the schedule. Review of the data shows that twice during the ten weeks no patrons used the library in this half-hour time period and twice four patrons used the library. Once the count is completed, relative probabilities are calculated for the expected arrival of the various numbers of patrons in the future. This empirical probability is determined by dividing the total number of weeks (ten) into the number of weeks that zero through four patrons were counted as arriving at the library. The results are shown in the far-right column, "Probability of Patron Usage." This is a probability based on the frequency of occurrence of an activity, which in this case is patron usage, during a specified time period. The probabilities indicate that there is a 20 percent chance that zero, one, or four patrons may use the library during this half-hour period; a 10 percent chance that two patrons will use the library; and a 30 percent chance that three patrons will arrive. Although the empirical probabilities for the Rexus Library (*see* Figure 7-12) are different than shown here, they were determined in the same manner. The determination of empirical probabilities is the first step in using this decision-making technique.

Once the empirical probabilities are determined, the expected number of patrons to be inconvenienced by finding the library closed in each of the three half-hour periods can be determined by multiplying the empirical probability by the expected arrivals for that probability.[4] These results are computed in Figure 7-12 under the heading "Expected Patrons Inconvenienced." During the first half-hour period when the library is closed, 1.75 patrons are expected to be inconvenienced. Similarly, for each of the next two half-hour periods, 2.45 and 3.5 patrons are expected to be inconvenienced by the later Saturday hours. At this point, it may be decided that it would be prudent to open the library at 10:00 A.M. instead of 10:30 to reduce the number of inconvenienced patrons and still curtail library hours and save budget dollars.

Case: The Rexus Library is considering changing its opening hours on Saturday morning from 9:00 to 10:30. The library director is attempting to estimate the number of patrons who would be inconvenienced by the later opening hours.

9:00–9:30 Arrivals		Empirical Probabilities		Expected Patrons Inconvenienced
0	×	.05	=	0.00
1	×	.60	=	0.60
2	×	.10	=	0.20
3	×	.10	=	0.30
4	×	.10	=	0.40
5	×	.05	=	0.25
			Expected total	1.75

9:30–10:00 Arrivals		Empirical Probabilities		Expected Patrons Inconvenienced
0	×	.08	=	0.00
1	×	.05	=	0.05
2	×	.30	=	0.60
3	×	.50	=	1.50
4	×	.05	=	0.20
5	×	.02	=	0.10
			Expected total	2.45

10:00–10:30 Arrivals		Empirical Probabilities		Expected Patrons Inconvenienced
0	×	.05	=	0.00
1	×	.05	=	0.05
2	×	.10	=	0.20
3	×	.15	=	0.45
4	×	.50	=	2.00
5	×	.10	=	0.50
6	×	.05	=	0.30
			Expected total	3.50

FIGURE 7-12   Illustrative example of the application of empirical probabilities in decision making

Subjective and empirical probabilities can be used in a number of different decision-making situations. Several of those situations have been illustrated in this chapter, but the illustrations are in no way all-inclusive. For example, subjective probabilities can be used in making budget estimates to determine the most probable increase necessary to counter the effects of inflation. Empirical probabilities can be used in any activity determination. For example, the probability of receiving overdue books from different patron classifications is essentially a measure of the risk of loss on loaned books. The application of these techniques is fairly extensive and only restricted by the limitations inherent in any estimation technique.

ESTIMATING COSTS WITH THE LEARNING CURVE

Although some managerial analysis techniques may not seem to be intuitive, most individuals would agree that when a task is completed the first time, it is usually more difficult to finish than the third or sixteenth time the same task is completed; and that agreement leads to a more intuitive method of cost analysis called the learning curve.

As staff members complete job functions, they learn more efficient techniques to complete the task. Thus, the worker who has performed a work-related task a number of times is more likely to complete it more efficiently and quickly than a new worker doing the same job. This learning process can be mathematically traced as a logarithm, and it is called the learning-curve effect.

The learning curve shows the relationship between the amount of time required to complete a task and the cumulative amount of items that are produced. It is a measure of efficiency. This curve can be related to more measurable librarianship or technician duties such as ordering books, maintaining the computer catalog, cataloging books, processing image files, shelf reading and other collection maintenance activities, and data mining of data warehouses.

The learning relationship is important where a new process is being introduced, especially when technology is involved. It provides an indication of how quickly staff will learn to operate the new process and improve their functioning from the first time they performed the task. It shows the rate of improvement in staff performance and cost reductions as the job is repeated. The learning curve is usually described as a percent represented by the following underlying formula:

$$Y = ax^b$$

Where Y = cumulative average hours required for a specified number of
    items to be completed
  a = the time required to complete the first item
  x = number of items completed in the process
  b = the learning rate exponent. It is the logarithm of the learning
    rate, divided by the log of 2 or the ratio of the natural
    logarithms.

Before applying the equation, the effect of the learning curve can most
easily be seen as the cumulative sequence of items doubles. In Figure 7-13,
items completed are shown as doubling with an 80 percent learning curve in
effect. The effect of the learning curve can be easily computed by multiplying 80 percent times the cumulative average time required to complete the
previous item. For example, the cumulative time to complete one item is fifty
hours, as shown in Figure 7-13. The cumulative time to complete two items
is forty hours each or a total of eighty hours for both items. The additional
time it took to produce the second item was thirty hours (eighty total hours
for two less the fifty hours for the first one). This information is shown in row
two in Figure 7-13.

When the number of items is doubled, as shown in Figure 7-13, the
learning-curve effect is easily determined. It is when the number of items
completed becomes three, five, six, or seven that the learning-curve equation
must be used to determine the learning-curve effect (i.e., when the rate is not

Cumulative Number of Items (Column 1)	Cumulative Average Time to Complete Each Item (Column 2)	Total Cumulative Time (Column 1 × Column 2 = 3)	Individual Item Time to Complete (Column 4)
1	50.0	50.0	50
2	40.0 (.80 × 40)	80.0	30*
4	32.0 (.80 × 40)	128.0	24†
8	25.6 (.80 × 32)	204.8	19.2‡

_____
*(80 − 50)/1 = 30
†(128 − 80)/2 = 24
‡(204.8 − 128)/4 = 19.2

FIGURE 7-13   The learning-curve effect with an 80 percent learning curve

doubled). The calculation of the cumulative average time at these points, beginning at three, is fairly straightforward and can be quickly done with any calculator that will compute logarithms.[5]

The learning rate itself can be computed based on historical data using either regression or the high-low method of analysis. Historical data showing the cumulative items completed and the corresponding average cumulative labor hours per unit can be converted to natural logs; then use linear regression to compute the slope from the data.[6] The slope is equal to the rate of learning.

The learning curve effect allows a library manager to determine how many hours it should take to complete a repetitive activity. Planning library work hours for an activity is important when a competitive grant application is being developed. Without the careful analysis of the cost of performing repetitive grant activities and their accurate costing, the grant may not be awarded. What may at first appear to be very expensive tasks may not be as expensive to perform if the effect of the learning curve is taken into account. The result may be that the budget in the grant application can be reduced so that the application is more competitive.

Further, if the effect of the learning curve is not properly considered, the library could be awarded the grant because of the low submission cost in the grant application. Thus, the library receives the grant, but its completion entails such high costs that the library must use up its own scarce resources in completing the grant activities.

When cost-conscious budgets need to be prepared either for grant applications or for the operating activities of the library, the learning curve is useful in providing more accurate cost projections. Expenditure estimates based on the initial cost of a new budget activity need to take into account the role of learning. Good time performance on a one-time job needs to be separated from the task performance that is repeated a number of times, and the reasons for the difference in such performance levels need to be understood by the manager.

Exercise 7-5

The Learning Curve

Edlinda Library Director Louise Phillips has recently heard about how people performing a repetitive new task learn to perform the task more efficiently as that task is repeated. The library has recently installed a new technology-based system to automate the circulation system with MARC records. All the books in the collection will have to be entered into the new system. Louise is trying to determine how long it will take to perform this task. She is assuming an 80 percent learning curve is in effect. During staff training to learn how to re-catalog books, the following trend was noted.

Number of Books Recataloged	Cumulative Average Time
1	45 minutes
2	36
3	28.8

Louise thinks that after recataloging 128 records, there would be little further improvement in staff time per record in completing the changeover.

1. If there are still 5,000 record entries that need to be made after each staff member reaches peak performance, how much staff time should be assigned to the task?

2. Assuming an average hourly rate of $18 per staff hour, how much will the automation project cost the library in staff time?

SUMMARY

The four managerial decision-making tools described in the chapter were used to forecast break-even points, differential costs, the probabilities of outcomes, and develop a learning curve for job functions. In this sense, they are all directed at forecasting future costs or events.

The methods described in this chapter are useful in helping managers make operating decisions in the library. The manager must operate within levels of uncertainty, and there is no surefire "cookbook" method or step-by-step procedure that can replace good managerial judgments. The techniques described here can only assist operating managers in decision making, and they should not be considered a cookbook approach to solving difficult problems.

Once a decision is reached by a manager and implemented, feedback should be used to evaluate the success of those outcomes. Without evaluating outcomes, no control can be exercised over managerial performance. This topic is addressed in the final chapter of this book, chapter 9.

Notes

1. Fixed and variable costs are discussed in detail in chapter 2. Briefly, *fixed costs* do not change as the level or volume of activity changes. An example of a fixed cost is

administrative salaries. *Variable costs* are costs that vary directly with the activity level. Supply costs are an example of a variable cost.

2. The high-low method, explained shortly, helps to separate variable and fixed costs from each other.

3. The following information is presented to illustrate how present value analysis would be used with the furnace example. The results are the same: purchase the new furnace, but the differential cost savings are now $84,172 ($2,458,000 − $2,373,828).

Old furnace:	Operating cost	$400,000 × 6.145*	=	$2,458,000

New furnace:	Operating cost	$275,000 × 8.514†	=	$2,341,350
	Old, disposal	2,000 × 1.00	=	(2,000)
	Cost of new	35,000 × 1.00	=	35,000
	New, disposal	3,500 × .149‡	=	(522)
				$2,373,828

*Table factor for an ordinary annuity: ten years at 10 percent
†Table factor for an ordinary annuity: twenty years at 10 percent
‡Table factor for a lump sum due at the end of twenty years at 10 percent. The amount shown is rounded.

(In appendix B, present value table factors are provided for up to ten periods. For periods longer than ten years, consult a finance or accounting book such as those listed in the references at the end of the chapter.)

4. For the earlier illustration in Figure 7-11, the calculation is made as follows:

$$0 \times .20 = 0.00$$
$$1 \times .20 = 0.20$$
$$2 \times .10 = 0.20$$
$$3 \times .30 = 0.90$$
$$4 \times .20 = 0.80$$

Expected total   2.10

This means that if the library is closed during this time period, 2.10 patrons are expected to be inconvenienced based on the activity sample taken for ten weeks.

5. Using the equation $y = ax^b$ and the data in Figure 7-13, the cumulative average time for three cumulative units is calculated as follows:

$$b = \frac{\ln (.80)}{\ln 2}$$

Calculator: A calculator with a "lnx" key will quickly compute b as follows:

$$b = \frac{-0.22314}{0.69414} = -0.3219$$

When x = 3, a = 50, and b = −0.3219, the cumulative average time (CAT) per unit is calculated as follows:

$$\text{CAT} = (50) (3^{-0.3219})$$
$$= 50 \times .70212$$
$$= 35.11$$

Calculator: Using the y^x key on the calculator raises the given number to any exponent.

Result: When the cumulative number of units is three, the cumulative average time is 35.11 hours, and the cumulative time to complete three units is 105.33 hours (35.11 × 3).

6. Assume that the following cumulative results had been collected from book cataloging activity in the past, and now the library was bidding on a grant that would allow for the purchase and shelving of a new series of books using an OCLC catalog classification that had not been used before. The library director wants to know the learning rate that exists in the book cataloging process for the library. Using the learning-curve equation ($Y = ax^b$), this can be determined. The historical data on cataloging rates follow:

Cumulative Items Cataloged (x)	Average Cumulative Labor Hours per Item (y)
10	1.0
20	0.8
30	0.6

In making this calculation, determine the natural log of the data points and enter them into a linear regression equation to determine the learning rate. Use the natural antilogarithm (the e^x button on the calculator) of the y-intercept to determine the time required to make the first unit—a. The learning rate—b—equals the slope of the linear regression line. For the above data, the time to complete the first item is 2.88 hours and the learning rate is 73.23 percent.

In general, most learning rates appear to fall within the 70 to 80 percent range. When the learning curve is equal to 1, no learning takes place. A learning rate of .5 results in a constant total time for production. This means that the actual total production of all new units is equal to the production time of the first item produced. This is the best rate that is obtainable because it would be unrealistic in most cases to assume that the total production time on new items would be less than the time it took to produce the first unit—by itself. In other words, a learning curve of less than .5 is probably unobtainable. It should be clear that as the learning curve is reduced, it shows better results from a highly trained and motivated staff.

Bibliography

Hilton, R. *Managerial Accounting: Creating Value in a Dynamic Business Environment.* Boston: McGraw-Hill/Irwin, 2002.

Horngren, C. T., G. Foster, and S. M. Datar. *Cost Accounting: A Managerial Emphasis.* Upper Saddle River, N.J.: Prentice-Hall, 2000.

McWatters, C. S., D. C. Morse, and J. L. Zimmerman. *Management Accounting: Analysis and Interpretation.* Boston: McGraw-Hill/Irwin, 2001.

CHAPTER

8

Leasing: Issues
and Analysis

Leases may allow a library to provide services to its patrons in a more cost-effective manner than other means, such as purchasing assets. A lease is a legal contract that allows a lessee—the library—the right to use assets such as equipment and buildings for a period specified by the lease. A leasing arrangement can be made for the services of personnel in addition to the services of assets. When libraries make a database search, they are leasing the right to have access to the information in the database. All these situations can be analyzed in essentially the same manner for their cost effects.

There are a number of reasons for leasing assets, information services, or personnel services. The major reason is that it allows the organization to provide services to patrons more efficiently than it could otherwise. How economical would it be for a library to develop its own database for literature searches rather than leasing access? With the use of a multiyear lease and fixed lease payments, it may be possible to temporarily hold costs in check at a time when inflation would normally increase the cost of operations. Many services that at one time would not be considered leaseable items are today under consideration as possible lease candidates. In some cases, this is being done so that the nonprofit organization, which is under serious budget stress, can receive a quick inflow of cash. For example, some universities are leasing their bookstores to corporations. The immediate effect of this change is that the university is paid millions for their book inventory and equipment, after which they receive annual payments without any headaches of managing a bookstore. Initially, this trade-off appears very appealing, but is it? It depends on the quality of services that are received by the faculty and students from the lessee. Quality is a nonfinancial factor that is mistakenly not taken into account in many quantitatively oriented decisions.

A number of factors must be taken into consideration when the possibility of leasing is under analysis to determine if leasing is a viable option for the library. To evaluate the leasing option from a financial viewpoint, current costs of operations must be analyzed and compared with lease costs to determine the savings, if any, that can occur through leasing. If the choice is made to lease, standards for performance need to be clearly outlined as well as compared with actual performance once the lease is in operation.

The objectives of this chapter are to describe two basic types of leases that can be negotiated and to evaluate the factors that need to be taken into account from a cost viewpoint when a lease is being considered as a means of service delivery. A secondary topic in this chapter is a consideration of certain qualitative factors that should be included in evaluating a leasing arrangement.

TYPES OF LEASES

The two basic types of leases that a lessor or lessee can sign are the operating lease and the capital lease.[1] An *operating lease* is the lease agreement that is used when an individual rents an apartment or leases a car for a business trip. The lease agreement provides for the use of property for a short or long period of time, after which the property is returned to the lessor. During the period that the lessee uses the property, lease payments are periodically made by the lessee to the lessor. Although the lease payment is the major cash outflow from the lessee, there may also be certain incidental payments made for utilities in the case of an apartment or gasoline with a leased car.

The second type of lease agreement is called a *capital lease,* and its terms are more complex than those of the operating lease. In this type of a lease agreement, the risks of ownership are transferred to the lessee as the lease is essentially an agreement to purchase the leased property by the end of the lease's term. Although for financial reporting purposes the lease is an asset, from a managerial viewpoint it is more important to understand the cash inflows and outflows that are related to this lease agreement.

The capital lease agreement is likely to include several options that are different from an operating lease. For example, the lease may include a bargain purchase option. A *bargain purchase option* allows the lessee to purchase the property at the end of the lease term at a price that is below the asset's fair market value. This option price is thus considered to be a bargain price, and the lessee will usually exercise the option. Payments typically made by the lessor in an operating lease must be paid by the lessee in a capital lease. Examples of such payments are insurance on the property, maintenance expenditures, and, possibly, property taxes. These two versions of leases are the types that are likely to be encountered in the library environment.[2]

Another leasing arrangement that can be used is called a sale and leaseback. Under this leasing arrangement, a library sells a building it owns to a private investor and immediately enters into an operating lease with the investor for the use of the building. Under a sale and leaseback, the library should only sell the building while retaining the use of the land to ensure its control over the building. This technique provides a fixed return to the investor and an immediate source of cash inflow for the library. Under this arrangement, the lessee pays all the costs of maintaining the facilities, such as utilities, maintenance, and, possibly, taxes. An option that allows the library to repurchase the building at the end of the lease term can be included in the initial lease agreement.

Sales and leasebacks are not extensively used in the library environment; therefore, the illustrations in this chapter are directed at operating and capital lease arrangements. The examples compare the leasing or purchasing costs of an asset or service.

Leases can be arranged for fixed assets such as buildings and equipment, but leasing of services such as maintenance or printing services or even the services of a library staff can be arranged. For example, the federal government has made contracting arrangements for library staff at some of its facilities.[3] Furthermore, it would be possible to arrange for leases of the library's circulating collection to reduce the investment in a collection of currently popular light fiction with a short life expectancy.

COST COMPARISONS OF LEASED ASSETS

To make cost comparisons between leasing and purchasing an asset, costs are compared over the same time periods, which are usually the term of the lease. To analyze the alternatives, present value analysis is usually used. (Appendix B should be reviewed by those unfamiliar with present value analysis.)

The periodic rental payments in a lease are treated as annuities. An *annuity* is an equal cash payment made at equal time periods that can be discounted to determine the present value of the series of payments. Lease payments can be separated into two types based on when the cash payment occurs, which is either at the beginning or the end of a period. Lease payments are usually made at the beginning of a period before the lessee takes control of the leased asset. Table 3 in appendix B lists the table factors necessary to use in making the calculations for lease payments made at the beginning of a period, which is an annuity due. Table 2, on the other hand, contains the table factors to use if lease payments are made at the end of a period, which is an ordinary annuity. In the analysis used here, periodic lease payments are assumed to occur at the beginning of a period rather than at the end. In lease analysis, Tables 2 or 3 are sometimes used in conjunction with Table 1, which is used to compute the present value of a lump sum payment such as an asset's salvage value or the present value of a bargain purchase option.

The examples in this chapter are used to analyze the decision between purchasing or leasing an asset, hiring a maintenance service or using an in-house maintenance staff for cleaning the library, and choosing between two different leasing contracts. The example in the chapter that deals with the choice between the purchasing or leasing of an asset is typical of any purchase/lease choice faced by a library manager. The other examples are also representative of the cost factors that would have to be analyzed in making an intelligent choice among the cost alternatives.

Leasing versus Purchasing an Asset

In this example, the director of a public library has a choice of purchasing a bookmobile for $95,000 or leasing one for $14,000 per year. The bookmobile is estimated to have a ten-year life. Annual depreciation on the bookmobile is $9,500 per year, but in choosing between purchasing and leasing, annual depreciation is irrelevant because the actual cash inflows or outflows are the only factors that need to be investigated.

The cost of maintaining the bookmobile is $1,500 per year. The lease agreement stipulates that this cost will be paid by the lessor. If the library purchases the bookmobile, maintenance expenditures will have to be paid by the library. If the library leases the bookmobile, the library will not be responsible for this cost. If the bookmobile is purchased, the $5,000 salvage value that will be received for the bookmobile at the end of its useful life must be taken into account.

The other expenses of operating a bookmobile will not change between the lease or purchase alternatives; therefore, they are not a consideration in the analysis. For example, the cost of gasoline and insurance will be paid by the library regardless of whether the bookmobile is leased or purchased. The difference in operating costs relates to the maintenance expenditures only.

Figure 8-1 shows how the calculations are made to determine which of the alternatives is the better choice for the library. Before reviewing this illustration, it should be noted that, as with the present value examples in chapter 6, this illustration assumes a discount rate of 10 percent.[4] Further, it should be noted that lease analysis also incorporates differential cost analysis (DCA), which was discussed in chapter 7, to analyze the costs that differ between the alternatives.

The information about the cost choices is divided into buy and lease options. The buy option shows the $95,000 purchase price of the bookmobile and the present value of the $1,500 maintenance costs as the two cash outflows that the library will make if the bookmobile is purchased. These outflows are reduced by the present value of the salvage value of $5,000 that the library will receive for the bookmobile at the end of its useful life. The $1,500 maintenance charges are likely to occur uniformly over the year, in actual practice, but for this illustration, they are assumed to occur at the end of the year. Thus, they become an ordinary annuity paid by the library. The table factor of 6.145 is obtained from Table 2 in appendix B at 10 percent for ten periods. It is multiplied times the $1,500 series of payments, an annuity, to obtain the present value of these series of payments, $9,217.50. The salvage value is not an annuity because it occurs only in one period at the end of the asset's life. Therefore, this is a lump sum payment, and the table factor for it is obtained at 10 percent and ten periods from Table 1 in appendix B.

1. Assumed discount rate = 10%	
2. Time period = 10 years	
Alternative One: Buy	
Purchase price	$ 95,000.00
Maintenance cost: present value ($1,500 × 6.145 table factor)	9,217.50
Salvage value: present value ($5,000 × .386 table factor)	(1,930.00)
Net present value	$102,287.50
Alternative Two: Lease	
Lease payment present value ($14,000 × 6.759)	$ 94,626.00

FIGURE 8-1   Analyzing the cost alternatives between buying and leasing a bookmobile

This cash inflow reduces the cost of the bookmobile and is deducted from the other two cash outflows.

Once the present values for the cash inflows and outflows in the purchase option are calculated, they are totaled to determine the net present value of this alternative. The net present value of the bookmobile is $102,287.50. To make the proper choice—least-cost alternative—for the library, the net present value of purchasing the asset must be compared with the present value of the lease payments.

The present value of the lease option is shown. The lease payments are an annuity due rather than an ordinary annuity because they are made at the beginning of each period. To calculate the present value of this series of payments, Table 3 must be used, "Present Value of an Annuity Due." The table factor at 10 percent and ten periods is 6.759. This amount is multiplied by the lease payments to determine the lease's present value of $94,626.

At this point, a managerial decision can be made as to which alternative is the least costly alternative for the library. Obviously, the best choice from a total cost perspective is to rent the bookmobile. However, there are qualitative considerations that will be considered later in the chapter that should also enter into this decision.

Exercise 8-1

Present Values and the Lease

The Mowry Library is considering signing a photocopy leasing agreement. Two companies have provided contracts with different terms, and the director is trying to determine which of the two contracts is the more cost-saving contract. ACME Business is offering a lease where the library will pay $125 quarterly for two years. Warren Business Supply is offering the same photocopy machine with two annual payments of $500.

Assume a discount rate of 10 percent and that the lease payments would be made at the beginning of the period. Which lease agreement is the most cost-effective choice, assuming all other characteristics of the two leases are the same?

Leasing or Contracting for Personnel Services versus In-House Personnel

It may be possible for a library to cut its operating costs by leasing or contracting for services rather than hiring employees to provide the services.

This does not necessarily mean that current employees need to be fired. It may be possible to transfer current employees to an employee leasing company then hire these employees back. In the process, money may be saved because the leasing company would handle payroll, federal and state compliance reporting, as well as unemployment expenses. The curtailment of record keeping by the library may mean it would also be able to save additional monies in the cost of maintaining personnel records and personnel administrative costs. In addition, labor problems over lack of adequate wage increases caused by a strained budget can be eliminated because the leasing company is responsible for wage increases. The elimination of these supplemental problems allows the library's administrative staff to concentrate on its primary mission objectives. These are some of the positive aspects for con sidering the leasing of services.

In Figure 8-2, a cost analysis is made between leasing maintenance services and using in-house employees. In the example, it is not necessary to

Cost of Maintenance Employees		
Salary		$12,500
Benefits		
Overtime premium	$ 500	
Holidays	570	
Vacation	950	
Accident and sick days	325	
Long-term disability insurance	350	
Medical costs	630	
Life insurance	180	
Health insurance	200	
Social security	950	
Unemployment	128	
Workers' compensation	75	
Pension plans	1,750	6,608
Total salary and benefits (for four employees)	$19,108 × 4 =	$76,432
Miscellaneous cost		
Elimination of one part-time position		$ 1,600
Annual cost of cleaning supplies		1,500
Cost of maintenance employees and miscellaneous items		$79,532

FIGURE 8-2   Cost comparison for leasing maintenance employees

use present value analysis because all cost data are based in the current time period; there are no timing differences. In making the comparison, the first step is to determine the costs of in-house personnel.

In the example, the ABC Library has a maintenance staff of four janitors who receive a yearly salary of $12,500 each. The library is considering converting to a leasing company for library maintenance services. The yearly charge for this service would be $75,000. If the total salary of $50,000 paid to the four members of the in-house maintenance crew is compared with the cost of leasing the maintenance service, it appears it is better to keep maintenance in-house. But, there are other costs that need to be taken into consideration. The cost of benefits paid to the in-house maintenance crew must be a consideration because these costs would be eliminated if the contract is signed with the leasing company—no crew, no benefits paid by the library.

A calculation is made to show the cost of salary and benefits currently paid to one member of the maintenance crew. Although the salary is $12,500, the cost of benefits paid directly to this employee is $6,608, which is more than half the salary the employee is receiving. As shown, benefit expenditures are composed of such items as overtime premiums, days off, insurance, social security, unemployment and workers' compensation payments, and payments into a pension plan. This total cost of one maintenance employee is $19,108. This total cost of the maintenance employees paid by the library needs to be taken into account when making the cost comparison between leasing a service and using in-house personnel.

In addition to salary and benefits, there are other cost considerations. For example, it may be possible to reduce the paperwork costs involved in payroll, hiring, and terminating functions. With maintenance personnel, steady turnover of employees is likely, and as a result there are paperwork costs for advertising and hiring new employees as well as orientation and termination costs. ABC Library assumes that one part-time employee involved in record-keeping functions will be released at an additional savings of $1,600. Also, included in this amount is the reduction in the costs of advertising for maintenance personnel. In addition to the personnel cost savings from this change, there will be a savings in the yearly cost of maintenance supplies used, $1,500 in this example. Any janitorial equipment that can be sold should also be included in the analysis as a one-time reduction of total lease costs.

The cost savings from eliminating one maintenance employee is $19,108 or a total cost savings of $76,432 for the four members of the maintenance crew. The total cost of the in-house maintenance for the ABC Library is $79,532. Therefore, if the leasing option is chosen, a yearly savings of $4,532 ($79,532 − $75,000) will occur. The best cost choice for the ABC

Library is to sign the lease agreement. If the lease includes a fixed five-year term, the total cost savings for the library is a significant amount. As noted earlier, there are other qualitative factors that must also be taken into consideration in making this decision, but from a cost perspective, it is wise to lease the janitorial-maintenance service.

Exercise 8-2

Book-Leasing Service

The Jones Library is considering using Moreland Book Servicing to provide leisure or popular titles for its circulating library. The annual fee for this service is $17,000, and a five-year lease will be signed. The books received from the service do not become the property of the library and must be returned to Moreland. Moreland pays for all return shipping costs. The service provides new titles on a monthly basis from selections made from its catalog.

The Jones Library has been purchasing these books for $28.50 per book on average (from purchase price to shelving the book). The library purchases 500 leisure titles annually. These titles can be sold after their use for an average price of $3.

1. What is the present value of the two options facing the Jones Library? Use a 10 percent discount rate.

2. What is the present value of the two options facing the Jones Library if it is assumed that book cataloging, purchasing, and receiving activities will be reduced enough to reduce staff and save $15,000 in payroll expenditures? Use a 10 percent discount rate.

LEASE COMPARISONS

The lease agreements that have been analyzed up to this point have had fixed annual payment schedules. A number of payment options can be incorporated into a lease agreement that make the task of determining the best cost alternative more complex. For example, lease agreements can call for graduated increases in payments tied to some outside factor such as inflation, or the agreement can call for stipulated annual fixed increases in payments over the lease term. In addition, the lease agreement can require that the lessee pay a damage deposit at the beginning of the lease. This deposit is returnable and may or may not earn interest. As previously stated, the lease agreement can provide the option for the lessee to take title to the asset at the end of the lease term at a bargain purchase price. Furthermore, the lease agreement may require that the leased asset have a stipulated market value at the end of the lease term. If it does not, the lessee is required to pay the difference between the leased asset's actual market value at the end of the lease and the fair market value it should have had as stated in the lease agreement.

In analyzing the cost differences between two leases, present values must always be used to determine which is the best cost choice for the library. Without the incorporation of present values, incorrect conclusions can be reached about the lease choices. Figure 8-3 provides an example of some of the variations that can arise in lease agreements, and the example illustrates how to identify the least-cost alternative for the library.

The XYZ Library has decided to rent an equipment system from a lessor. Normally, the cash purchase price for this library equipment system is $18,000. There are two companies that are willing to provide the equipment under a leasing agreement, but the terms of the two lease agreements differ substantially from each other. The director is uncertain as to which lease would be the better cost choice for the library.

The first lease, from Acme Leasing, provides for five fixed lease payments of $3,200 for five periods beginning at the inception of the lease. In addition, the agreement calls for an $8,000 damage deposit that will be returned at the termination of the lease. The library does not anticipate that any damages will occur and therefore expects to receive the entire $8,000 back at the end of the lease term. The second lease, from E–Z Leasing, provides for graduated increases in the lease payments of $500 after the first payment of $3,000 is made at the beginning of the lease. In addition, this lease contains a bargain purchase option that provides that at the end of the lease the library may purchase the system for $1,000. The XYZ Library uses a 10 percent discount rate to analyze the present value implications of the two leases.

In analyzing the leases, draw a time line that outlines the payments as they occur. This schedule is provided at the top of Figure 8-3. The lease payments are shown above the time line, and the lease periods are shown below the line. Although not shown on the time line, the deposit is returned at the end of the fifth period. If the total amount of the lease payments made under both of the leases is computed, it can be seen that $16,000 would be paid under the Acme lease ($3,200 × five periods) and $20,000 under the E-Z lease ($3,000 + $3,500 + $4,000 + $4,500 + $5,000). From this perspective, the best choice for the library seems to be the Acme lease by $4,000 ($20,000 − $16,000).

Time Schedule

| 1 | 2 | 3 | 4 | 5 | Lease payments |

| 1 | 2 | 3 | 4 | 5 | Periods |

Acme Lease

Lease term = 5 years Assumed discount rate = 10%
Total payments = $16,000 Deposit required = $8,000
Annual payments = $3,200

Acme Lease Analysis

	Present Value
Deposit cash outflow	$ 8,000.00
Present value of lease payments	
($3,200 × 4.170)	13,344.00
Present value of returned deposit	
($8,000 × .621)	(4,968.00)
Net present value of lease agreement	$16,376.00

E-Z Lease

Lease term = 5 years Assumed discount rate = 10%
Bargain purchase option = $1,000 Deposit required: None
Total payments = $20,000
Annual payments = Begin at $3,000 and increase in increments of $500 over the term of the lease

E-Z Lease Analysis

Payment Number	Payment Amount		Table Factor		Present Value
1	$3,000	×	1.000	=	$3,000.00
2	3,500	×	.909	=	3,181.50
3	4,000	×	.826	=	3,304.00
4	4,500	×	.751	=	3,379.50
5	5,000	×	.683	=	3,415.00

Present value of lease payments	$16,280.00
Present value of bargain purchase option	
($1,000 × .621)	621.00
Net present value of lease agreement	$16,901.00

FIGURE 8-3 Lease alternatives

The analysis of the Acme lease includes the initial deposit, the fixed lease payments, and the return of the deposit. The initial deposit at the beginning of the lease is a cash outflow, and even though it will be returned to the library at the end of the lease, its effect on cash costs must be taken into account. As the deposit is paid at the beginning of the lease, it is not adjusted for the time value of money effect. The present value of the lease payments of $3,200 is calculated using the table factor from Table 3 in appendix B at 10 percent for five periods. This amount is $13,344. The present value of the deposit that is returned at the end of the lease must be calculated to determine the full effect of making an $8,000 deposit with the lessor for five years. The deposit being returned at the end of the lease term is similar to the salvage value received from a fixed asset, and the table factor from Table 1 for 10 percent and five periods is used to determine its present value of $4,968. Even though the deposit is returned to the library, there is an opportunity cost in foregone interest to the library of $3,032 ($8,000 − $4,968) for making the deposit.[5] These three factors are summed to determine the cost of the Acme lease. This total, $16,376, is the net present value of the lease. This amount must now be compared with the net present value of the E–Z lease agreement.

The E–Z lease agreement includes graduated lease payments. There are several ways in which the net present value of graduated lease payments can be determined. Figure 8-3 presents one such method, whereby the five lease payments are separately analyzed. Because the first payment of $3,000 is made at the inception of the lease, it does not need to be adjusted for the time value of money as it is already in the current period. The other lease payments need to be adjusted for time-value effects. Rather than using the annuity tables with this series of graduated annuities, each payment, after the first, is considered to be a separate lump sum payment, and the table factors from Table 1 are used to determine the present value of this series of payments.

The first table factor in the calculation, .909, is taken from Table 1 for 10 percent and one period. One period is used because this amount is paid, as shown in the time line, at the end of the first period, and this is the assumption in Table 1—lump sum payments occurring at the end of a period. The same sequence is followed for the remaining lease payments. These lease payments are multiplied times the table factors to determine the present value of the total series of payments, or $16,280.

The last item that has to be considered in the E–Z lease agreement is the bargain purchase option that allows the library to take title to the asset in return for $1,000. It is assumed that this is an attractive offer for the library and that the library will exercise its option to purchase the equipment. For this reason, the results must be put into the calculation. The $1,000 payment, which is a lump sum payment, is to be made at the end of period five of the lease term. To determine the present value of the $1,000, the table factor from Table 1 for 10 percent at five periods is multiplied times the $1,000 option payment. The result, $621, is added to the present value of the lease payments to determine the net present value of all the payments. The net present value of the E-Z lease agreement is equal to $16,901.

After this analysis is completed, the best choice from a total cost perspective is with Acme. By signing this lease, the library will save $525 ($16,901 – $16,376). This conclusion shows that the lease agreement does not favor Acme by $4,000, but by only $525, and there is another consideration. With the E-Z lease, the XYZ Library can acquire the entire equipment system for an additional $525 (in terms of present value dollars). The normal acquisition purchase price of this system is $18,000. Therefore, a decision needs to be made as to whether the lower price for the system is worthwhile in light of the slightly higher level of lease payments required by E-Z. For a nonprofit organization, this may not be an easy decision as the budgeted dollars appropriated for leasing may be exceeded if the E-Z lease agreement is chosen.

When lease agreements have terms and stipulations that differ significantly from one another, it is necessary to carefully analyze these differences using time-value concepts. Without present value analysis, library resources can be wasted when they are particularly difficult to obtain. It is helpful to use a checklist to identify the costs, stated or unstated, in a lease. Cost factors that can increase or decrease the cost of a lease include whether installation costs, insurance, maintenance expenditures, shipping charges, auxiliary supplies, and upgrades to the asset are going to be paid for by the lessor or the library. Figure 8-4 provides a beginning checklist for such an inventory of lease costs. Once a yes or no determination and its amount is checked on each cost item, the total cost of leasing becomes more apparent. In Figure 8-4, the most favorable lease characteristics for the library are checked.

As with all financial decisions, qualitative factors related to leasing must also be considered. The next section looks at some qualitative factors.

Exercise 8-3

Variations on the Book Service Lease

On November 1, 20xx, the Markell Book Servicing Company developed a book servicing plan for the Kennywood Library. The library wants to rent second copies of very popular titles from Markell rather than purchase a second copy of the title. Based on usage studies of

Lease Characteristic Questions	Yes	No
Does the lease provide for auxiliary supplies (photocopy toner, etc.)?	√	
Can the library request direct service from the manufacturing warranty of the leased asset?	√	
Does the library pay maintenance costs?		√
Does the library pay the installation costs?		√
Does the library pay for asset upgrades (PC memory, etc.)?		√
Does the library pay for insurance?		√
Does the library incur any costs if the leased asset is rejected as unsatisfactory?		√
Is the library financially responsible if the leased asset is damaged or destroyed?		√
Is there a lease-purchase option?	√	
Is there a charge for the early termination of the lease?		√
Can the item be subleased within the library system?	√	
Can the item be subleased to an outside third party?	√	
Is the library responsible for the return of the asset at the end of the lease?		√
Is there a maximum yearly maintenance fee provided by the lessor?		√
Is the lease assignable to a third party by the lessor?		√
Is the lessor responsible for any sales and use taxes generated by the lease?	√	
Is there a penalty because of default?		√
If lessor alterations to the asset create increases in lessee maintenance costs, is the lessor responsible for the increase in these costs?	√	

FIGURE 8-4 Cost checklist for a library lease

leisure books by patrons, the number of second titles is estimated to have a seasonal trend, with the highest usage occurring in the months of June, July, and August.

Under the lease, the total annual number of second titles required would be 600, or 50 per month, on average. Because of the seasonal demand for titles, 65 titles would be purchased in the months of June, July, and August if the lease is not signed. In no case, however, could the total number of second titles exceed 600 during the year. The lease agreement with Markell will provide for 50 books every month over the lease term without variation.

Assume that Markell will provide the service at the maximum annual charge of $18,000, or $28 per book. The payment to Markell will be on a monthly basis, with the first payment made at the beginning of the lease term. For Kennywood, the net shelf cost of purchasing these books is $26 per title. The net shelf cost is the total of all costs to get the book onto a library shelf.

Determine the present value of the two alternatives for Kennywood—continue purchasing or leasing—from November 1 to August 31. Remember that during an annual period only 600 titles can be purchased. Assume a 10 percent discount rate and that the number of titles purchased is 41 in December; otherwise, 44 titles will be purchased except for the months of June, July, and August, when 65 are purchased in each of the three months.

TRADE-OFFS IN LEASING

One advantage of leasing is that it allows libraries to stay current with the most recent technologies. With computer technology, for example, new developments occur so quickly that purchasing computer facilities can result in a financial commitment to outmoded and outdated equipment. In many cases, this equipment becomes more and more difficult and expensive to service. Leasing provides the library with the most recent technology, and therefore leasing may be the better choice from both cost and quality perspectives.

In a leasing arrangement, it is important to select a lessor with a good reputation for quality service. Factors such as the downtime on equipment from initial call to repair, the quality of the equipment and supplies provided, and the general attitude of the lessor are important considerations in evaluating the lessor's reputation. The reputation of the lessor will affect the quality of the service regardless of whether equipment or personnel services are leased. Many times the best way to determine the quality of a lessor's reputation is to contact other lessees who have a current lease with the lessor and to ask them about the quality of service delivery from the lessor.

Although leasing personnel services may result in less paperwork for the organization, a lease requires added administrative effort to negotiate and possibly renegotiate terms. Lease negotiations, and possibly locating new lessors, are added efforts not required when the assets are owned or services are provided by in-house personnel. Therefore, the initial advantages of less paperwork and less time devoted to the personnel problems of the organization have to be measured against the search for an acceptable lessor and the time devoted to negotiating a lease agreement. In addition, all the paperwork that was associated with an in-house maintenance workforce or a purchased asset probably will not be eliminated once a leasing company provides the service. It is still important to evaluate the quality of the leased services being provided, and this function may take time away from the primary mission objectives of the library. In fact, leased assets may require more work of this nature than a purchased asset. So, it cannot be assumed that the advantages in time savings only favor leasing arrangements.

Once in-house employees or an asset are no longer under the complete control of the library—when they are leased—any inflationary cost increases are sure to be passed on by the lessor. Therefore, decision makers need estimates of whether the future salary increases of in-house employees would be as great as the increase in annual lease payments that may occur. With leased personnel services, flexibility may exist in the face of substantial increases in lease payments because it is possible to rehire internal staff, but with equipment leases, it may not be possible to pay for an expensive piece of equipment at the time lease payments are increased. Therefore, the flexibility of entering and terminating a lease agreement should be a consideration, separate from costs, prior to signing any lease agreement.

Another aspect of lease flexibility is related to the range and quality of tasks performed by leased personnel. The additional services provided by in-house maintenance personnel, for example, are not always available with leased personnel. This is another aspect of leasing that needs to be explicitly considered. In-house personnel may feel they are significant to the organization, and as a result, they may expand their duties beyond their formal job descriptions. This can be particularly important if emergency work, such as fixing leaks, needs to be performed by maintenance personnel. In-house personnel may not question the fact that they need to fix the roof during a rainstorm, but leased personnel may not have this written into their job functions so that it would be necessary to phone for emergency services. In-house personnel may be willing to perform other miscellaneous activities that are not part of a leasing arrangement. The lease agreement will need to spell out all auxiliary activities or services that are to be provided or not provided under the terms of the lease. This is also true for leased assets. The service and warranty arrangements for assets need to be clearly delineated in the lease agreement.

A Final Consideration: Monitoring Lease Performance

The monitoring of lease performance has already been mentioned as an administrative duty required to evaluate lease activities. But, this topic needs to be mentioned in more detail.

Leasing may be a viable alternative to purchasing a new asset or may improve the manner in which current services are delivered. But, without the proper monitoring of performance, it cannot be determined if the correct choice was made. Furthermore, if a lease was selected as the most cost-effective choice, monitoring must be instituted to ensure that previous standards of service are being met.

When a lease is signed, there are some "hidden costs" that should be taken into account in analyzing the total cost of the lease. These costs include the continuous monitoring of service standards and the changeover costs that may occur at the time the service is changed from an in-house operation to a lease arrangement. Monitoring costs are a permanent cost of the lease; changeover costs would normally only cause a small temporary increase in costs.

Monitoring costs occur as administrative time is devoted to evaluating lease activities. These costs are not additional costs caused by signing a lease. They are monitoring costs already incurred within the organization and reassigned to monitor lease performance. For this reason, they were not included in the cost calculations in Figures 8-1, 8-2, and 8-3. If it were necessary to add more personnel to the library staff to monitor lease standards, then these new costs should be included in comparing leasing with other alternatives. The temporary costs related to the changeover are considered insignificant in the examples, and they are not included in the analysis either.

Before signing a lease agreement, it is important to determine how the lease contractor intends to monitor its employees to ensure that acceptable service standards are being followed. If these monitoring procedures are not acceptable to the library, negotiating for changes in the lease contract may be necessary. The standards for performance need to be clearly written into the lease agreement to ensure that the library is receiving the services for which it is paying.

Library monitoring functions also need to be in place. These functions include spot checks to ensure standards are being met relative to such factors as the speed of service, how well the service is provided, courteousness of lease employees on library premises, response of lease organization to emergencies, and flexibility to changes in scheduling caused by possible conflicts with community activities, for example. In addition to spot checks, the lease services should be monitored according to a preplanned schedule. The easiest technique to use in making these evaluations is a survey checklist. This checklist serves as the library's documentation for any later disagreements about the level of service or nonservice provided by the lessor. If the terms of the contract are not being met, the lessor needs to be notified, which may require a lessor-lessee conference. If differences cannot be worked out, legal action may be necessary, but this step should only be used as a last resort.

The signing of a lease should not be considered an easy way to eliminate administrative responsibility. The patrons of the library will not bring their complaints to the lessor; these complaints will still have to be handled by the director and library staff. The director and staff of the library still have ultimate responsibility to the public, and to ensure those responsibilities are being met, a systematic method for monitoring all leased functions needs to be carefully developed.

Exercise 8-4

Buying a Bookmobile?

The Rexus Creek Library has partnered with Rexus County to obtain a bookmobile using a tax-exempt municipal lease-purchase agreement. The bookmobile is state of the art and valued at a $150,000 cash price. The lease agreement is structured as a series of one-year renewable obligations subject to Rexus County government's ability to appropriate funds as well as an underlying financial payment commitment from the library. Besides making the annual lease payments, the library is responsible for all annual maintenance, insurance, taxes, and operating expenses of the bookmobile. The county can obtain this financing from investors and record it as a "nondebt obligation." A local for-profit bank-leasing subsidiary is providing the funding for the bookmobile and will receive state and federal nontaxable interest payments at 6 percent annually. This rate is 1 percent lower than the county and library would be able to arrange with short-term borrowing. The bank-leasing company will act as a broker and place portions of the lease obligation with other institutional investors.

1. Assume that there are ten annual payments under the lease.
   (a) How much are the annual payments?
   (b) What is the total amount that the library is paying for the bookmobile?
   (c) How much interest is the library paying?
2. Assume that there are ten annual payments under the lease, but the library had to use short-term borrowing to obtain financing.
   (a) How much are the annual payments?
   (b) What is the total amount that the library is paying for the bookmobile?
   (c) How much interest is the library paying?
   (d) How much more would the library pay for the bookmobile with short-term financing than with the tax-exempt lease agreement?

SUMMARY

This chapter has used present value analysis to analyze the cost of leasing as a viable alternative to purchasing assets or maintaining in-house service personnel. These leasing-versus-purchasing alternatives are available choices for most libraries. Although for-profit organizations have the third alternative of borrowing funds and using those funds to purchase assets, most nonprofit organizations such as libraries are not authorized to incur debt. Therefore, the two practical approaches for acquiring personnel services or the service potential of an asset are either to lease or purchase them.

Besides the cost considerations associated with leasing, other factors need to be taken into account, such as the quality of the service provided by the lessor and the hidden costs—lease monitoring costs—of leasing. Leasing can be a viable alternative to purchasing assets or using in-house personnel, but *all* factors—cost and quality—must be considered when this alternative is under consideration by library managers.

Notes

1. The analysis here concentrates on the effect these leases have on managerial decision making and is not concerned with their financial statement effects. The reporting

differences between these two leases are significant when they are recorded in the financial statements. From a managerial viewpoint, the differences are not as important.

2. Other types of lease agreements should be briefly mentioned. Leveraged leases are an example of a lease that can be used to finance large purchases running into the millions of dollars. To finance this transaction, the financial backing of a third-party lender is required. The typical leveraged lease involves three parties. A lender loans funds to the lessor, who proceeds to purchase the capital asset and lease it to the lessee—the library. The lessee makes lease payments back to the lessor, and these lease payments are used by the lessor to pay principal and interest on the amount borrowed from the lender. Any amounts not paid to the lender are kept by the lessor.

3. From a managerial viewpoint, contracting out and leasing are the same activity and are analyzed in the same manner.

4. The examples in chapter 6 did not go beyond a five-year time frame, but Figure 8-1 incorporates a ten-year period. The reason for this difference is that cash flows in a lease agreement are set according to a legal contract, whereas many of the cash flow estimates in chapter 6 could be subject to a high level of uncertainty as the time frame of the cost projections extends beyond five years.

5. An opportunity cost is the value attributed to the next best alternative that was foregone or, in this case, not obtainable because of the managerial choices actually made. In this case, an opportunity was missed to earn at least 10 percent on the funds deposited over the five years. Essentially, this is a cash flow that was foregone.

CHAPTER

9

Performance Analysis:
The Evaluation of Administrators

Once the best analytical techniques have been applied to solving managerial problems and the corresponding operating decision has been made and implemented, evaluating the performance of those who are responsible for successful outcomes is necessary. The previous chapters have explained the analytical techniques and illustrated their applications to solving managerial problems in libraries. This chapter is not concerned with specific managerial techniques that can be applied to ensure the more efficient use of library resources. Instead, it is devoted to discussing issues that surround the evaluation of the higher-level administrator (HLA). HLAs are the individuals who have the responsibility and authority to use and apply the managerial techniques for making operating and strategic decisions within the library.

In general, performance evaluations relate to the performance of the library, its departments and programs, and the individuals responsible for the operation of these departments and programs. Performance evaluation is a form of managerial control over objectives or goals and initiatives. These objectives and initiatives may be either quantitatively or qualitatively oriented.

Performance evaluation must be directed at all organizational levels in the library for it to work. Several methods are suggested here for evaluating performance. These methods include simple activity counts to contract plans for HLA performance outcomes.

Some general criteria of evaluation should be met by all performance evaluation systems. First, they should provide current data in a timely manner. If the feedback on performance objectives is out of date, it is useless to the manager, who cannot take effective corrective actions. Therefore, timeliness is an important criterion. Data provided on performance also should be shown in a comparative format in order for the manager to determine the level of change from previous periods. This provides clear answers to the question, How well or how poorly am I doing?

Any performance objectives that have a direct effect on behavior and motivation should be carefully considered before they are implemented. If a performance objective is established that is too "ideal" or unreachable, it can seriously decrease employee motivation. Although it is acceptable to establish performance within attainable standards, the establishment of unattainable objectives only causes decreased employee morale as employees realize that they cannot achieve the objective—so why try?

Another factor to consider is the use of a mixture of performance criteria instead of stressing just one or two important evaluators. Without a mixture of performance criteria for the evaluation, a manager's behavior will be directed at achieving success on a narrow range of evaluators, which may have unintended consequences that are detrimental to the library. For example, when service counts are made without considering the quality of the service being provided, the performance goal in terms of numbers can be met, but the quality of that service may be poor because it was provided in such a hurried manner. This can result in growing patron dissatisfaction at a time when it appears that the library's objectives are being achieved. Furthermore, when new technology is adopted, its successful use is dependent on adequate employee training. Neither employee learning nor patron satisfaction is measured with traditional financial measures.

A methodology that does use a mixture of performance evaluators to review overall strategic performance is called the balanced scorecard (BSC). The methodology used with the balanced scorecard incorporates a wide range of measures, including financial, for evaluating performance in a comprehensive manner. R. S. Kaplan and D. P. Norton have written extensively about the use of the balanced scorecard adapted to both corporations and nonprofit organizations.[1] A common theme for usage of the balanced scorecard within both types of organizations is to develop a series of performance measures that evaluate financial, customer, internal processes, and employee learning and growth measures into a combination that helps the organization successfully achieve its strategic initiatives. These measures have to be tied together in a way that allows for success in one area to be translated into success in another area at the same time. The balanced scorecard will be discussed more fully later in the chapter.

Timeliness of data, comparative data, attainable standards, and a mixture of performance criteria are some of the primary considerations in establishing any performance criteria for managerial control and goal achievement. Because material is already available for evaluations of output measures in libraries, the emphasis here is specifically directed at describing performance evaluators that have a potential for controlling the activities of HLAs.

GENERAL PERFORMANCE MEASURES

Activity counts are the simplest method that can be used for evaluating performance. When this method is used, it is a gauge of workload incurred in a library unit, or department. For example, in the Reference Department, workload numbers can be provided about the number of reference questions answered as well as periodical, index, database, and microfilm usage. Such data provide information about the demand for services but little else. This information is helpful, but it does not provide information about the efficiency and effectiveness of operations nor does it indicate whether strategic initiatives are being met. In addition, such measures are based on historical data that provide very little insight into future trends.

Measures of efficiency and effectiveness are a step up from simple counts of performance. Efficiency measures weigh the amount of resources used to achieve outcomes or results. More efficient operations are marked by demonstrating higher levels of output for a given set of input or using the minimum amount of input to achieve a preset output level. Many performance measures established to measure efficiency are based on cost-per-item calculations. When there is a decrease in the cost per item of output, it is interpreted as an increase in the efficiency of operations. In a Reference Department, such a measure might be the cost-per-reference question. Measures such as the cost per volume, circulated by the Circulation Department, could be considered a measure of performance efficiency. Efficiency measures can be established with targets for future performance, thus influencing future trends. Regardless of how efficiency measures are used, they are better measures of performance than simple workload counts.

Although efficiency measures appear to be a useful method to control managerial performance, caution should be exercised in their use to ensure that the measure is controllable by the manager. For example, efficiency can be affected by cutbacks in the budget that are imposed on a departmental manager and over which he or she has no control. As a result, the manager's performance evaluation is affected through no fault of his or her own. When this occurs, the performance evaluation system begins to lose its credibility, and if the trend continues without adjustments, its ability to motivate managers and to control operations is lost.

Efficiency criteria should be used with caution and in combination with other performance criteria that measure effectiveness. Effectiveness is the extent to which policy results are achieved. These policies can include objectives that are to be attained in the future, such as yearly service objectives. These objectives should be established with enough specificity that they are truly measurable as performance criteria. To do this, they must have a program or departmental objective orientation and still be tied to the library's mission. Many times librarywide objectives are not specific enough to have a serious impact on changing behavior. A 2 percent increase in patrons helped is not as specific as the departmental goal of a 2 percent increase in reference questions answered. Examples of performance measures based on effectiveness are the percentage of reference questions answered successfully or the percentage of patrons satisfied with the reference service. These objectives are directed at quality of service issues as they relate to library mission objectives.

This information needs to be presented in a format that is useful for managerial decision making. Without proper presentation of the information, it is difficult or impossible for managers to analyze the results. In addition, care must be taken to ensure that employees do not fudge data to make their performance look good. This behavior could result in less success in overall library operations. For example, if the Circulation Department is not mailing overdue notices on a timely basis, then a way to correct the situation may be to evaluate the circulation staff by counting the number of overdue notices mailed within a specific time period. However, the evaluation method, counts of mailed overdue notices, may result in a blizzard of overdue notices being issued but still not improve library service. This would occur if, in an effort to mail as many overdue notices as possible, the Circulation Department mails overdue notices to patrons who still have several days left to hold borrowed materials. Essentially, data have been fudged to meet the evaluation criteria, and, until patrons begin to complain, the results look good.

One important difference between efficiency and effectiveness measures is that the data for calculating efficiency measures are usually collected within the library's established internal data collection system—cost-per-item information—whereas a significant portion of the data needed for effectiveness measures may be collected from external data sources. For example, data on patron satisfaction with service or speed are collected through surveying patrons—a data source outside the library's established data collection system. These performance measures focus on the quality—observed outcome—of a service as rated by those individuals using the service. These quality measures may rate outcomes without considering the inputs that caused those outcomes. When efficiency is rated, the inputs must be related to the outputs to calculate the measure of performance.

There are several reasons for this focus on the outcome or the result of actions. First, the outcome evaluator is used in conjunction with an efficiency measure that provides input/output relationships, achieving a balanced approach. Second, it may be impossible to directly trace the relationship between the efforts expended and the outcome.

Although all library activities have an input/output relationship, there are variations in how accurately this relationship can be measured. For example, if a staff member is checking shelves, it is possible to determine his or her rate of speed and then use an efficiency measure such as the cost relationship between feet of shelving and the staff member's salary. This cost relationship—input/output—can be used with many repetitive activities such as number of books shelved, number of books checked out, cost of processing new books, and so forth. But, with the nonrepetitive, long-range objectives that tend to occur at higher administrative levels these efficiency measures are difficult or impossible to develop, and as a result, if HLAs are to be evaluated, it must be done with comprehensive outcome measurement that includes both measures of effectiveness and efficiency.

Outcome measurement is the evaluation of administrative input to determine the value generated from that input. This evaluation is usually oriented toward long-term strategic initiatives that are difficult to meaningfully relate directly to single financial measures. In addition, the final outcome of administrative input is, in many cases, difficult to relate to intermediate or short-term objectives. Administrative outcome measurement is essentially a series of program effectiveness measures with a long-term, mission-based orientation.

Exercise 9-1

The Focus for Performance Measures

The Broken Creek Community Library is a medium-sized library in a rural community. Based on benchmark measures for similar libraries, Broken Creek is on the lowest end of all measures related to patron service. Myra Ewol, the head of Circulation, has often brought up the topic of developing patron performance measures to better serve the community. Although other staff, including the director, have supported her suggestions at staff meetings, no progress has ever been made toward the development of performance metrics.

Can you offer suggestions as to why, even when there is support for performance evaluation at Broken Creek, no progress has been made for the adoption of any measures?

LONG-RANGE OUTCOME MEASURES

Several examples of outcome measures have been briefly described. Outcome measurement has the potential to assess the quality of long-term results when it is difficult to measure short-term input/output relationships. In this way, a means to evaluate the performance of HLAs can be developed because many of the functions they perform are long-term in nature. For example, the desired outcome of a program may be to increase the access of the library to one-parent families in the community. The success of outcomes can be measured by surveying one-parent families and evaluating this externally generated information. This is a long-term initiative that is controllable by HLAs in the library. For outcome measurement to have an effect on employee and managerial behavior, performance outcomes must fit within a controllable range for the HLA. A controllable range of influence is one that may not show a direct relationship between input and output; however, it is still clear that the HLA has responsibility for this area and can exercise control to achieve the long-term objective. Without HLA controllability, outcome measurement is in an "open loop," making change impossible to implement. If the outcome measure is clearly uncontrollable by the manager, it should not be used to evaluate that manager's performance.

Many times the data used to evaluate outcomes achieved by administrators must be collected from external sources—the group to whom the program is directed, such as patrons or employee groups—which is another characteristic of HLA outcome measurement. For example, evaluative information can be collected with mail surveys or telephone interviews questioning such issues as the friendliness of library personnel; the convenience of library hours; the usage that is made of library facilities by age, sex, household location within a city, race, and physical handicap; and so forth.

External data can also be collected by using observers who evaluate library outcomes controllable by HLAs, such as the neatness and quietness of library facilities, the correctness of books shelved in the stacks, the ability of library personnel to answer questions, or the availability of current periodicals that are expected to be in the library's collection. The outcomes under evaluation by trained observers are different than those evaluated by the general public. Trained observers have the ability to provide more in depth information about complex outcomes than the general public. For example, patrons may not have a clear concept of the completeness of a library's periodical collection, but a trained observer would be expected to have sufficient knowledge to judge the collection's completeness. The use of trained observers is similar to requesting an independent peer review of administrative performance. Under peer review, librarians from a consortium of regional libraries or possibly an accreditation committee would evaluate administrative success in meeting a series of selected quality outcomes. Again, these reviews may not be able to trace an administrator's input directly to the outcome, but they may be able to determine if success was achieved in meeting outcomes. The organization's internal auditors are another group that can help to evaluate some of these quality measures. Internal auditors evaluate management performance as part of their regular audit functions.

The purpose of these evaluations is to obtain and judge feedback on selected administration-level outcomes. By their very nature, these outcomes have an extended time period orientation when compared with typical efficiency measures and counts of performance. As a result of their long-term orientation, changes to outcomes can only be slowly implemented. With an efficiency measure, if the cost per item is too high, costs can be cut immediately, but with an outcome measure such as courteousness of personnel or the cleanliness of facilities, the rate of improvement is going to occur at a slower pace than with immediate 10 percent budget cuts.

Although it has been emphasized that outcome measurement is directed at successful outcomes, this is not always the case. Outcome measurement can also be directed at measuring negative outcomes. This information can be just as important as successful outcomes, for example, HLA actions in a failed fund-raising campaign.

ADMINISTRATORS AND LONG-RANGE OUTCOME MEASUREMENT

As stated, the tasks of many lower-level employees can be measured by counts of activities. These counts can include information about new library cards issued, number of books processed, and so forth. These measures can be combined with cost data to develop efficiency measures. But, when it comes to HLAs, how can their performance be evaluated? They are concerned with long-range programs, and they do not, usually, perform activities that can be counted. Furthermore, an HLA's performance evaluation should be based on more than simply not exceeding budgetary allocations.

An HLA's performance should be evaluated, but evaluative measures for HLAs are difficult to develop because it is hard to relate outcomes to efforts. For example, if the director of a library is sitting behind his or her desk reading the newspaper's comics, how is this observable? And is this behavior decreasing the productivity of the organization or is it providing a necessary break for the director after which productivity will increase? There is the story of a public library director who took an hour each afternoon to do "reading and paperwork" in his office. During this time, he closed the door to his office and left word that he was not to be disturbed. His staff assumed he was conducting library business until one wintry afternoon he ran out of his office with his shoes burning. He had fallen asleep with his feet on an electric heater, leading to the questions, When is a respite turned into goldbricking and slacking? And how can such behaviors be observed in an HLA?

The work activities of HLAs are not highly structured, and there are imperfect data about the level of effort expended to achieve long-term program initiatives. Therefore, yearly performance measures may not properly reflect achievement or nonachievement of these initiatives. As an example, consider the effects of lack of maintenance on a facility, such as a leaking roof or cracked pipes that are not usually reported until the water damage becomes apparent, which may be years after maintenance was curtailed by administrative decision. Yet, good performance measures would detect such dysfunctional managerial behavior prior to it occurring.

To help prevent the occurrence of these behavior patterns, performance measurement should be focused in two directions. First, performance data can be collected about administrative activities that were actually performed. The accounting system records cost information on most actions taken by managers. But, managers should be responsible for actions they have not taken as well as actions they have taken that may negatively affect the achievement of the library's mission. Data on the former outcomes are usually not recorded within the organization's accounting system.

The Balanced Scorecard

One method that is useful in collecting all performance information and relating it to long-term strategic initiatives is the BSC. The BSC provides the tools for managers to tie financial and nonfinancial performance evaluation to the mission and strategic initiatives of the organization. The BSC process allows for the monitoring of operating activities in a way to ensure that library staff and management are performing daily activities that contribute to the achievement of long-term initiatives. As the BSC is a very open approach, it also provides a way to communicate strategic initiatives to all levels in the library. The BSC looks beyond the financial objectives and incorporates learning and growth targets, the development of internal organization processes, and customer objectives that all align with each other as well as the organization's financial objectives. Figure 9-1 introduces the matrix relationship between these four performance evaluation areas.

Even without defining objectives, performance measures, targets, or initial initiatives for Figure 9-1, it still can be seen that once these factors are selected, their correlation with one another becomes implicit under the BSC. For the library and HLAs, financial targets may mean ensuring that the library is financially viable. Measures of patron satisfaction include evaluators of those initiatives used to increase patron satisfaction. Internal processes relate performance measurement to those areas where the organization must be successful in order to achieve its strategic initiatives. Thus, managers become aware of those organizational processes that contribute to long-term organizational success and how to advance those processes to a higher level of achievement. Learning and growth measurements relate to employees. For the organization to successfully achieve its long-term initiatives, its employees must be adequately trained and skilled. Normal financial measures look at employee training as a cost that reduces available revenues.

HLA coordination of these four areas within a set of objectives, measures, targets, and initiatives is vital for the success of the organization. Therefore, it needs to be determined whether the HLA is providing the guidance needed to achieve the library's strategic goals, not just its operating objectives.

Perspective	Objective	Performance Measure	Target	Initial Initiative
Financial				
Patron				
Internal Processes				
Learning and Growth				

FIGURE 9-1 The outline for the BSC

BSC at the Department Level

The starting point for using the BSC in library management begins with the mission statement and the objectives that flow from it. For example, assume that the Perry Library has a mission of "providing high-quality service to patrons." If the mission statement stops there, it is soon only used when it is necessary to show others that a mission statement exists. Therefore, the mission statement must serve as the guide for each department; and, it is hoped, as a departmental employee finishes a task, he or she, too, can see how it contributed to the mission.

For such coordination to occur, all departments in the Perry Library need to relate their activities to the main library's mission. For example, in the Collection Services Department the "sub" mission is "to provide high-quality collection services to patrons." Once such a guiding mission is selected, financial, patron, internal processes, and learning and growth objectives, measures, targets, and initiatives must be determined and tracked.

The Collection Services Department in the Perry Library wants to use the BSC matrix as outlined in Figure 9-1. The department wants to determine how the purchase of new collection cataloging software called ADM will interact with its mission statement. In the past, purchasing new technology or software meant an interdepartmental committee reviewed the library criteria requirements and the characteristics and capabilities of the new technology to try to find the best match within the budgeted cost. Once the technology with the closest match was selected, the committee was disbanded and the technology was purchased and put into use. This approach has lead to difficulties and protracted time periods in trying to successfully implement new software in the past.

At this point, the committee has decided that ADM software was the best purchase choice within budget guidelines and that ADM meets the department's mission of providing high-quality collection services to its patrons. The committee now is selecting financial, patron, internal processes, and learning and growth criteria that will ensure that the software is closely tied to the Collection Services Department's strategic mission. Figure 9-2 is the result of their deliberations on the BSC.

Figure 9-2 shows that the committee has done more than simply recommend the purchase of new software. It has adapted the purchase to the department's strategic mission. In the financial area, it is expected that the use of ADM will reduce the cataloging costs on a per-book basis. The future financial target is to reduce the unit cost of items cataloged by 10 percent. The initiative used to accomplish this goal is ADM software. It is hoped that when a new book is requested by a patron, ADM's speed in purchasing and cata-

Perry Library BSC Collection Services Department				
Perspective	Objective	Performance Measure	Target	Initial Initiative
Financial	Reduce collection maintenance costs	Cost per item cataloged	−10%	Use ADM
Patron	Increase satisfaction	Survey responses	4.1 average score on responses related to collection requests by patrons	Use ADM
Internal Processes	Temporary reassignment of IT to ADM implementation	IT hours devoted to ADM	IT hours equal to one new part-time employee	Use ADM
Learning and Growth	Retraining of employees to use ADM	Number of seminars attended by employees	Two full-day seminars per employee	Schedule ADM training

FIGURE 9-2 Using the BSC at the department level

loging the book will translate into increasing satisfied responses from patrons on the patron satisfaction survey. The target score on the patron survey for collection services questions are expected to average 4.1, which is an increase over the 3.7 average received in the past. To make ADM a success, internal information technology (IT) services and employee training need to be expanded. Two measures for determining whether this occurs are the number of hours devoted to ADM by internal IT staff and the amount of training provided for employees so that they can effectively use the ADM system. The internal processes target is an increase in IT hours devoted to ADM equal to twenty hours per week, or one part-time employee. Under learning and growth targets, collection services employees are to have two full days of seminar training on the ADM system.

Once this BSC is set up for the Collection Services Department's ADM initiative, the performance measures must be monitored to determine if the targets for each measure are being achieved. If the measures have been carefully considered to meet mission guidelines, the department's long-term initiatives are achievable. The BSC provides a means for individual departmental activities to be linked to strategic library initiatives. For example, when a staff member attends training, it may be considered to be an interruption in his or her daily activities, but within the BSC matrix, such training contributes to achieving the long-term initiatives of the unit and the library. Of course, underlying this entire process is the mission statement of providing high-quality service to patrons.

Exercise 9-2

BSC at the Departmental Level

The Markus Wellmen Free Library's mission statement states that the library will serve a culturally diverse community by promoting lifelong learning and cultural development with high-quality service. The library has recently set up Coffee and Cushions, a retreat area within the library for purchasing coffee and bakery products. The manager hired to run Coffee and Cushions comes from a commercial background and insists on establishing performance goals for the shop before accepting the management position.

Using the BSC approach, develop a mission statement and financial, patron, internal processes, and learning and growth goals for Coffee and Cushions. Be certain that your goals integrate with one another and the mission statement that you have written.

BSC at the HLA Level

As previously stated, the performance of HLAs is more difficult to trace because their activities are related to achieving long-term initiatives. It would be expected that HLAs' strategic impact on financial, patron, and learning and growths measures could be evaluated without too much difficulty. For examples of such evaluators, see the following section, "Examples of Performance Evaluators." Many times the effect that HLAs have on internal processes is more difficult to evaluate. Also, the way HLAs affect internal processes can be of significant importance to the overall well-being of the library. Therefore, this section specifically reviews two measures that may be used with the BSC to evaluate HLAs using the internal processes perspective. Measures based on the following two areas are suggested for incorporating HLA internal processes evaluation into the BSC.

1. Deferred item maintenance
2. HLA value-lost and value-gained determinations

1. *Deferred Item Maintenance.* Deferred items can be used as an outcome measure for HLA performance evaluation. The recording of deferred items in a managerial report can provide an indication of nonaction on the part of an HLA. The typical emphasis in a managerial performance evaluation is on reviewing actions *taken* by managers. For example, the cost of data on new programs is analyzed in great detail. But, little attention is paid to managerial actions that should have been taken and were not. One area where deliberate nonaction may occur is in the proper maintenance of assets or in the proper training of employees to ensure that full use is being made of new technologies and better library services are actually being provided as new technologies are introduced into the library. Nonaction by management in areas such as these is not identified in any reports, and as a result, resources deteriorate and are wasted. Managers should be held accountable for actions they did not take just as they are held accountable for those they did take.

Maintenance spending is used here as an illustration of nonaction decision making by HLAs. When budget cutting occurs in a library or any nonprofit organization, one of the most common cuts is in maintenance expenditures. These cuts can go unnoticed for long periods of time, but eventually funds must be provided to make up for years of neglect. These funds are used for extensive renovation or the rebuilding of prematurely deteriorated facilities.

One long-term performance measure for HLAs can be related to the proper maintenance of facilities. If maintenance is inadequate to the point of deterioration, a question arises as to the administrator's ability to raise supplemental funds to make up for the accelerated payments that will be required to rebuild facilities. An administrator could have a benefactor willing to provide these monies at a future date so that premature obsolescence and deterioration of facilities is not a serious problem. So, improper maintenance may be compensated for by a generous benefactor . . . possibly.

The first step in evaluating performance outcomes related to deferred maintenance is to determine the difference, if any, between the expenditures that should be made for proper maintenance of assets and the actual amount expended for maintenance. Are these expenditures adequate or is there a shortfall? Information from vendors is usually available regarding the amount of yearly maintenance charges needed to properly maintain equipment and other assets. If this information is not available from vendors, the cost of proper maintenance of buildings, vehicles, and equipment can be estimated.

Using these estimates and the amounts actually spent—as recorded in the accounting records—a deferred maintenance charge can be calculated. The charge is a variance that is equal to the difference between the amount of maintenance expenditures actually spent and the dollar amount that maintenance guidelines indicate should be expended. When less is expended than should have been to maintain the facilities properly, the difference is a curtailed maintenance expenditure. If the balance in this off-the-books account continues to increase, it is likely to be a sign of prematurely deteriorating assets.[2]

A shortfall in maintenance of facilities provides an indication of nonaction by an HLA. Yet, as previously noted, a second factor in this evaluation can be directed at the ability of the administrator to attract funds to make up for the shortfall. The shortfall, by itself, is an indication of a problem. But, the problem can be corrected by the library administrator's actions in successfully attracting supplemental funds to replace assets that have prematurely deteriorated. If the administrator is responsible for inadequate maintenance on assets and does not have the ability to attract funds to the library to make up for this shortfall, then the performance of that administrator is inadequate. Corrective controls need to be established to ensure that future monies are not taken away from maintenance at a rate that causes premature deterioration of assets. Figure 9-3 provides a means to incorporate deferred maintenance and the generation of external funding into the BSC.

Figure 9-3 shows the interaction of three measures as related to maintenance on library assets that are already in place. If the level of deferred maintenance is found to be increasing (row one measures), it would be expected that a successful HLA would obtain increased external funding to make up for the shortfall (row two measures). Furthermore, it would be important to determine if any additional external funding was being used to make up for the deferred maintenance shortfall. The minimum target ratio for supplemental funding when deferred maintenance is occurring is shown in Figure 9-3 as a target measure of one. This relationship means that each dollar of underspending on recommended maintenance is being made up for with a dollar of supplemental support obtained by the HLA.

Over the short-term, it may be possible to curtail maintenance expenditures and use these monies for new initiatives in the library that make a library director appear to be a dynamic leader. In these cases, the director can find a new position before the deterioration becomes apparent. The reporting system should raise red flags early to make the board and other interested parties aware of the situation occurring through administrative nonaction or

Objective	Performance Measure	Target	Initial Initiative
Maintain Working Facility Assets	Recommended maintenance dollars less current maintenance in budgeted dollars = deferred maintenance*	Zero difference in the measure	Request for maintenance expenditures in budget
Increase External Funding	External funding dollars received	Annual dollars of external funding equal to 5% of total budget	Formulation of a library advisory committee formed from community leaders for supplemental support
Supplemental Support for Maintenance	Dollars of external supplemental support/deferred maintenance charge	Should be equal to one	Formulation of a library advisory committee formed from community leaders for supplemental support

*This is the deferred maintenance charge.

FIGURE 9-3 The internal process perspective for HLAs as related to deferred maintenance recognition

contriving behavior. Nonactions are usually not evaluated but should be if a true picture of administrative performance is to develop.

In the current curtailed funding environment, a manager may have to make a choice between drastically cutting maintenance or services, but regardless, the fact that maintenance has been cut should not go unreported. The current savings in maintenance expenditures may result in unanticipated and accelerated increases in future expenditures.[3]

The typical accounting system also does not record information about deferred maintenance charges.[4] Therefore, this information must be collected outside the accounting records. One way to collect deferred maintenance information is with the performance audit. A performance audit is conducted by the internal audit department to ensure that operations have been carried out efficiently. The audit can investigate any activities to determine if specified program objectives have been accomplished in a prescribed manner. With a performance audit, information can be collected to determine if there is a shortfall in maintenance expenditures. The board of directors of a library can request that a performance audit be conducted, and, furthermore, they can specifically request that certain programs or administrator's activities be evaluated as part of that process. In this way, information can be collected about whether facilities are being properly maintained.

A performance audit provides an excellent means for assessing and evaluating actions taken and not taken by HLAs. The tools of a performance audit can include conducting surveys of patrons, interviewing patrons and employees, and preparing reports for managerial purposes rather than financial reports for external reporting.

2. *HLA Value-Lost and Value-Gained Determinations.* Another aspect of HLA evaluation that can fit within the BSC format is an evaluation of HLA decision-making effectiveness. Here, a determination is made as to whether the HLA is providing input, or decision support, that increases the library's service to the public. In other words, the most valuable contribution from HLAs is their input into decision making. HLA decision input should result in higher levels of service to the public. Of course, it could occur that HLA input is detrimental to decision making in the organization, resulting in less service provided to the public.[5] Good HLA decisions result in a value gain as identified by service provided to the public; and poorly formulated HLA decisions, for whatever reason, result in value loss through lower levels of public service.

Value determination relates to the value lost or gained by the public in terms of service levels provided by the library resulting from HLA inputs. If an administrator has been directly involved in problem definition, choice identification, and final selection of a solution to a long-term problem, are the results better? Is better service the consequence of that administrator's input? Has value been added to the services provided by the library because of administrative input? A value determination question can be answered in several ways by employees who have participated directly in the program, project, initiative, or activity under review:

1. No administrative input was received—no service value was lost. (HLA input not needed. Slacking behavior possible.)
2. Little administrative input was received—service value was lost. (Slacking behavior possible.)

3. Administrative input was received—service value was lost. (Incompetence/self-interest possible.)
4. Administrative input was received—service value was gained. (Success possible.)

As previously stated, HLA input into the organization cannot be counted in terms of widgets produced. Instead, it must be measured in terms of long-term outcomes, and value determination is a method that can be adopted to evaluate those outcomes. In conjunction with a performance audit, a series of confidential survey questions administered by the internal audit staff and asked of employees can help determine where HLA input has been successfully applied.

In response to a value determination question, an employee may make this statement: "No administrative input was received—no service value was lost." This response indicates that the administrator had no input into the work activity, and it was completed successfully. There is more than one possible reason for this response. It may be that the HLA should have been involved in providing direction in this project or activity, but the HLA was involved in slacking behavior. Even when an administrator is slacking, however, library employees may have been able to exercise enough initiative to prevent lost service value from occurring.

The response to the question may indicate something altogether different. A number of activities in the library can be completed successfully without HLA input, such as book purchasing decisions and staff scheduling. The response to this question may indicate that the surveyed activity was one such area. It is not necessary for HLAs to be involved in many day-to-day library activities. In fact, if these administrators are involved in these activities, a question arises as to why their efforts are misdirected.

The second response to a value determination question may be "Little administrative input was received—service value was lost." This employee response identifies an activity or project that has been neglected by the administrator but viewed by the employees interviewed in a performance audit as an area where administrative input could have increased patron service levels. If this is an activity—book purchases, for example—that should be handled by employees without administrative input, then the fault lies with the employees and not with the administrator.

On the other hand, consider another example of lost service value. An annex is built by a library. The top administrator on the building committee did not take an active interest in the construction, resulting in poorly executed construction and lost value. This administrator may not have properly organized his or her time or may have been involved in slacking behavior. The overseeing of the construction was not an activity that employees would be expected to direct without close input from an HLA.

Of course, the employee responses regarding administrative input on a building project could have been "Administrative input was received—service value was lost." This third response indicates something quite different. In this case, the HLA contributed to the problem. The HLA was either incompetent—lacked ability—or affected the building project in some other negative manner, such as through promoting his or her self-interest. Self-interest behavior in an HLA occurs when decisions are made that further the HLA's interests over those of the organization. In the building construction example, the requirements for such an overly large HLA office area could cause a reduction in the ability of library departments to provide adequate services because of a lack of floor space. As a result, the organization's resources may be wasted. Personal long-distance calls, travel junkets, and personal use of library assets are other examples of wasting organizational assets to further HLA self-interests.

During the performance audit, the internal auditors conducting the survey of employees need to be aware of several factors. First, they should become aware of any concerted effort by employees to "get" an unpopular administrator. If such a process is occurring, they should attempt to determine the cause for this employee action. Second, all individual employee information must be kept confidential and only released in a form that cannot be identified with any particular employee. Furthermore, any value loss or value gain that is reported should be of a significant nature.

There will always be minor problems with any project or activity. The internal auditors conducting the performance audit are trying to evaluate overall HLA performance to determine if selected outcomes are being achieved successfully, and the surrogate for success is value—service value—gained or lost as determined by the survey instrument.

Some administrators are oriented only toward those initiatives outside of the library, and although internal operations may proceed satisfactorily for a time without higher-level input, a balanced administrative style must exist in order to achieve sustained performance. The purpose of auditing administrative behavior is primarily to determine if the administrator is trying to lead the library or department and secondarily to determine if the administrator is successfully providing that leadership. The audit can be completed through sample HLA decision inputs to gain a perspective on the HLA's decision-making abilities. The performance audit is not performed to assign blame but to help in improving HLA decision-making skills.

The final employee response to the interview question regarding administrative input may be "Administrative input was received—service value was gained." This response indicates that favorable HLA decision making is occurring in the organization. The employees view HLA inputs as positive and helpful in achieving higher levels of service for patrons. It is important to note whether these project activities are ones in which an HLA should be participating. If the administrator is involved in the normal day-to-day selection of books for the collection and the employees surveyed respond that service-level value was gained, this is still unsatisfactory. An HLA is not retained to make decisions about book selections; therefore, the positive response needs to be coupled with the activity to determine if true value has been received by the library from the services of the HLA.

As stated, value determinations can be performed during a performance audit. The independence of the internal auditor performing the audit is expected to result in nonbiased survey data. It is not unusual for employees to be asked a series of confidential questions during a performance audit.

The format for a series of employee survey questions that could highlight these aspects of HLA functions is illustrated in Figure 9-4. In Figure 9-4, it can be seen that the type of HLA function is first described. This description provides an indication as to whether the HLA should be involved with the activity in the first place. Next, the HLA's contributions to the activity are rated by the employees. If the HLA had input into the activity, was the input useful (question 2)? If the HLA did not have input into the activity, would such input have been useful if it had been made (question 3)? The employees make their evaluation on a Likert scale ranked from one to five. In both questions 2 and 3, it is expected that HLA activities are directed toward long-term planning and their input improves the process.

Again, note that the orientation of the HLA's evaluation under a performance audit is directed at long-term changes. The results cannot be evaluated within a short-term time frame. In addition, as with any employee survey, care must be taken in interpreting the responses to avoid the distortions that can develop from employees who are "out to get an administrator."

Yet, if this behavior is manifested by a number of employees, it needs to be determined why employees are acting this way. Therefore, a performance audit can be used as a diagnostic tool to evaluate and, if necessary, offer suggestions for improving HLA input into organizational activities and projects.

Although HLA performance can be evaluated during a performance audit, an internal audit department may not be available to the library's board or scheduling problems may make it impossible to arrange for the internal audit staff to audit the library. In these cases, an independent peer review

Describe the activity, project, or initiative that is being evaluated.

_____

_____

_____

_____

_____

_____

_____

1. Was administrative input received about the described activity?
   Please circle one: Yes   No

Note: If you answered *Yes* to Question 1, answer Question 2; otherwise, answer Question 3.

Instructions

Answer Question 2 or 3 using a five-point scale ranging from "strongly disagree" (SD) for 1 to "strongly agree" (SA) for 4. If you are unsure, please mark item 5 "uncertain."

2. Administrative input was helpful in completing the described activity.

SD	D	A	SA	Uncertain
1	2	3	4	5

3. Administrative input would have been helpful in completing the described activity.

SD	D	A	SA	Uncertain
1	2	3	4	5

FIGURE 9-4   Partial survey questions about HLA performance

committee may be used. The peer review committee should be composed of a group of nonpolitical and knowledgeable professionals from outside the library. A peer review committee of library professionals may be formed from a group of regional libraries.

Exercise 9-3

BSC for Overall Library Initiatives

The director of the Markus Wellmen Free Library is very pleased with the way the Coffee and Cushions manager developed a BSC. The library director has recently begun two initiatives. The first initiative is to act as a partner with the local school in developing technological competencies for the community, and the second initiative is to promote staff-community collaborative activities.

1. Under the following BSC matrix, develop performance measures that would strengthen each initiative without detracting from the other.

Perspectives	Develop Community Technological Competencies	Promote Staff-Community Collaborative Activities
Financial		
Patron		
Internal processes		
Learning and growth		

2. Once these performance measures are established, what should the library director do to ensure their success?

Examples of Performance Evaluators

The type of performance indicators for the four areas—financial, patron, internal processes, and learning and growth—varies with the mission of the organization as well as those processes in which the organization needs to excel. Therefore, there is no acceptable list of evaluators that will provide for the requirements of each library. Throughout the previous chapters, numerous managerial performance measures have been described for evaluating financial performance. Those measures can be selected to act as evaluators depending on the needs of the organization.

With this qualification, a list of overall library—not departmental—evaluators is provided in Figure 9-5, but they should only be considered as illustrative for the four areas. Furthermore, the list contains evaluators that lag performance. If possible, it is best to have evaluators that lead performance

Financial	Patron	Internal Processes	Learning and Growth
Governmental budget dollars received divided by patrons	Number and trend of patrons using the library	Administrative costs/total appropriation	Hours of technology training per employee
Increasing in budgeted funding from previous year	Satisfaction index scores on patron service satisfaction survey	Average time for decision making in days	Share of employees below the age of forty
Total cost of operations divided by patrons	Number and trend of complaints	New books/total collection	Satisfaction index scores on employee work satisfaction survey
Total cost of operations divided by total books in collection	Trend of collection use	Dollars spent on new technology	Number and type of suggestions in employee suggestion box
Variances from budgeted amounts	Number and trend of overdue books	Administrative cost per employee	Number of part-time and temporary employees/total employees
Annual life cycle cost of equipment divided by total life cycle costs of equipment	Demographics of patrons using the library as compared with demographics of the community	Successful achievement of HLA strategic initiatives	Employee turnover rates

FIGURE 9-5   General BSC library evaluators

trends. For example, survey responses are more likely to provide leading indications of future trends than are metrics taken off the financial report. A timely analysis from a survey will show potential changes in patrons' attitudes beginning to occur, whereas financial ratios from the last year only show what has happened in the past, not future trends. It should also be noted that these measures appear as surrogates for the performance that is being evaluated.

In Figure 9-5, the financial measures are directed toward evaluating the overall viability of the library. Variance measures are included under the financial heading to determine how well the overall finances of the library are managed. Life cycle cost trends are important to determine (row six). If the library is purchasing equipment that will contribute to excessive and unsustainable future fixed costs, it needs to be shown. Remember, these are general measures. A specific library would be expected to have specified strategic initiatives developed under an overall mission statement. Therefore, all measures should be directed at providing support for the organization's mission.

The measures under internal processes in Figure 9-5 are general illustrative measures. For example, two of the measures review the trend in administrative costs as a percentage of total appropriations and from the number of employees administered. The actual costs considered to be part of the *administrative costs* category would have to be determined by each library.

Many of the patron and employee measures indicate how these groups view the organization as well as provide indications of the trends in those areas. All comparisons should be done with data from previous periods to determine the trend that is taking place.

CONTRACTS FOR PERFORMANCE

If administrative performance can be determined through evaluation of long-term outcomes based on surveys of employees who are involved in achieving those outcomes, then it is possible to contract for administrative performance and outcomes. This allows HLA performance to be evaluated based on how well contracted outcomes were achieved. A contract for long-term performance should be agreed upon by the administrator and his or her superior. The contract should have specific outcomes against which performance can be evaluated, and the goals of the contract should be directed at a long enough time period for the outcome to be realized. HLAs should exercise authority to control contracted performance outcomes as they cannot be evaluated against performance outcomes over which they have no control. Through this system of contracts at all organizational levels, goals can be harmonized and tied to the mission. As administrators explain these goals to managers and staff within the nonprofit hierarchy, they can develop a cooperative network of interacting BSC objectives.

Unlike short-term monthly performance evaluators, for example, HLA feedback must be aggregated over longer periods. In many cases, determinations of HLA performance may only be available when the final outcome is reached. Unfortunately, daily information cannot be effectively provided about these long-term goals and outcomes. The smaller the time segment used for evaluation, the more difficult it is to judge the HLA's true performance.

Therefore, a criterion of contracts for performance is that the outcomes should be controllable, long-term in nature, and specified in enough detail to determine whether they have been achieved. The administrator must be given enough leeway with the organization's resources to allow those resources to be used in the most efficient manner possible. This latter requirement means that very tight restrictions on the use of funds need to be eliminated. These managers must have full control over resources that have been allocated to them. In this way, they have full responsibility to achieve contracted outcomes and the ability to use the resources at their disposal in the best manner for achieving those outcomes.

The concept of contracting for performance is to provide a clear and realistic definition of the job that an administrator is requested to perform and to outline clearly the HLA's accountability for long-term objectives. It also gives that administrator the ability to change the resource mix of his or her department in a manner that best achieves that outcome. Good management cannot concentrate operational decisions in the short-term. Short-term managing needs to be supplemented with longer-term objectives in order for the library to have consistency in achieving its goals. HLA success in achieving short-term goals may not necessarily lead to success with long-term outcomes. Many times there is no clear way to trace short-term goals to important long-term outcomes. It is good to have short-term goals, but the organization cannot successfully function without long-term objectives and initiatives. Contracting for performance is one method that can be specifically targeted for long-term objectives.

Exercise 9-4

Evaluating BSC Performance Measures

J. Bunyan Library is using the BSC to help it achieve its strategic initiatives (for an example of initiatives, see those listed for the Markus Wellmen Free Library in Exercise 9-3). The library's strategic policy statement lists its strategic initiatives directly under the library's mission statement of "providing a literate, safe, and intellectually stimulating environment for its patrons." The library has described its primary initiative as "Increase the J. Bunyan Library's capacity to accomplish its strategic initiatives." The library director and staff have developed the following BSC framework for enhancing the library's ability to achieve its primary initiative.

Comment on the purpose and value of the performance measures that have been selected to achieve the J. Bunyan Library's primary initiative.

Perspectives   Primary initiative: increase the J. Bunyan Library's capacity to accomplish its strategic initiatives

Financial   Cost dollars devoted to new strategic initiatives/number of new initiatives (financial report classifications)

Patron   Patron satisfaction survey results compared internally and externally with existing national/regional norms (patron survey results)

Internal processes   The contribution that HLAs make to the strategic decision-making process (employee survey results)

Learning and growth   Employee understanding regarding how their daily activities contribute to achieving strategic library initiatives (subjective evaluation)

SUMMARY

Most of the chapters in this book have described the tools of managerial decision making. Unlike those chapters, chapter 9 is concerned with how to evaluate decision makers who use analytical methods to make operating decisions. This evaluation is directed at evaluating long-term initiatives that are difficult to measure on an output-per-unit basis. As a result, surrogates for HLA outcome measures have to be evaluated, and the BSC provides a means to make such an evaluation.

Regardless of the projected outcomes from using analytical techniques, the final responsibility for decision outcomes rests with the administrator. Organizational initiatives and the progress toward their achievement provide a means for evaluating HLA decision making. Many of the activities with which top-level administrators are involved are difficult to evaluate with the typical evaluative procedures used in rating other staff members. Furthermore, it is difficult to establish short-term goals for HLAs that are directly related to strategic long-term initiatives. For this reason, it is necessary to use evaluative techniques that focus on the initiatives resulting from HLA decision-making input.

In this chapter, the BSC is suggested as a means of evaluating actions taken and not taken by HLAs. Specific departmental and project objectives related to HLA input are evaluated for success through these employee interviews. Deferred maintenance and employee interviews are indicative of areas that may be used to evaluate the effectiveness of leadership in the library, but they should not be considered to be the only way.

Finally, HLA performance can be measured in terms of preset goals established through a series of organization-wide contracts with HLAs. These contracts are outlines of long-range goals. They allow for an organization-wide BSC orientation and continuity toward achieving the organization's mission.

Notes

1. *See* articles and books by R. S. Kaplan and D. P. Norton such as *The Balanced Scorecard: Translating Strategy into Action* (Boston: Harvard Business School Press, 1996); and *The Strategy-Focused Organization: How Balanced Scorecard Companies Thrive in the New Business Environment* (Boston: Harvard Business School Press, 2001).

2. Deferred maintenance is not related to depreciation. If deferred maintenance were reported on the financial statements (currently, it is not), it would be shown as an increase in a liability account and as a reduction in the organization's net worth. The reduction should recognize the deterioration of the library's assets, and a liability should be recognized for the potential liability owed to the public for the premature replacement of assets that will occur.

3. Although deferred maintenance has been mainly related to equipment and buildings, it can be related to personnel as well. In a library, one of the most important assets is human resources, and human resources can deteriorate in the same manner as physical assets through obsolescence of skills. There is an annual "maintenance" charge in terms of training human resources to ensure that when new technology is introduced into the library it is fully utilized and maximum services are provided to the public.

4. At most, an accounting system records depreciation expense, but even when depreciation is recorded, it does not provide any indication about the correct amount of maintenance expenditures on fixed assets. On the income statement or other similar statements, maintenance expenditures are aggregated with other expenditures, and even if maintenance expenditures are listed separately, this does not determine whether *adequate* expenditures are being made to maintain assets properly.

5. The HLA may be interested in expending the absolute minimum of effort needed to retain his or her position. This behavior is considered to be "slacking behavior."

Bibliography

Kaplan, R. S., and D. P. Norton. *The Balanced Scorecard: Translating Strategy into Action.* Boston: Harvard Business School Press, 1996.

Kaplan, R. S., and D. P. Norton. *The Strategy-Focused Organization: How Balanced Scorecard Companies Thrive in the New Business Environment.* Boston: Harvard Business School Press, 2001.

Olve, N., J. Roy, and M. Wetter. *Performance Drivers: A Practical Guide to Using the Balanced Scorecard.* Chichester, England: John Wiley & Sons, 1999.

Zweizig, D., and E. J. Rodger. *Output Measures for Public Libraries: A Manual of Standardized Procedures.* Chicago: American Library Association, 1987.

APPENDIX

A

The Methods of Accounting Used in Libraries

The recording of financial data for nonprofit organizations is based on one of three different accounting methods. Without basic adjustments from one system to another, the data in these systems are not comparable. The three methods in use are cash, accrual, or modified accrual. Under these systems, the timing for recording an entry in the ledgers differs along with the dollar amount being recorded. Therefore, expenditure levels under one system will not be comparable with the expenditures made under another system. Accounting methods for financial reporting to parties outside the organization are developed and prescribed by various accounting bodies. These prescribed procedures are considered to be the authoritative methods acceptable for use.

If a library is very small, the differences in the methods may not be significant, but as transactions increase in number and complexity, material differences between the systems become apparent. The systems are in use because some libraries may be part of a city or state government entity, whereas other libraries may be research libraries in a corporation or law or accounting firm. The parent organization, of which these libraries are a part, uses a different basis of accounting to recognize transactions. A city or state may use the modified accrual basis of accounting as prescribed by the Governmental Accounting Standards Board (GASB), and a corporation uses the accrual basis of accounting.[1] The GASB is the accounting board that prescribes the methods of accounting for libraries in state and local governments' financial reports.

Even with the prescribed methods of accounting of procedures in effect, the cash method may still be used. The cash basis of accounting is a system that records a transaction in the accounting system when cash flows into or out of the organization.

The method is very simple to use and requires fewer journal entries when compared with the accrual basis. This is in contrast with the accrual method of accounting. Under full accrual accounting, expenses and revenues are recorded in the time period that they are incurred or earned, rather than when the cash is paid out or received.

Another accounting system that may be used in a library is called the modified accrual system. This method adopts a combination of both the cash and accrual basis, and the actual journal entry varies with the specific transaction. For example, revenues that are likely to be received up to 60 days into the new year are still considered revenues of the previous period under modified accrual accounting. This is described as the "availability" criterion used in recognizing revenues under modified accrual accounting. Under modified accrual, most expenses (expenditures) are recorded using the approach followed in the accrual method. But, currently, there are exceptions made concerning supplies and other inventory assets. At the present time, these assets can be expensed when they are purchased or when they are used. The expensed-when-used method follows accrual accounting, and the expensed-when-purchased method follows cash accounting. Also, under modified accrual, a special situation exists for the recognition of interest expense owed at the end of a fiscal year. Interest expense may not be recorded as an expense and a liability of the current fiscal period unless budget monies are set aside for the payment of the interest expense. Some of these differences will now be expanded upon in more detail.

Examples of Journal Entries and Their Effect on Financial Reporting under the Different Systems of Accounting

Inventories

A library must deal with inventories of supplies and materials. Depending on the system of accounting in use, the amount of supplies and material expenditures will differ. This difference is not based on actual use, but on the method of accounting used.

Assume that on July 1, 20x1, the beginning of the fiscal year, the Stat Library receives an invoice from Texas Vending for the purchase of $4,500 of supplies for the current year. There were no supplies available from last year—they had been used up. On August 1, 20x1, the invoice is paid by the library. During the current year, the library uses $4,000 of supplies. Therefore, at the end of the year, on June 30, 20x2, $500 of supplies are left in the storeroom. The entries for this transaction would be recorded as shown in Figure A-1 for each of the methods.

Review of the transactions shows the cost of supplies is $4,500 and $4,000 under the cash and accrual basis, respectively. The question is asked: What is the cost of supplies used by the library during the year? The answer has to be $4,000 because $500 of supplies are still left over in the storeroom. This means that *cost* and *expenses* may not be synonymous terms under all systems of accounting. Therefore, the accrual method of accounting assigns a truer measure of the actual costs of a library's programs. Furthermore, without adjusting entries to reconcile the systems, it

<hr>

Cash Basis

July 1, 20x1	No entry		
August 1, 20x1	Supplies expense	$4,500	
	Cash		$4,500
June 30, 20x2	No entry		

Total supplies expense for the year: $4,500

Accrual Basis

July 1, 20x1	Supplies expense	$4,500	
	Accounts payable		$4,500
August 1, 20x1	Accounts payable	$4,500	
	Cash		$4,500
June 30, 20x2	Inventory of supplies	$500	
	Supplies expense		$500

Total supplies expense for the year: $4,000 ($4,500 – $500)

Modified Accrual Basis

Currently, the modified accrual basis can use either basis for recognizing this transaction. The choice is left to the organization.

<hr>

FIGURE A-1   Journal entries for recognizing supplies expense

is impossible to compare the costs of running two similar libraries that use different methods of accounting.

Revenues

The amount of revenues or contributions received by a library can differ depending on the system of accounting in use. These differences make it difficult to make revenue or contribution comparisons between similar-sized libraries unless adjusting entries are made to reconcile the difference in the basis of accounting.

In the first revenue example, assume that on September 30, 20x2, the Stat Library is notified that they have earned interest of $10,000 on their investment portfolio for the three-month period from July 1 through September 30. On October 7, 20x1, the library received a check for $10,000.

In Figure A-2, the amount of revenue recognized under each method is the same. This is true, in this case, because the cash was received in the same period that the library was notified it was going to be receiving investment revenue. In other words, there were no timing differences between the systems. Note that if the cash had not been received in the same fiscal period as the notification period, the cash basis would not have recognized any revenue.

As another example of recording revenues, assume that on June 30, 20x2, the library's year end, the library was notified that it was awarded an unrestricted grant of $50,000 that could be spent on expenditures for operations. The grant monies are forwarded to the library on August 28.

In Figure A-3, it can be seen that the initial entries and revenues recognized are the same under the accrual and modified accrual basis, but with the cash basis, there is no entry because there is no cash inflow. There is a $50,000 difference between revenues under the cash basis and the other two methods. But, if the grant was expected to be received on August 30, more than sixty days after the library's year end, it would not be recognized as revenue under the modified accrual basis. Under the modified accrual basis, revenue is not recognized if it is not considered to be available for use. Currently, revenue is considered available if it is received within sixty days of the year end to pay liabilities of the just completed fiscal year. The GASB's availability recognition is defined as "collected within sixty days of the entity's year end." After the complete implementation of Statement 34, many of the differences between modified and accrual accounting will no longer exist.

Cash Basis			
September 30, 20x1	No entry		
October 7, 20x1	Cash	$10,000	
	Interest revenue		$10,000
Total revenue recognized: $10,000			

Accrual Basis			
September 30, 20x1	Interest receivable	$10,000	
	Interest income		$10,000
October 7, 20x1	Cash	$10,000	
	Interest receivable		$10,000
Total revenue recognized: $10,000			

Modified Accrual Basis

Same entries as under the accrual basis. Total revenue recognized is $10,000.

FIGURE A-2   Journal entries recognizing revenues in the same fiscal period as the revenues are received

	Cash Basis		
June 30, 20x2	No entry		
Total revenues: None			
	Accrual Basis		
June 30, 20x2	Grants receivable	$50,000	
	Grant revenues		$50,000
Total revenues: $50,000			
	Modified Accrual Basis		
June 30, 20x2	Grants receivable	$50,000	
	Grant revenues		$50,000
Total revenues: $50,000			

FIGURE A-3   Journal entries recognizing grant revenues in a different fiscal period than that in which the revenues are received

The collection of fines provides another example of the "availability" criteria that controls the recognition of revenues under the modified accrual basis. Assume that from the year end of June 30 through August 29, 20x2, $3,000 of book fines are collected in cash. Under the modified accrual basis, these fines are recognized as revenue in the previous year because these amounts were collected within sixty days of the year end. The entries for the modified accrual basis as of June 30, 20x2, are shown in Figure A-4.

The revenue under the modified accrual basis for the year ended June 30, 20x2, is $3,000 higher than the revenue shown under the cash and accrual basis. Again, this difference is because of the application of an "availability" criterion in the recognition of revenues.

The Significance of the Differences

These examples should make it apparent that the different methods of accounting result in different dollar amounts being recorded as expenditures and revenues on the financial statements. In addition, the amounts shown on budgetary statements may also differ. It is possible to make adjusting entries at the end of the year to avoid these differences. The reconciling entries should be made to convert the accounting records to an accrual basis if that basis is not already in use. Without knowing whether the same basis of accounting is being used in different libraries, it is useless to make program cost comparisons among them.

Cash Basis		
June 30, 20x2	No adjusting entry	
Total revenues: None		
Accrual Basis		
June 30, 20x2	No adjusting entry	
Total revenues: None		
Modified Accrual Basis		
June 30, 20x2	Cash	$3,000
	Book fines revenue	$3,000
Total revenues: $3,000		

FIGURE A-4   Journal entries illustrating the effect of the "availability" criterion

For further examples of the differences between the methods of accounting, *see* G. Stevenson Smith, *Accounting for Libraries and Other Not-for-Profit Organizations, Second Edition* (Chicago: American Library Association, 1999), chapter 3, "Which Accounting System Are We Using?"

Note

1. Modified accrual and accrual accounting are becoming similar. Statement No. 34, *Basic Financial Statements—and Management's Discussion and Analysis—for State and Local Governments* (Norwalk, Conn.: GASB, 1999), adopted by the GASB in June 1999, is making these formerly diverse methods of accounting more similar. The standard should be totally implemented for all applicable organizations by June 15, 2003.

APPENDIX

$\boxed{\text{B}}$

Time Value of Money Concepts and Discounted Cash Flows

Time value of money concepts are related to the idea that an individual will set aside current earnings in the form of savings if interest can be earned on this foregone consumption. The amount saved today will grow in value as interest is earned. Furthermore, the interest earnings will accumulate and earn interest on that unwithdrawn, previously earned interest. In effect, there is a compounding of interest earnings. Therefore, a sum saved today is greater in one year by the interest earned on it, and at the end of a second year, it accumulates to a larger increment because of the interest earned on previous interest earnings that were not withdrawn.

The importance of the time value of money concept is that it allows cash flows made in different time periods to be made comparable. It is difficult to make managerial decisions about the purchase and the cost of operating assets without the ability to make cash flows in different time periods comparable. The time value of money concept allows comparisons to be made as to whether cash outflows today or in the future are more costly to the organization. By just simply comparing the total dollar amounts, this determination cannot be made.

The time value of money concepts, by themselves, are not intended to incorporate the effects of inflation. Time-value concepts are only intended to account for the ability of an organization to earn interest on its financial investments. This technique clearly shows that a dollar paid out or earned today is not equal to a dollar paid out or earned one year from now.

As an example of how the compounding of interest works consider Figure B-1. Assume that $1.00 is invested in a savings account earning 5 percent interest per year

Year	Amount Invested at Beginning of Year	5% Interest Earned during the Year	Total Invested at End of Years 1, 2, and 3
1	$1.00	$0.05000	$1.05000
2	1.05	0.05250	1.10250
3	1.1025	0.55125	1.15763

FIGURE B-1 The compounding of interest

for three years. As shown above, the dollar would accumulate to a sum of $1.16 (rounded) at the end of three years.

This example illustrates the compounding of interest, and it shows how interest is also earned on previously earned interest. In terms of decision-making alternatives, this illustration shows that there is no difference between receiving $1.00 today and receiving $1.16 three years from today, assuming a discount rate of 5 percent. On the other hand, if someone were willing to give you $1.25 three years from now or $1.00 today, you would be better off to take $1.25 in three years. The potential for managerial decision making should be apparent. By using the idea of compounding interest to determine a future amount such as $1.16, the reverse can also be computed. The reverse shows a current value of $1.00 is the same value as $1.16 receivable in three years. This current value is called the *present value* of a sum.

It has been illustrated that $1.16 three years from now is worth $1.00 today. This means that the present value of $1.16 is $1.00 assuming a compound interest rate of 5 percent over a three-year period. Compounding is presented here as a means of understanding present value and discounted cash flow analysis.

A series of cash flows is illustrative of the periodic cash payments related to maintaining equipment, or the series may be related to lease payments. A single cash payment may be related to the amount paid for a new asset or the amount received at the end of the asset's useful life from salvage. All these amounts need to be compared on an equal basis. Discounted cash flow analysis allows that comparison to be made. In nonprofit organizations, discounted cash flow analysis emphasizes the selection of the least-cost alternative for the entity, or the present value of the minimum cash outflow. Most of the examples in the book deal with outflows rather than both an inflow and outflow of cash as would occur in a corporation.

Finally, note that cash comparisons are being made here. If figures are taken directly off the entity's financial statements, they must be converted to a cash basis before time-value concepts can be applied. Appendix A discusses the differences between the cash basis and other accounting methods used to prepare the financial statements.

Determining the Present Value of Cash Outflows

Determining the present value of the cash flows that occur in the future is called *discounting the cash flows*. The present value of an amount to be received in the future is always less than the future amount because of the discounting that occurs.

Cash flows are evaluated differently depending on whether they are a periodic series of cash flows or a single cash amount. A single cash payment is referred to here as a *lump sum,* and periodic series of cash flows are called *annuities.* A determination must be made as to whether a cash flow is a lump sum or an annuity of cash payments. Without the proper determination, it is not possible to select the correct present value table.

The table factors in Tables 1 through 3 allow one to determine the present value of these cash flows. The present value tables allow for the reversal of the compounding previously illustrated. Three tables for determining present values are included in this appendix. Tables for compound amounts are not included here because the illustrations in the chapters do not deal with the accumulation of future amounts. (*See* the

Table 1. Present Value of a Lump Sum

Periods	5%	6%	7%	8%	9%	10%
			Table Factors			
1	0.952	0.943	0.935	0.926	0.917	0.909
2	0.907	0.890	0.873	0.857	0.842	0.826
3	0.864	0.842	0.816	0.794	0.772	0.751
4	0.823	0.792	0.763	0.735	0.708	0.683
5	0.784	0.747	0.713	0.681	0.650	0.621
6	0.746	0.705	0.666	0.630	0.596	0.564
7	0.711	0.665	0.623	0.583	0.547	0.513
8	0.677	0.627	0.582	0.540	0.502	0.467
9	0.645	0.592	0.544	0.500	0.460	0.424
10	0.614	0.558	0.508	0.463	0.422	0.386

Table 2. Present Value of an Ordinary Annuity

Periods	5%	6%	7%	8%	9%	10%
			Table Factors			
1	0.952	0.943	0.935	0.926	0.917	0.909
2	1.859	1.833	1.808	1.783	1.759	1.736
3	2.723	2.673	2.624	2.577	2.531	2.487
4	3.546	3.465	3.387	3.312	3.240	3.170
5	4.329	4.212	4.100	3.993	3.890	3.791
6	5.076	4.917	4.767	4.623	4.486	4.355
7	5.786	5.582	5.389	5.206	5.033	4.868
8	6.463	6.210	5.971	5.747	5.535	5.335
9	7.108	6.802	6.515	6.247	5.995	5.759
10	7.722	7.360	7.024	6.710	6.418	6.145

Table 3. Present Value of an Annuity Due

Periods	5%	6%	7%	8%	9%	10%
			Table Factors			
1	1.000	1.000	1.000	1.000	1.000	1.000
2	1.952	1.943	1.935	1.926	1.917	1.909
3	2.859	2.833	2.808	2.783	2.759	2.736
4	3.723	3.673	3.624	3.577	3.531	3.487
5	4.546	4.465	4.387	4.312	4.240	4.170
6	5.329	5.212	5.100	4.993	4.890	4.791
7	6.076	5.917	5.767	5.623	5.486	5.355
8	6.786	6.582	6.389	6.206	6.033	5.868
9	7.463	7.210	6.971	6.747	6.535	6.335
10	8.108	7.802	7.515	7.247	6.995	6.759

additional readings referred to in the bibliography at the end of this appendix for a more detailed discussion about the compounding of interest.)

Lump Sums

Lump sums are amounts that are paid out or are received at the end of a specified time period. Cash outflows of this nature could be cash deposits that are returned or the salvage value received for an asset at the end of its useful life. If these amounts are illustrated on a time line, they appear as in Figure B-2.

To determine the present value of a lump sum, the factors in Table 1 are multiplied times the lump sum cash inflow or outflow. The purpose of this calculation is to take the time factor out of the analysis and allow a comparison to be made between a future cash flow and current cash flows—the "now" time point in the time line.

As an example of determining the present value of a cash receipt to be received in the future, assume that $5,000 in cash will be received five years from now and an

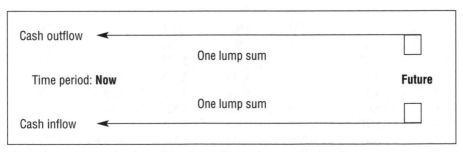

Figure B-2   Lump sum cash outflow and inflow at the end of a time line

8 percent discount rate is used. An implicit assumption in this illustration is that compounding occurs on an annual basis; therefore, five periods are used. If interest were compounded quarterly, twenty compounding periods would be used (five years × four quarters). Another assumption in the analysis is that the discount rate will remain constant at 8 percent over the five-year period.

The first step in determining the present value of this cash receipt is to find the table factor (.681) for five periods at 8 percent in Table 1, "Present Value of a Lump Sum." The second step is to make the present value calculation as follows:

$$\text{Future sum} \times \text{Table factor} = \text{Present value}$$
$$(5 \text{ periods, } 8\%)$$
$$\$5,000 \times .681 = \$3,405$$

This calculation shows that there is no difference between receiving $3,405 today or $5,000 in five years assuming that $3,405 can be invested at 8 percent during the five-year period. Using this analysis, it is possible to compare $3,405 with all other amounts received today or "now" in making managerial decisions. Without taking the time value of money concepts into account, it is impossible to compare $5,000 receivable five years from now with current cash flows.

Annuities

When a periodic series of cash flows is received or paid over a specified time period, the cash flows are called an *annuity.* The time line in Figure B-3 illustrates two different types of annuities. The first series is called an *ordinary annuity* because the cash inflows, represented by vertical lines, occur at the end of each period. Loan agreements that provide for no payments for thirty days are examples of ordinary annuities. The second series is called an *annuity due* because the cash flows occur at the beginning of the period. Lease payments are typical of cash outflows that occur at the beginning of a period.

Each payment, either at the beginning or end of the periods, must be adjusted for the time differences over which it is received or paid. The payments are adjusted to the current period using the present value factors in either Table 2 or Table 3. Table 2

Time Line: **Four Periods; Four Payments**

Ordinary annuity

Annuity due

FIGURE B-3 Examples of two different annuity payment schedules

is used with ordinary annuities, and Table 3 is used with annuities due. As an example of how to use these tables, assume that each of the periodic payments, shown as vertical lines in the time schedule, is equal to $1,000 over four periods. Furthermore, assume that the discount rate is 5 percent.

The present value of an annuity due over the same time period and at the same discount rate will always be higher than the present value of an ordinary annuity, assuming equal cash payments. With an annuity due, the first payment is made at the beginning of the time line; therefore, this initial $1,000 cash payment, which is received earlier, has a significant effect in increasing the present value of the series of payments.

It is not necessary to have an annuity due table to make these calculations; table factors in an ordinary annuity table can be converted to those in an annuity due table. In many cases, this may be necessary because it is more common to find ordinary annuity tables than annuity due tables in books that explain the calculation of present values. The method of conversion from one table to the other is to deduct 1 from the number of periods for an ordinary annuity and add 1 to the table factor at that point in the ordinary annuity table. For example, in the previous illustration, deducting 1 from four periods results in looking for the table factor in the ordinary annuity table, Table 2, at three periods and 5 percent. This table factor is equal to 2.723. When 1 is added to this table factor, the result is the same table factor, 3.723, as found in Table 3 for four periods and 5 percent. The calculation for determining the present value of an ordinary annuity and an annuity due is shown in Figure B-4.

At this point, present value analysis may appear to be a mechanical process in which a table factor is multiplied by either a lump sum or periodic cash flows, but the process becomes much more complicated when applied to real-world situations. It is difficult to project cash flows into the future on many projects. Unless these projections are based on legally fixed payments such as those occurring in a lease or mortgage, the estimates become more inaccurate as the time periods are extended. For this reason, large variations can occur in results that are generated using present value analysis, or discounted cash flows.

	Annuity	×	Table Factor (Four Periods, 5%)	=	Present Value
Ordinary annuity (Table 2)	$1,000	×	3.546	=	$3,546
Annuity due (Table 3)	$1,000	×	3.723	=	$3,723

FIGURE B-4   Calculating the present value of an annuity of $1,000

Another difficulty in applying present value analysis is the problem that arises in selecting the proper discount rate. In the corporate area, the discount rate generally used is the corporation's cost of capital, but that rate may be adjusted to take into account various additional factors that are determined to be important by managerial decision makers. In general, the cost of capital is the rate of return that is expected to be received by those who provide capital funds to the corporation. The providers of capital generally expect to receive interest or dividend income from their investments in addition to possible appreciation in their stock portfolios.

Determination of the Discount Rate

With nonprofit organizations such as libraries, there is little agreement as to how to determine the proper discount rate. To overcome the problem, some governments adopt a policy of using a discount rate of 10 percent for analyzing projects, for example; this rate is used in the illustrations in the chapters. Whatever rate is chosen, it should be used consistently throughout the organization.

The discount rate should be based on a pretax average opportunity cost with adjustments for fund-raising costs for some sources of funds. An opportunity cost is the value attributed to the next-best alternative that was foregone or not obtainable because of the managerial choices actually made. As the term applies to the discount rate, it means the interest rate that was foregone to provide funds to the nonprofit organization. This interest cost is directly related to the source that provided the funds. For example, private donor contributions and state funding are seen as having different opportunity costs. The interest cost of state funds might be related to the long-term rate of interest paid by the state to borrow these funds. But there is more controversy surrounding the rate to use for monies received from donor's contributions. Although an alternative rate could be earned on a donor's contributions, it is not completely agreed upon as to how that rate should be determined. The two interest costs are seen as being different, and therefore the best option is to determine both of them and then weigh them together to obtain an average discount rate for the entire library.

In a corporation, if the cash inflows are less than the cash outflows from an investment—a negative net cash flow—the decision criteria requires that the investment be rejected. Unlike the analysis for a corporation, in a nonprofit organization usually all cash flows are negative or outflows. The selection of a discount rate will not make the present value of the cash flows become negative as the cash flows are likely to be negative already. Therefore, at least from this point of view, the effect on decision making from using an incorrect discount rate is not likely to result in a negative outflow and trigger the decision criteria of rejecting a program or library initiative. But, using the incorrect discount rate can make the present value of the cash outflows from a project appear more or less favorable than it actually is, resulting in the possible cancellation of programs or projects. In addition, the analysis can result in one project being chosen over another based on its lower cost outflows.

Limitations of Present Value Method

The application of present value analysis in nonprofit entities suffers from the same major limitation that occurs in the corporate area. The problem with this technique is that if the payment schedules are not fixed in a legal agreement, it is difficult to make accurate forecasts of future cash flows. As the period of time under analysis becomes more extended into the future, the reliability of projected cash flows becomes more inaccurate.

From a theoretical point of view, projecting cash flows into the future for fifty years or more and applying the concept of discounted cash flows is possible. In this way, the value of long-lived assets can easily be compared with one another to determine which is the least costly alternative for the nonprofit organization. Difficulties begin to arise when these cash projections are taken out of a theoretical context and applied to real-world situations. In real-world situations, many times it is very difficult to extend cash flow projections out into the distant future because of the difficulty of accurately predicting the cash flows from a project. Theoretically, this technique is applicable to long-range analysis, but in practice, long-range cash flow projections are known to be inaccurate. As a consequence, the application of real option methodologies have been applied to these situations.[1] In many cases, real option methods suffer from some of the same limitations facing present value methods.

Net Present Value

Net present value (NPV) calculations are used as a decision-making technique to select between alternative capital investments. The NPV is the summation of the present value of the annual net cash flows of a project: the present value of total cash inflows less the present value of the initial cost of an investment project and other cash outflows. If the net cash flow is positive, then this project should be considered as a possible investment. In a corporate setting, if the difference is positive it means cash inflows have a higher present value than cash outflows, and depending on the amount of investment funds available, the corporation may decide to make the investment.

For a nonprofit organization, NPV has a reduced impact on decision making. The reason for this difference between the corporate and nonprofit setting is that in most nonprofit evaluations the cash flows are all outflows. Although a nonprofit organization's assets may generate revenue, in some situations, usually the asset is purchased to provide a service to the public rather than to create profits. Therefore, in most cases, all cash outflows are negative, and NPV analysis cannot be used for decision making as it is used in for-profit organizations, where there is both a cash inflow and outflow. If the same decision criterion—only accept projects with a positive NPV—were used in a nonprofit context as it is in a corporate context, no nonprofit investments would be made because the NPV of most nonprofit investments is negative. In these situations, societal goals override the pure profit decision criteria. This does not mean that present value analysis has no place in nonprofit organizations.

Present value analysis can still help identify the least-cost alternative even if NPV results are negative.

Note

1. For example, *see* M. Amram and N. Kulatilaka, *Real Options: Managing Strategic Investment in an Uncertain World* (Boston: Harvard Business School Press, 1999).

Bibliography

Most beginning management accounting, finance, or intermediate accounting textbooks have a section that deals with present value analysis. For example, *see* chapter 16 in R. Hilton, *Managerial Accounting: Creating Value in a Dynamic Business Environment* (Boston: McGraw-Hill/Irwin, 2002). Also, *see* chapter 7 in J. Jiambalvo, *Managerial Accounting* (New York: John Wiley & Sons, 2001).

C

Solutions to Chapter Exercises

Exercise 2-1. Thinking about Overhead Costs

The costs incurred to operate the Moreover Library's Human Resources (HR) Department are considered to be overhead (indirect) costs of the Reference Department as long as HR provides services to the Reference Department. A reasonable method of allocating the HR costs to the Reference Department needs to be determined. Although several methods can be used, one of the more common ways to allocate these costs is by assigning them based on the number of employees in the Reference Department prorated over all library employees.

Exercise 2-2. Why Am I in Trouble?

The Cost Report prepared by the Accounting Department has the objective of assigning all costs to the departments that provide services to library patrons. This approach is used to determine the full cost of these operations. As a result, the Reference Department is assigned a slice of all overhead costs that are incurred in the library. Three such costs are the charges for the library's phone charges, depreciation and maintenance related to operating the library building, and a portion of administrative costs. The head of reference is concerned because the method of allocating overhead costs to the department does not seem to correspond with the level of services provided. For example, the library director does not have much contact with the Reference Department. Yet, the Reference Department is allocated a $15,000 charge for administrative services. As a result, the department head feels that little control exists over these allocated costs, and therefore the department should not be held accountable for them. Although no one is "in trouble" yet for exceeding cost guidelines, these allocated costs can lead to misleading conclusions as to the full cost of operations.

Exercise 2-3. *Some Simple Cost Patterns*

1.

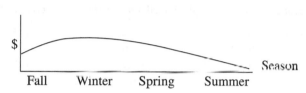

Fall   Winter   Spring   Summer

It would be expected that the cost line would be the highest during the winter season and lowest during the summer.

2.

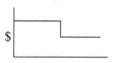

It would be expected that the costs of online periodicals are not as high as printed periodicals, and that is one of the reasons for changing to the online format.

Exercise 2-4. *Budget Cuts*

1. The full cost of operating the Reference Department is $241,000, and a 10 percent budget reduction is $24,100. Unfortunately, a large portion of the full costs of operations is allocated costs ($36,000), and they are not going to change. The head of the Reference Department has no control over these allocated costs, and they will continue to be allocated to the Reference Department close to the same dollar level even after the 10 percent budget reduction takes place. Therefore, if reference is required to reduce its budget by $24,100, this is 11.75 percent of those costs that are controllable by the department head ($24,100/205,000 = 11.75 percent). The only means for the Reference Department to reduce its full costs by $24,100 is to take the entire reduction from controllable costs. In this case, those are the costs of personnel, equipment purchases, and supplies.

2. For the reason above, the reference head might try to restrict the 10 percent budget cut to "controllable costs." Total controllable costs are $205,000, and a 10 percent reduction of those costs would be $20,500. The department head can make an argument that these are the only costs that can really be reduced, whereas those costs assigned by the library's Accounting Department are not controllable by the department head.

Exercise 3-1. Calculate Performance Ratios Based on Cost Data

1.

	Actual Year-to-Date	/	Budgeted Year-to-Date	=	Percent (%)
Administration	$15,700	/	$15,000		105
Technical Services	25,820	/	26,110		98
Public Relations	8,800	/	7,500		117
Human Resources	6,600	/	6,600		100

2. Amounts budgeted for personnel salaries and wages in human resources are not likely to change from the original budget unless a new person is hired or an employee leaves. If the human resources line is overspent, it means that someone was hired without additional budget authorization or possibly someone received a raise again without authorization—two changes that are unlikely to occur if budget guidelines are being followed.

Exercise 3-2. Cost Allocations

1. STEP 1: Base Distribution

			Technical	Programs			Totals
Base	Admin.	Custodial	Services	1	2	3	
No. of employees	—	2	2	4	2	4	14
Square footage	—	—	800	4,000	1,500	3,500	9,800
Books cataloged	—	—	—	11,000	3,000	7,000	21,000

STEP 2: Percentage Distribution

Service	Base	Custodial	Technical Services	Programs		
				1	2	3
Admin.	14	.1428	.1428	.28571	.1428	.28571
Square footage	9,800	—	.082	.408	.153	.357
Tech. Serv.	21,000	—	—	.524	.143	.333

STEP 3: Cost Allocation

Step	Service Departments			Programs			Totals
	Admin.	Custodial	Tech. Serv.	1	2	3	
	$60,000.00	$16,000.00	$23,000.00	$60,000.00	$18,000.00	$65,000.00	
1	(60,000)	+8,568.00	+8568.00	+17,142.00	+8,568.00	+17,142.00	$59,988.00*
		$24,568.00					
2		(24,568.00)	+2,014.58	+10,023.74	+3,758.90	+8,770.78	$24,568.00
			$33,582.58				
3			(33,582.58)	+17,597.27	+4,802.31	+11,183.00	$33,582.58
Full Program Costs:				**$104,763.01**	**$35,129.21**	**$102,095.78**	

*The difference is because of rounding

2. (a)

Item	Programs		
	1	2	3
Program costs	$104,763.01	$35,129.21	$102,095.78
Books cataloged	11,000	3,000	7,000
Cost per book cataloged	$9.52	$11.71	$14.59

(b)

No. of patrons	12,000	15,000	16,000
Cost per person	$8.73	$2.34	$6.38

(c) The results in Part (a) indicate that Program 3 has the highest costs per book cataloged and Program 1 has the lowest costs. In Part (b), the results indicate that Program 1 has the highest costs and Program 2 has the lowest costs per patron using the collection. The difference is because of the per-unit base measures chosen.

(d) The results in Parts (a) and (b) illustrate that care has to be taken in choosing a per-unit variable (base) because the per-unit measure can result in very different views as to the performance of programs. It is important to choose a per-unit variable (base) that is closely reflective of the strategic objectives that the organization is following. In this case, one objective might be to encourage patron use; therefore, the second per-unit measure based on the number of patrons using each of the collections in the program areas is a better measure upon which to base per-unit costs.

3. (a) STEP 1

Service or Activity	Allocation Base	Service Departments				Programs			
		Maintenance & Custodial	*Accounting*	*Administration*	*Technical Services*	*Circulation*	*Reference*	*Children's Library*	*Regional History*
Depreciation	$210,000	.124	.057	.086	.105	.271	.152	.119	.086
Administration	28*	—	.179	.107	.179	.214	.107	.143	.071
Maintenance & Custodial	213,750†	—	—	.0082	.014	.5474	.14	.2667	.0234
Accounting	154,000‡	—	—	—	.143	.37	.208	.162	.117
Technical Services	101,000	—	—	—	—	.595	.129	.198	.079

*Includes all employees except those in Administration
†Includes all square footage except that in Administration and Accounting
‡Excludes Maintenance & Custodial, Accounting, and Administration

STEP 2

Step No.	Service Departments Costs					Program Costs and Allocated Overhead				
	Depreciation	Administration	Maintenance & Custodial	Accounting	Technical Services	Circulation	Reference	Children's Library	Regional History	Totals Allocated
	$89,000.00*	$26,000.00	$12,000.00	$18,000.00	$22,000.00	$57,000.00	$32,000.00	$25,000.00	$18,000.00	
1	(89,000.00)	+11,036.00	+5,073.00	+7,654.00	+9,345.00	+24,119.00	+13,528.00	+10,591.00	+7,654.00	$89,000.00
		$37,036.00								
2		(37,036.00)	+6,629.44	+3,962.85	+6,629.44	+7,925.70	+3,962.85	+5,296.15	+2,629.56	$37,035.99*
			$23,702.44							
3			(23,702.44)	+194.36	+331.83	+12,974.72	+3,318.34	+6,321.44	+554.64	$23,595.33*
				$29,811.21						
4				(29,811.21)	+4,263.00	+11,030.15	+6,200.73	+4,829.42	+3,487.91	$29,811.21
					$42,569.27					
5					(42,569.27)	+25,328.72	+5,491.44	+8,428.72	+3,362.97	$42,611.85*
Full Cost of Programs:						**$138,378.29**	**$64,501.36**	**$60,466.73**	**$35,689.08**	

*The difference is because of rounding the percentages in Step 1

3. (b) All cost allocation methods are somewhat inaccurate. The differences are not usually very significant when per-unit calculations are made. This does not mean that allocation is useless. The important point is to have consistently comparative dollar information about the organization's programs. When a logical method of cost allocation is chosen, the comparative differences become apparent regardless of how the overhead costs are "stepped down."

Exercise 3-3. *Determine Returns on Revenue Centers*

1. If only the new equipment is considered as the investment, then the return on investment is calculated as follows:

$$\frac{\$25,000 \text{ profit}}{\$125,000 \text{ investment}} = 20\% \text{ return on investment}$$

2. If the new equipment and a reasonable charge for the use of the building are considered to be the investment, then the return on the investment is calculated as follows:

$$\frac{\$25,000 \text{ profit}}{\$125,000 + \$500,000^* \text{ building charge}} = 4\% \text{ return on investment}$$

---

*The building charge should be based on the current value of the building, $25,000,000, not the original purchase price of $5,000,000. A reasonable charge could be based on the space used by the gift shop times the building's fair value.

$$\frac{2,000 \text{ sq. feet in gift shop}}{100,000 \text{ sq. feet in entire building}} \times \$25,000,000 = \$500,000$$

3. There is a significant difference between 4 and 20 percent. The higher rate looks better. The more realistic return would include a charge for the space occupied. The $25,000 profit is not going to change in either case. It would be a judgmental decision for the director to make. Knowing the board, this library director chose the 20 percent solution.

Exercise 4-1. *Identifying Cost-Creating Activities*

The following suggestions may help Max get started in determining the cost-creating activities that occur within the library. First, Max needs to realize that not everyone's activities need to be determined. The level of detail in a specific library does not require that every employee's activities be identified and documented. Those activities that are significant cost-generating activities (i.e., cost drivers) are the most important activities that need to be identified. Therefore, the job may not be as large as it at first appears. A focused way to start the analysis of cost-generating activities is to review the forms and requests that are used between departments and the public. This is a good place to identify cost-creating activities on an interdepartmental basis and between the library and segments of the public that are being served.

Once the analysis has been completed up to this point, Max should determine whether all the staff or only certain portions of the library staff will need to complete a self-survey to identify their specific functions and activities. After this information is collected, it should become much more apparent to Max what has been done in the library, by which department, and the interrelationships among the departments themselves and the public.

Exercise 4-2. *Interlibrary Loans and Activity-Based Accounting Methods*

One of the first steps in helping the director of Essex University Library and the head of ILL work with activity-based costing methods is to determine the salary and mailing costs that are related to ILL activities.

Assigning Salary Expenditures to ILL Activities

Based on the information provided in the problem, the following schedule shows a method of salary allocation to the ILL.

	ILL	Non-ILL
Librarian's salary—$45,000	$27,000 (60%)	$18,000 (40%)
Staff salary—$47,000	42,300 (90%)	4,700 (10%)
Totals	$69,300	$22,700

Salary costs related to ILL activities are $69,300.

Assigning Mailing Expenditures to Internal and External Functions

A second step would be to determine how the mailing expenditures are assigned to various activities in the ILL Department. Mailing costs are divided between internal requests from patrons at Essex University and requests from external libraries for materials on a 70/30 split. Using that information, it can be determined that the mailing costs of $35,000 are divided between external and internal requests as follows:

$35,000 × .70 = $24,500 internal requests from patrons
$35,000 × .30 = $10,500 external library requests for materials

The head of the ILL has provided a list of activities that are performed within the ILL, but she has not assigned any times required to perform the activities. If the number of minutes for each activity were known, it would be possible to determine costs on a worked-minute basis.

Without any information on work minutes, it is still possible to assign salary and mailing costs to the number of books and articles processed through the ILL based on activities. The following costs provide a method to allocate these costs to book- and article-processing activities.

Mailing Expenditures and Activities

1. *Internal requests from patrons:* assigned mailing costs: $24,500

   The mailing costs are all assigned to books and articles using the following ratios tied to mailing activities. As the head of ILL has not time-weighted these activities, each activity is given an equal weight:

Activity	Mailing request for *article*	(1)
	Mailing request for *book*	(1)
	Mailing *book* back after loan period	(1)
		3

   In the schedule, two activities are related to books and one is related to articles. For this reason, the ratios used to allocate costs are 2/3 and 1/3, as follows:

Books	2/3 × $24,500 =	$16,333
Articles	1/3 × $24,500 =	8,167
Total		$24,500

2. *External for materials:* assigned mailing costs: $10,500

Activity	Mailing *article* to requesting library	(1)
	Mailing *book* to requesting library	(1)
		2

   In the schedule, the activities are equally divided between books and articles. For this reason, the ratios used to allocate costs are 1/2 and 1/2, as follows:

Books	1/2 × $10,500 =	$ 5,250
Articles	1/2 × $10,500 =	5,250
Total		$10,500

   The total estimated cost for mailing books is $21,583 ($16,333 + $5,250), and the total mailing cost for articles is $13,417 ($8,167 + $5,250).

Salary Expenditures and Activities

Now the question arises as to how to assign the salary expenditures of $69,300 to the processing of books and articles. When all the activities are reviewed, it can be seen that some activities relate to both the processing of books and articles, whereas other activities are only related to books or articles. For example, photocopying articles for external requests is only performed for article requests. The only way to classify these activities into internal and external activities is by giving them an equal weight. Therefore, the number of activities that are performed, for either external or internal requests, are counted and classified. Although it would be better to assign activity weights on minutes worked, pages copied, or other similar measures, this information is currently not available.

1. Internal Requesting Activities
   (a) Both (6)
       Check current collection for books
       Check current collection for journals
       Mail request to loaning library
       Check receipt of item
       Notify patron
       Record pickup by patron
   (b) Books, only (3)
       Receive returned book from patron
       Follow-up on nonreturn
       Return book to loaning library

2. External Requesting Activities
   (a) Both (2)
       Mail out book or article request
       Collect fee on loaned materials
   (b) Books, only (5)
       Locate book
       Document loaned material
       Check returned loaned materials
       Record returned book
       Reshelve book
   (c) Articles, only (1)
       Photocopying article

Matrix of Activities

	Both	Books	Articles	
Internal from patrons	6	3	0	
External for own materials	2	5	1	
Totals	8	8	1	= 17 total activities

Total salary costs $69,300/17 = $4,076.47 salary cost per activity

Salary costs of $69,300 are assigned to common activities (both), books, and articles.

	Both	Books	Articles	Total
Internal	$24,459	$12,229	0	$36,688
External	8,153	20,382	$4,076	32,611
Total	$32,612	$32,611	$4,076	$69,299

The result of the review of activities, as related to books and articles, results in the following cost assignments.

Total Costs Related to Internal Requesting Activities

(a) Total

	Both	Books	Articles	Total
Mailing	$ 0	$16,333	$8,167	$24,500
Salary	24,459	12,229	0	36,688
Total	$24,459	$28,562	$8,167	$61,188

The ILL Department has information about usage statistics: the average number of internal (9,750: books, 6,000, and articles, 3,750) and external requests (5,500: books, 4,500, and articles 1,000) along with data on the average number of articles and articles requested by these groups.

(b) Per Unit

$Total/Units

Both	$24,459/9,750 = $2.51
Books	$28,562/6,000 = $4.76
Articles	$8,167/3,750 = $2.18

Total Cost Related to External Requesting Activities

(a) Total

	Both	Books	Articles	Total
Mailing	$ 0	$ 5,250	$5,250	$10,500
Salary	8,153	20,382	4,076	32,611
Total	$8,153	$25,632	$9,326	$43,111

(b) Per Unit

$Total/Units

Both	$8,153/5,500 = $1.48
Books	$25,632/4,500 = $5.70
Articles	$9,326/1,000 = $9.33

Per-Unit Cost of Internal and External Activities

Request Area	Both	Books	Articles
Internal	$2.51	$ 4.76	$ 2.18
External	$1.48	$ 5.70	$ 9.33
Total	$3.99	$10.46	$11.51

Summary

The results of the activity analysis have raised a lot of questions. The most expensive area appears to be external requests for articles at $9.33 per request. It also becomes apparent that the cost of article requests is much higher than external requests for books on a per-unit basis. In addition, there is a relatively high cost for serving book requests from internal patrons, at $4.76 per book. The director and Alice are surprised to see such a large dollar difference in per-unit costs as it was always thought the servicing of external book and article requests had the same costs.

The director and the head of ILL would like to reduce or combine activities in order to reduce costs but not the quality of the services. The director would also like to know how to better assign the costs of activities related to "both" internal and external requests to a specific ILL activity. The table showing per-unit costs does not assign any clear responsibility for these costs in column two, "Both."

At this point, the director has asked Alice to conduct a survey of employees to determine the time that they spend on the various departmental activities that have been identified. It is hoped that through a more detailed investigation of activities, it might be possible to curtail activities that are not really contributing value to the department's services.

Exercise 4-3. Applying Activity Accounting in Acquisitions

1. Books

	Dept. and Tech. Charges		Book Time per Activity		Per-Unit Cost
Ordering	$15.75	×	.50	=	$ 7.875
Processing invoices	12.60	×	.50	=	6.300
Accession/processing	34.24	×	.30	=	10.272
Cancellations	21.00	×	.10	=	2.100
Cost per book acquired and processed					$ 26.55*

Articles

	Dept. and Tech. Charges		Book Time per Activity		Per-Unit Cost
Ordering	$15.75	×	.80	=	$12.600
Processing invoices	12.60	×	.50	=	6.300
Accession/processing	34.24	×	.80	=	27.392
Cancellations	21.00	×	1.00	=	21.000
Cost per article acquired and processed					$67.290*

*Rounded

2. The following table compares actual costs with activity accounting costs and technology charges in columns one and two, respectively, in order to determine the variances from activity cost levels.

	Actual Cost	Activity Accounting Cost	Variance* U(F)
Ordering	$ 7,500	$ 7,875	$ 375
Processing invoices	13,000	12,600	(400)
Accession/processing	14,000	13,695	(305)
Cancellations	1,500	1,050	(450)
Totals	$36,000	$35,220	$(780)

*(U) Unfavorable; F Favorable. If the actual costs are more than the activity costs, it is an unfavorable variance because the actual costs incurred are more than those that were planned to be incurred for each activity. If actual costs are less than activity costs, the variance is favorable.

Exercise 4-4.   *Nonvalue-Added and Value-Added Activities*

The identification of nonvalue-added activities depends if or how those activities may be dealt with in an alternative manner. For example, if technology can replace several employee functions without a decrease in quality, then those employee activities may be nonvalue-added activities.

In the Essex Library several activities may be considered nonvalue-added activities:

1. Alice's non-ILL activities (i.e., 40 percent of her time) spent outside the ILL do not add value to the services provided by the ILL. It should be determined if the level of outside functions can be reduced.

2. The additional requests sent to patrons requesting the return of loaned materials to the ILL does not add value to the services provided by the ILL, and the number of requests needs to be reduced. Faculty members have the worst record for returning materials to the ILL.

3. If article mailing can be replaced with the use of online e-mailing, then the slow receipt of items through the mail would be considered a nonvalue-added activity that should be eliminated, along with the cost of photocopying articles.

4. The checking of the collection to determine if the patron-requested item is in the collection is a nonvalue-added activity. The patron should fill out the request in a system that automatically checks the library's collection. Such a system would eliminate paperwork and checking activities of the ILL staff.

Exercise 5-1.   *Working with Budget Reports*

1. The current budget answers only one question: Are our expenditures within our legal guidelines? It does not provide any managerial information about whether operations are being efficiently or effectively performed.

2. There might be factors that could also be considered cost drivers other than those explained here.

    Ordering: This cost driver is probably the number of purchase orders issued by the Acquisitions Department. The staff time involved in preparing purchase orders would determine most of the cost of ordering materials for the library. The staff time would vary depending on if this were an automated or manual, paper-driven operation.

Supplier-Related Costs: These costs are likely to be driven by the number of vendor's invoices received by the Acquisitions Department. Again, the actual cost of labor time related to this activity would vary depending on if the operation were automated or manually driven.

Accessioning of Materials: The actual number of items received is the cost driver here. It would be expected that the number of items received would be different from the number of items ordered with purchase orders.

Cancellations: The cost of processing cancellations is likely to be driven by the number of cancellation request forms completed by library personnel and other units.

3. No, the current accounting system cannot reallocate the costs to the four areas of cost accumulation that are required by the Acquisitions Department.

   If the Business Office were receptive to Alice's needs, it would be possible to change the accounting cost codes so that salaries, wages, supplies, and photocopying expenditures were reassigned to ordering, supplier, accessioning, and cancellation costs.

Exercise 5-2. Analyzing Cost Patterns within a Library Department

1. The functions performed within a department determine which base should be used as a cost driver for that department. There is no one base that is always the best cost driver. With the IT Department, either labor hours or logged computer time should be used as the cost driver. Although it may be argued that the combination of the two together would be the best method, the IT Department is a small department, and thus it would be better to choose one or the other, but do not use both.

2. Good performance should not simply be based on past performance levels. Good performance should be based on a standard for good performance (i.e., a benchmark). It is assumed the consultant is providing such a benchmark. For this reason, either 15,000 hours of direct labor or 110,000 hours of computer time should be used as a standard for good performance in the IT Department.

3. Using Figure 5-8 as a model, the following calculations are determined:

Cost Patterns

Variable Costs

Salary for part-time	$24,000	
Computer maintenance costs	5,000	
Supplies	6,000	$35,000

Fixed Costs

Salaries for full-time	$54,000	
Equipment/software	12,000	66,000
Totals		$101,000

Per-Unit Costs per Computer Hour

Variable Costs

Salary for part-time	$24,000/110,000 =	$0.22
Computer maintenance costs	5,000/110,000 =	0.05
Supplies	6,000/110,000 =	0.05
Total variable cost per hour		$0.32

Fixed Costs

Salaries for full-time	$54,000/110,000 =	$0.49
Equipment/software	12,000/110,000 =	0.11
Fixed costs per hour		$0.60

4. The problem with the analysis in question 3 is that no standards have been established for the dollar amounts shown for fixed costs ($66,000) and variable costs ($35,000). Are these dollar totals acceptable for good performance in the IT Department? As the department has been under review by a consultant, who has not made any comments about these costs, it will be assumed that the costs of IT operations are acceptable for good performance in the department. If they were not acceptable as standards, then new standard costs would have to be determined in the calculations used in question 3.

Exercise 5-3. *Nonfinancial Performance Measures*

The exercise identifies three distinct areas where nonfinancial performance measures can be integrated with financial measures to provide a more comprehensive perspective on departmental performance. The three areas are (1) patron or customer satisfaction, (2) employee contributions, and (3) the effective meeting of internal policy goals. With employees, their contributions are strongly influenced by the level of training; therefore, employee training and learning must be evaluated first.

Patron Satisfaction

Satisfaction survey from patrons

Reduce number of complaints

Employee Contributions (Based around Learning Levels)

Staff training programs and attendance levels

Reduce staff turnover levels

Increase percentage of staff using new technology for answering appropriate questions

Meeting Internal Policy Goals

Analyze satisfaction survey for responses to level-of-quality issues

Decrease time required to receive requested materials

Develop measures to trace the relationship between policy plans and their implementation

In some cases, these measures would be turned into ratios. In most cases, they would not be based on the data collected in the financial statements or budget reports. If they are not based on data previously collected by the financial system, the cost of developing these measures must be compared with the benefits that are received from their use in assisting managers in the decision-making process.

Exercise 5-4.   *Analyzing Spending, Usage, and Time Variances*

The following schematic outlines the variances for question numbers 1 and 3. The 200 hours (shown in bold type) needs to be determined first ($4,600/$23).

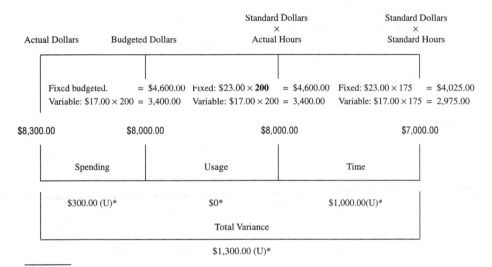

		Standard Dollars × Actual Hours	Standard Dollars × Standard Hours
Actual Dollars	Budgeted Dollars		

Fixed budgeted. = $4,600.00   Fixed: $23.00 × **200** = $4,600.00   Fixed: $23.00 × 175   = $4,025.00
Variable: $17.00 × 200 = 3,400.00   Variable: $17.00 × 200 = 3,400.00   Variable: $17.00 × 175 = 2,975.00

$8,300.00 $8,000.00 $8,000.00 $7,000.00

Spending   Usage   Time

$300.00 (U)* $0* $1,000.00(U)*

Total Variance

$1,300.00 (U)*

----
*(U) Unfavorable

2. There are several reasons that the spending variance was unfavorable. The spending variance may have occurred because part-time labor is being paid too high an hourly rate. To correct the problem the rate needs to be reduced, or part-time employees who receive a lower hourly rate need to replace the full-time workers currently working on the project. This spending variance may have occurred because employees with the skills to catalog books are being used to shelve the books, and it would be better to use lower-skilled employees for shelving tasks.

4. The usage variance is zero because no supplies or materials were used in the project. The project has only used labor up to this point.

5. The librarian-manager needs to reduce the hourly rate paid to part-time employees to get the spending variance under control. In addition, the hours (time variance) used to complete the project are excessive compared with good standards for completion. The librarian-manager should more closely supervise the project

to determine why it is taking so much longer than necessary to complete the cataloging and shelving. It may be that the extra time is necessary, but the reasons need to be investigated.

Exercise 6-1. Calculating the Cost of Lightbulbs

In making the calculation, it must be realized that it will take thirteen incandescent bulbs to be used for every one fluorescent bulb (10,000/760 = 13). The following table outlines the life cycle costs over 10,000 hours.

	Incandescent*	Fluorescent
Purchase Cost	$ 1.00	$15.00
Operating cost per kWh		
Incandescent: (.76 kWh × 60 watts		
× $0.10 per kWh) × 13	$ 59.00	
Fluorescent: (10 kWh × 15 watts		
× $0.10) × 1		$15.00
Replacement cost over 10,000 hours		
Incandescent: $4.75 × 13	$ 62.00	
Fluorescent: $3.00 × 1		$ 3.00
Total life cycle cost	$122.00	$33.00

* The numbers are rounded

The difference in cost over the life cycle of the two bulbs is $89.00 for one bulb. Although the initial cost for the fluorescent bulb is higher, it incurs lower costs over its life cycle. Most annual budgets do not allow for these sorts of savings as the expenditure line for the purchase only looks at the asset's current cost.

Exercise 6-2. A Heating System Replacement

1. Using the data presented in the problem and the table factors in appendix B for ten years and a 9 percent discount rate, the following comparison can be made.

New System

	Ordinary Annuity Cash Outflow	Lump Sum Cash Inflow	Present Value
Year 1			
Purchase price			$ 30,000
Installation cost			4,000
Years 1–10			
Electricity use*	$5,000 × 6.418[†]		$ 32,090
Gas use	$7,000 × 6.418[†]		$ 44,926
Annual maintenance	$1,000 × 6.418[†]		$ 6,418
Year 10			
Less salvage value	$2,000 × .422[‡]		844
Net cash outflow			$116,590

Old System

	Ordinary Annuity Cash Outflow	Lump Sum Cash Inflow	Present Value
Years 1–10			
Electricity use‡	$16,000 × 6.418†		$102,688.00
Annual maintenance	800 × 6.418†		5,134.40
Net cash outflow			$107,822.40

*50,000kWh × .10 = $5,000; same method used for old system
†Table factor for an ordinary annuity for ten periods with a discount rate of 9 percent
‡Table factor for a lump sum cash inflow in Year 10 with a discount rate of 9 percent

Result: The analysis shows that in this case the old system should not be replaced because it is more costly to replace it than to keep it over the ten-year period.

2. In the next case, the analysis period would have to change to eight years as the library would no longer be in the building after the eight-year period was over. The analysis is the same except for the change in the time period.

New System

	Ordinary Annuity Cash Outflow	Lump Sum Cash Inflow	Present Value
Year 1			
Purchase price			$ 30,000
Installation cost			4,000
Years 1–8			
Electricity use*	$5,000 × 5.535†		$ 27,675
Gas use	$7,000 × 5.535†		$ 38,745
Annual maintenance	$1,000 × 5.535†		$ 5,535
Year 8			
Less salvage value	$2,000 × .502‡		1,004
Net cash outflow			$104,951

Old System

	Ordinary Annuity Cash Outflow	Lump Sum Cash Inflow	Present Value
Years 1–10			
Electricity use‡	$16,000 × 5.535†		$88,560
Annual maintenance	800 × 5.535†		4,428
Net cash outflow			$92,988

*50,000kWh × .10 = $5,000; same method used for old system
†Table factor for an ordinary annuity for eight periods with a discount rate of 9 percent
‡Table factor for a lump sum cash inflow in Year 8 with a discount rate of 9 percent

Result: In number 1, the net cash outflow between the two heating systems is even greater than in case number 2. This reflects the time value of money in the shorter period.

Exercise 6-3. Starting a Revenue Venture

1. The present value of all costs required to start up the Book Nook need to be computed.

   (a) Immediate cash outlay and the present value of part-time salary:

Espresso machine	$10,000
Cups, saucers, etc.	200
Tables, chairs, etc.	1,500
Present value of PT salary ($15,000 × 5.786*)	86,790
Present value of costs	$98,490

   ---

   *Table factor for an ordinary annuity for seven periods at 5 percent

   (b) Cash profit from coffee sales:

   Profit per cup × cups per day × days in month × months in year = total annual cash profit
   $1.50 × 50 × 30 × 12 = $27,000

   Present value of ordinary annuity of $27,000 for seven years with a 5 percent discount rate:
   $27,000 × 5.786* = $156,222

   (c) The cash profit for the Book Nook over the seven years would be

   Present value of cash profits − present value of costs = cash profit
   $156,222 − $98,490 = $57,732

   In this case, the cash profits could be used to purchase new equipment worth $57,732 at the end of the seven-year period.

2. Here, the director wants to know what is the minimum number of cups that would have to be sold to ensure that the cash profit was not negative and thus equal to $98,490. The easiest way to make this determination is to combine and reverse the formulas in number 1 (b) and solve for the number of cups per day when the present value of the cash profit equals $98,490.

   (a) (Unknown cash profit) × 5.786* = $98,490; $98,490/5.786 = $17,022 cash profit

   (b) $1.50 × (unknown number of cups) × 30 × 12 = $17,022

   $17,022/540 = 32 minimum number of cups that need to be sold per day over the seven-year period

   Joe should consider whether it will be possible to sell on average thirty-two cups of coffee per day.

   ---

   *Table factor for an ordinary annuity for seven periods at 5 percent

Exercise 6-4. Nonfinancial Performance Measures

There are many correct answers to this question. Some of the nonfinancial measures that might be used follow:

- Patron satisfaction survey on the ease of use and library support and help in using the PCs
- Measures to evaluate the training provided to the library staff so that they can efficiently help patrons with the new PCs and the software on them
- Measures to determine how the board is functioning now that it no longer has a designated meeting room
- Time measures to determine the downtime on the PCs and the LAN
- Time to access the Internet, slow or fast access, and so forth

The relationship between the measures selected should support patron satisfaction or employee training.

Exercise 7-1. Break-Even Analysis

1. How many coffee cups will the library have to sell?

$$\text{BE units} = \frac{\$3,600}{\$5 - \$2}$$

$$= 1,200 \text{ cups}$$

2. What selling price should the library charge?

$$\text{x} = \text{selling price}$$

$$1,200 \text{ cups} = \frac{\$7,200}{\text{x} - \$2}$$

$$\text{x} = \$8$$

Exercise 7-2. High-Low Analysis

1. Equation for a straight line.

$$\text{Variable cost} = \frac{\$7,500 - \$1,000}{35,000 - 5,500}$$

$$= \frac{\$6,500}{29,500}$$

$$= .2203$$

Fixed Costs   (a) $1,000 - 5,500\ (.2203) = -211.65*$

(b) $7,500 - 35,000\ (.2203) = -210.50*$

Total cost estimate $= -\$211 + .2203$ (searches)

*The difference is because of rounding

2. In this example, the fixed cost reduces the total cost of operating the databases by $211. In any cost line, this is a very unusual relationship. It may be that the database service is returning a portion of the total costs to the library after a specified number of searches are made.

3. If the number of searches increased by 10 percent, there would be 38,500 searches made in the coming year. Using the total cost equation, it would indicate that the cost of providing databases would be $8,271, as follows:

Total cost estimate = −$211 + .2203 (38,500 searches)
$$= -\$211 + \$8,482$$
$$= \$8,271$$

Exercise 7-3.   Ethics and Grants

There are a number of acceptable answers to this question depending on how the answer is justified. Each answer should incorporate a break-even aspect to it.

Break-even analysis can help show how much of a surplus would be available as well as how much and how quickly a deficit would develop for the library. *See* the accompanying chart.

If the director allowed 500 participants in the program, the deficit would be $25,000. Can the library afford to help this many people and incur this deficit?

If the program were limited to 200 participants, the library would have a surplus of $5,000 to purchase new equipment for the literacy program and the library.

With all choices, the break-even chart helps the library director readily see these relationships.

What is the ethical choice? Each choice can be argued as being ethical.

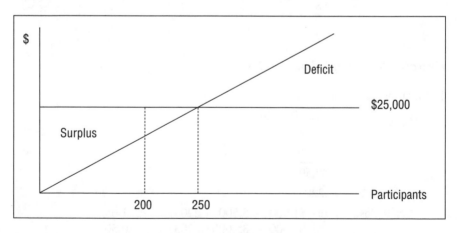

Exercise 7-4.   Differential Cost-Decision Analysis

1. Only the differential costs should be considered in making this decision. It should be noted that overhead is not one of those costs. The differential cost analysis follows:

	Costs Saved— Drop Janitors	Cost of Clean-All
Salaries	$40,000	
Supplies	2,200	
Maintenance	1,000	
Service cost per sq. ft.		$50,000
Severance pay		10,000
Less: gift shop revenue		(12,000)
	$43,200	$48,000

From the analysis, it appears better from a single-cost viewpoint not to fire Lou and Fred at this time.

2. Besides the dollar cost of the change, other factors might be considered:

How much of an increase in Clean-All's service fee will occur in the future?

Do Lou and Fred provide services—such as repairs—that Clean-All would not provide in their package?

How much is it going to cost to replace library-owned janitorial equipment in the future?

Are there intangible costs (nonfinancial) associated with Lou and Fred? Are they a personnel problem, for example?

Exercise 7-5.   The Learning Curve

1. The first step is to determine the cumulative average time at 128 records. This can be done with the learning curve equation or by multiplying by 80 percent. In either case, record completion would be 9.5 (rounded) minutes. As there are 5,000 records remaining to be completed, it would require 792 hours.

   5,000 books × 9.5 minutes = 47,500 minutes/60 minutes = 792 hours

   If three staff members were assigned to this task, it would take 6.6 weeks to complete the recataloging. With this time commitment, it is important to ensure the best training is being provided to reduce the records per minute as much as possible.

   792 hours/40 hours per week = 19.8 weeks/3 staff members = 6.6 weeks

2. The dollar cost of developing the automated circulation system using an $18 average rate of pay would be $14,256.

   792 hours × $18 = $14,256

   Now is the time to ask for library volunteers.

Exercise 8-1. Present Values and the Lease

Use the factors in Table 3 in appendix B in the following computation.

	10% Table Factor				
ACME (8 periods)	5.868	×	$125	=	$733.50
Warren (2 periods)	1.909	×	$500	=	$954.50

The most cost-effective choice is the lease agreement with ACME. This choice would save the library $221 over the two-year period.

Exercise 8-2. Book-Leasing Service

1. The net price the Jones Library is paying for the books is $25.50 ($28.50 – $3.00). The total annual cost to the library is $12,750 ($25.50 × 500). The present value of the two alternatives—continue to purchase or lease—is calculated using Table 3 in appendix B, as follows:

		10% Table Factor		**Present Value**
Continue purchasing	$12,750	×	4.170	= $53,168
Moreland lease	17,000	×	4.170	= 70,890

The cost of the lease is $17,722 more expensive than continuing to purchase the books as had been done in the past.

2. If $15,000 can be saved in payroll cuts by signing the lease, the total cash outlay on the lease is only $2,000 ($17,000 – $15,000). In this case, the cost of the lease becomes very attractive.

		10% Table Factor		**Present Value**
Continue purchasing	$12,750	×	4.170	= $53,168
Moreland lease	2,000	×	4.170	= $ 8,340

By signing the lease, the Jones Library will save $44,828 over the five-year term of the lease.

Exercise 8-3. Variations on the Book Service Lease

The time period for the analysis is ten months—from November 1 to August 31—and the first payment under the lease is assumed to occur at the beginning of the lease or on November 1. The first payment does not have to be discounted as it is already in the current time period. The subsequent payments are discounted using the lump sum present value factors (Table 1). There are other ways to make this computation using Table 3, but it is shown here using the lump sum factors. During this ten-month period, only 500 titles can be purchased (10/12 × 600). The results follow.

Alternative 1: Continue Purchasing as in the Past

Month	No. of Titles × $ Cost	Total Cost × PV Factor	Present Values
November	44 × $26 =	$1,144 × 1.00 =	$1,144
December	41 × $26 =	$1,066 × 0.909 =	$969
January	44 × $26 =	$1,144 × 0.826 =	$945
February	44 × $26 =	$1,144 × 0.751 =	$859
March	44 × $26 =	$1,144 × 0.683 =	$781
April	44 × $26 =	$1,144 × 0.621 =	$710
May	44 × $26 =	$1,144 × 0.564 =	$645
June	65 × $26 =	$1,690 × 0.513 =	$867
July	65 × $26 =	$1,690 × 0.467 =	$789
August	65 × $26 =	$1,690 × 0.424 =	$717
Total	500 titles		$8,426

Alternative 2: Leasing Alternative

Month	No. of Titles × $ Cost	Total Cost × PV Factor	Present Values
November	50 × $28 =	$1,400 × 1.00 =	$1,400
December	50 × $28 =	$1,400 × 0.909 =	$1,273
January	50 × $28 =	$1,400 × 0.826 =	$1,156
February	50 × $28 =	$1,400 × 0.751 =	$1,051
March	50 × $28 =	$1,400 × 0.683 =	$956
April	50 × $28 =	$1,400 × 0.621 =	$869
May	50 × $28 =	$1,400 × 0.564 =	$790
June	50 × $28 =	$1,400 × 0.513 =	$718
July	50 × $28 =	$1,400 × 0.467 =	$654
August	50 × $28 =	$1,400 × 0.424 =	$594
Total	500 titles		$9,461

The leasing alternative costs $1,035 ($9,461 − $8,426) more than continuing with internal purchasing. This difference is even more than the differences between the nondiscounted costs of the two alternatives of $1,000 ($14,000 − $13,000). This analysis does not take into account any of the qualitative factors between the two choices.

Exercise 8-4. *Buying a Bookmobile?*

1. (a)

$$\frac{\$150,000 \text{ cash price}}{7.8 \text{ (10 periods/6\% Table 3 factor)}} = \$19,230 \text{ annual payment}$$

(b) $19,230 × 10 = $192,300 total cost of the bookmobile

(c) $192,300 − $150,000 = $42,300 additional cost of interest expense

2. (a) $$\frac{\$150,000 \text{ cash price}}{7.515 \text{ (10 periods/7\% Table 3 factor)}} = \$19,960 \text{ annual payment}$$

(b) $19,960 × 10 = $199,960 total cost of the bookmobile

(c) $199,960 − $150,000 = $49,600 additional cost of interest expense

(d) $49,600 − $42,300 = $7,300 in additional interest without the lease agreement

Exercise 9-1. The Focus for Performance Measures

The number-one difficulty in the successful implementation of performance measures is support from higher-level management. Without strong support from the top-level library managers, it is unlikely that performance measures will be successfully adopted. At Broken Creek, there is "support," but it is tepid support. The support at Broken Creek does not extend outside staff meetings. Organizational cultural change involves risk. Consequently, without a starting initiative for using performance measures from higher-level managers, there is little chance of performance measures being used at Broken Creek.

Exercise 9-2. BSC at the Departmental Level

The following BSC is one suggested approach for the Coffee and Cushions retreat in the Markus Wellmen Free Library.

Perspective	Objective	Performance Measure	Target
Financial	Positive return	Positive net income	5% return above all costs in the first year
Patron	Satisfaction with retreat	Increasing levels of patron use	Trend of monthly use increasing by 2% in the first year
Internal processes	Developing organizational efficiency	Meeting financial, patron, and learning and growth goals	Meet stated goals within first year
Learning and growth	Trained staff	Employee turnover	Only replace two part-time counter persons within first year

Exercise 9-3.   BSC for Overall Library Initiatives

1. Suggestions for the BSC Matrix

Perspectives	Develop Community Technological Competencies	Promote Staff/ Community Collaborative Activities
Financial	Total tech. cost/patron usage levels (per-unit measure)	Leave time granted for community-based activities (hours)
Patron	Satisfied patron index (based on surveys and possible focus group)	Number of interactions with community in hosting community events in the library (simple count)
		Response from community members on survey sheets after meetings (satisfaction survey)
Internal processes	Subjective evaluation by administrators of the culture of the library and how it relates to technological change	Adaptation of library facilities for better hosting of community events (memo requests and type of request for room changes, for example)
Learning and growth	Hours of employee technology training (hours)	Number of staff participating in community forums, etc. (counts)
	Percentage level of participation = number participating staff/total staff	Staff-level participation: attendance at local meetings—becoming an officer in community-based organization— attendance at regional or national meetings

2. Once performance measures are agreed upon, targets need to be set for each of them; later, feedback needs to be collected to determine how successfully they are being met. Rewards for successful performance should also be incorporated into the library.

Exercise 9-4. Evaluating BSC Performance Measures

The following comments provide a review of the BSC primary initiative selected for increasing the J. Bunyan Library's capacity to accomplish its strategic initiatives.

Financial: The purpose of this measure is to determine the costs being devoted to support the new initiatives adopted in the library. The value of this measure depends on how easy it is to collect this information. Some organizations will develop new initiatives at an alarming rate. These initiatives have little financial support or chance of succeeding. The relationship between financial support for new initiatives and the number of new initiatives shows whether the library is overreaching toward initiatives and goals that will never be accomplished.

Patron: The satisfaction index is being compared with previous results from the library itself. Importantly, independent benchmarks are also being used for comparative purposes. It is always better to use national or regional standards as measures of comparison if they are available.

Internal Processes: The HLAs have the most influence in affecting strategic decision making. Therefore, it is important to evaluate their contributions to the achievement of the J. Bunyan Library's primary initiative. A survey response to a questionnaire, such as the one illustrated in Figure 9-4, will help answer questions about the level of HLA input. There are no external benchmarks for making this type of comparison, so careful judgment will have to be applied to the results.

Learning and Growth: All employees in the J. Bunyan Library should understand how their daily activities contribute to achieving the library's initiatives. Such employee understanding can be evaluated through interview sampling of employee opinions, surveys, and a sampling of HLA communication to employees regarding the relationship between their tasks and strategic initiatives.

GLOSSARY

Accrual method of accounting An accounting method that focuses primarily on the passage of time to recognize revenues and expenses rather than on the flow of resources or cash.

Activity-based costing (ABC) A system of costing that uses detailed identification of activities as a way to trace costs to services and products. It, like traditional-based costing, uses allocations to assign costs to cost objects, but it uses a more detailed analysis of activities or cost drivers.

Allocation A method of assigning costs, usually overhead, to cost objects to determine their full costs. Overhead is assigned using a surrogate to assign the costs. Commonly used surrogates or cost drivers are direct labor, number of personnel, or floor space, for example.

Analysis of variance The determination of the difference between actual costs and standard costs (established as projections before the activity began) to evaluate performance. If actual costs are less than the standard established, the variance is favorable. If the actual costs are more than the standard costs, the variance is unfavorable

Appropriations An appropriation is a legal authorization for making expenditures within set dollar amounts, time periods, and specified purposes.

Assets Items with a determinable future value and that are owned by the organization.

Balanced scorecard (BSC) A method to evaluate progress toward strategic initiatives that coordinates objectives, performance measures, and targets for meeting the organization's long-term mission. The BSC does not simply measure financial targets. It combines financial targets with patron, internal processes, and learning and growth targets to achieve a more holistic view of the organization's progress.

Book value The book value of an asset is the asset's net value. Book value is determined by deducting all the accumulated depreciation recorded on an asset from its purchase price.

Break-even analysis (cost-volume-profit analysis) A methodology that identifies the point, in total units or dollars, where the total revenues exactly equal the total costs of a profit-generating activity.

Budget   An annual planning tool used to match financial resources with financial expenditures. The budget provides a means to achieve the organization's stated mission.

Capital lease   A lease that allows the lessee to control a leased asset for a specified time period under a financing plan. A capital lease allows the lessee to finance the purchase of a leased asset through a series of lease payments over a specified time period. The final outcome is that the leased asset is purchased by the lessee.

Cash basis of accounting   A method of accounting that only records business transactions when a cash exchange has occurred. It emphasizes the flow of cash rather than the passage of time or the flow of resources for transaction recognition.

Contracts for performance   These are agreements between higher-level administrators (HLAs) and the organization. The contract is signed prior to the HLA accepting a new position. It provides contractual terms upon which the HLA will be evaluated after a specified time period. Failure to live up to the agreed-upon terms can result in termination or reassignment.

Contribution margin   The contribution margin is the difference between the selling price and the variable costs of a unit. It measures the per-unit contribution to profit or the reduction of total fixed costs.

Controllable cost   A controllable cost is one that can be influenced by the decisions made by a manager. Thus, the cost is defined as controllable.

Cost driver   A cost driver is the activity that causes costs to increase over time.

Cost object   A cost object is an activity or project upon which the cost analysis is focused and consequently upon which costs are separately accumulated and reported.

Current cost   When inflation occurs over a time period, the repurchase cost of all assets increase (for example, a car purchased in 1966 compared with a car in 1999). The current cost is the purchase price today for a comparable asset as one currently owned by the organization and actually purchased in an earlier time period.

Deferred maintenance   If maintenance expenditures are not made on a routine basis to keep the organization's fixed assets in proper working order, the maintenance has been deferred. As a result, the service potential of the asset has been reduced. The gap between the maintenance performed and maintenance required to keep the asset in proper working order can be measured and recorded, and it is called deferred maintenance.

Depreciation   The allocation of the purchase price of a long-term fixed asset to the time periods to which the asset provides benefits. Depreciation is the accounting recognition of the usage or obsolescence of the asset. It is recorded as an expense, but unlike other expenses, it does not create a cash or resource outflow.

Differential cost The costs that differ between two alternatives are known as differential costs. Differential costs are important for choosing between alternatives. Sometimes differential costs are called marginal costs.

Direct cost Those costs such as direct labor and direct materials that can be easily traced to a cost-generating project or activity.

Direct method of cost allocation A method of cost allocation whereby the cost of all support departments are directly allocated to producing departments in order to determine the full cost of the producing departments. The direct method does not use allocations and reallocations of costs to determine the full costs as is done in the step-down method of cost allocation.

Discount rate The interest rate that is used in calculating the present value of cash flows. It is a rate that is assumed to remain constant over the life of the cash flows.

Discounted cash flow This is a methodology that takes into account the cash flows generated by an activity or project within the context of present value analysis. It allows for the comparability of cash flows among alternative choices where the cash flows are of differing amounts and are realized over different time periods.

Discretionary cost Although discretionary costs can be variable, fixed, or mixed, their distinguishing characteristic is that they are incurred at the discretion of higher-level managers in the organization. These costs may be expended for additional staff training, for example.

Encumbrance An encumbrance discloses a commitment of budgetary monies for an anticipated purchase. It is recorded at the time the purchase order is issued by the organization. An encumbrance is not a liability.

Expenditure Expended resource outflows during the current period. Expenditures include most expenses.

Expense Expiration of resources, or the incurrence of a liability recognized by the passage of time, or the incurrence of the actual expenditure used to generate revenues and provide services in the current period.

Financial Accounting Standards Board (FASB) This is the accounting body that sets accounting principles, rules, and standards that are to be used in accrual accounting.

Fiscal period A twelve-month period used in tabulating financial reports. A calendar period is from January to December, but a fiscal period may be any twelve-month time period. Most government organizations in the United States use a fiscal period from July to June.

Fixed cost Total fixed costs stay constant over increasing volume levels, and per-unit fixed costs decrease as volume or units increase. An example of a fixed cost is a supervisor's salary.

Flexible budget A budget whose dollar allocations change as the volume level, such as number of patrons, upon which it is based increases or decreases. A static budget's dollar allocations remain constant regardless of the level of volume changes.

Full cost The full cost of a project or activity includes all the direct costs such as direct labor and direct materials as well as an allocation for overhead.

Generally accepted accounting principles (GAAP) The principles, standards, and interpretations that are followed, used, and accepted in preparing financial statements.

Governmental Accounting Standards Board (GASB) This is the accounting body that sets the accounting principles, rules, and standards that are to be followed by state governments.

High-low analysis A simple method of finding the linear equation for two plotted points on a graph. It provides the equation for a straight line.

Historical cost The original purchase price of an asset is its historical cost.

Indirect cost Another term used to describe overhead costs. *See* Overhead.

Inventory Amounts such as supplies that are held in storage and not yet used but classified separately from other long-lived assets because of their shorter-term nature.

Investment center An organization division that provides a return on the cost dollars invested in the center. The center has its own revenues and expenses and investment base. *See* Return on investment.

Learning curve The learning curve measures the relationship between the amount of cumulative labor time required to perform a task or make a unit and the learning that takes place as that task is repeated many times. The curve traces the increase in worker skill development that occurs as a task or job is repeatedly performed. The curve is particularly useful in making future labor cost estimates when a new task or function is begun.

Lease term The time period over which the leased asset will be used.

Leaseback Leaseback arrangements usually provide tax advantages to one of the parties to the lease and an immediate cash flow for the other party. In a basic leaseback arrangement, an asset is sold to a third party who immediately leases the asset back to the selling party.

Lessee The party leasing an asset.

Lessor The party who owns the asset and leases it to another party.

Life cycle costs After an asset is purchased, costs continue to be generated by that asset over its entire life. These costs include maintenance expenditures, for example. When all such costs are considered, they are called the life cycle costs of the asset.

Life cycle management A method of asset selection and decision making that is closely tied to the total life cycle cost of the asset being purchased.

Long-lived assets Assets that have a life over one year or longer than the current fiscal period. Such assets are usually equipment or property.

Market value This is the price at which an asset will sell in an open market. With many assets, this is difficult to determine. Market value is also called fair market value.

Mission statement Organizations develop a mission statement for guiding their employees toward a unified vision. The method in which the mission is integrated into an organization can vary from none to incorporating it into the daily activities of each employee.

Mixed cost A mixed cost is one that has the attributes of both variable and fixed costs.

Modified accrual accounting An accounting method that uses a combination of accrual and cash-based accounting methods. It focuses on the flow of resources through funds rather than the passage of time to recognize business transactions.

Net present value The difference between the present value of cash inflows from an activity or project and the costs incurred to generate those cash inflows (purchase cost, for example).

Noncontrollable cost Costs that cannot be controlled by a specific manager at their hierarchical level in the organization are considered to be noncontrollable costs. At a higher organizational level in the organization, these costs may be controllable. *See* Controllable cost.

Nonfinancial performance measures Many performance measures are developed from financial reports and budgets. When other sources of information are used for the development of performance measures, such as surveys, they are called nonfinancial performance measures.

Nontraceable costs With some overhead costs, the cost-benefit relationship in finding a cost driver that causes the incurrence of these overhead costs is not worth the effort to identify the relationship. Additionally, the relationship may be so tenuous as to not be meaningful. These costs are considered to be nontraceable costs.

Nonvalue-added activity Activities that are performed that add no value to the outcome of a task. For example, waiting is not a value-added activity. Such wait times may occur during committee meetings that add little or no direct value to the quality of patron services.

Object of expenditure Objects of expenditure represent the items upon which the annual approved budget is allocated. With objects of expenditure, the allocation is directed toward a specific item, such as equipment or periodicals. Such allocations are good for checking budget allocations for specific expenditures, but they are difficult to use if it is important to cost out project activities such as the cost of bibliographical searches.

Operating lease A lease that allows the lessee to rent the specified asset for a specific time period, after which the asset is returned to the lessor.

Operational planning Operational plans are short-term or tactical plans for organizational activities. Operational plans occur within a time horizon of months up to one year.

Opportunity cost This is the cost of the next-best alternative. It is not a cost that is recorded in the accounting records, but it is a cost that influences decision-making choices.

Original cost The purchase price of an asset is referred to as its original cost.

Overhead These costs are associated with the general activities of the organization and must be incurred but are difficult to identify directly to a specific activity. These costs are the opposite of direct costs, which are closely associated with a project or activity. Under activity-based costing, the objective is to reduce overhead costs to a smaller percentage of the total costs of operations.

Present value analysis A methodology used for comparing the cash flows from an activity or project with the initial cost of the activity or project. Present value tables are used in conjunction with an interest rate and the time periods over which the cash flows occur to find the present value of the activity or project.

Price index The price index provides a means to measure the change that has occurred in purchasing power as caused by the effect of inflation or deflation. These changes usually cause erosion in the purchasing power of the dollar. There are a number of price indexes to use to determine the effect of inflation on purchasing power.

Profit center An organization division that acts as a profit-generating unit with its own revenues and expenses.

Relevant range The range of normal operations within the break-even curves. It is the unit range the organization has operated within before. It helps to provide assurances that costs will behave linearly within the range and that the cost relationships will remain consistent.

Responsibility accounting A system of performance evaluation that assigns cost-control responsibility to a specific functional manager in the library. The manager is responsible for costs at the point where they are incurred in the organization. Responsibility accounting provides for more detailed control at the point of cost incurrence rather than later as costs are accumulated in the financial reports.

Return on investment (ROI) This calculation represents the percentage of return (a ratio) from the capital investment made in a project or activity. It is based in an investment center within the organization, such as a gift or coffee shop. ROI is calculated by dividing the annual net profit by the cost of project investment.

Revenues Amounts that are realized or owed as earned. The definition of "earned" can vary with the method of accounting being used.

Salvage value The estimated value remaining in an asset at the end of its useful life. This is the estimated price at which an asset can be sold when it is retired.

Sensitivity analysis Sensitivity analysis has applications to many situations. It is applied to a set of data relationships by varying one factor and then another to determine how sensitive the factors are in changing the project outcomes.

Spending variance One of a trio of variances that are used to evaluate efficient operations. It arises from the difference between the actual costs incurred and the summation of budgeted fixed dollars and standard variable cost per unit times the number of actual hours used.

Standard cost Costs that are preset at efficient levels within attainable limits. These costs are set to achieve cost control over cost-incurring processes. They can be used as an evaluation of managerial performance in achieving the standards.

Static budget A budget whose dollar allocations do not change as the volume level, such as number of patrons, upon which it is based increases or decreases. The annual library budget is a static budget because the various line item allocations remain constant regardless of the level of change in library activity. The static budget and the legal budget are synonymous.

Step-down method of cost allocation A method of cost allocation whereby the cost of all support departments are allocated to producing departments to determine the full cost of the producing departments. The step-down method uses allocations and reallocations among service and production departments to determine the full-cost activities.

Strategic planning Strategic plans are long-term plans for organizational activities. Strategic plans are more difficult to achieve than operational plans because they occur in a time horizon of one year and beyond.

Sunk costs Costs that continue regardless of the managerial decision that is made. For example, the price paid for an asset and in some cases directors' salaries are considered sunk costs. These costs should not be a factor in managerial decision making.

Time variance One of a trio of variances that are used to evaluate efficient operations. It arises from the difference between the standard rate times the actual hours used and the standard rate times the standard hours used.

Usage variance One of a trio of variances that are used to evaluate efficient operations. It arises from the difference between the summation of budgeted fixed dollars and standard variable cost per unit times the number of hours used and the standard rate times the actual hours used.

Value-added activity   Value-added activities refer to those functions that add value to the direct outcome of an activity. Time spent increasing the quality of an outcome is a value-added activity. Not all activities add value to a process.

Value gains   Value gains relates to higher-level administrator contributions to the long-term decision-making process as determined by employee surveys. If the higher-level administrators' contributions add to the value of the decision-making process as reflected in the final outcome of the decision, it is referred to as value gains.

Value lost   Value lost relates to higher-level administrator (HLA) contributions to the long-term decision-making process as determined by employee surveys. If the HLAs' contributions detract from the value of the decision-making process as reflected in the final outcome of the decision, it is referred to as value lost.

Variable cost   Total variable costs increase over increasing volume levels and per-unit fixed costs remain constant as volume or units increase. An example of a variable cost is direct materials such as supplies.

Variance   Variances record the difference between two sets of numbers. In accounting, variances record the difference between budgeted dollars and the actual spending, for example. The reporting of variances shows how closely actual spending conformed with projected spending. Thus, variances provide evaluations on managerial performance.

INDEX

Page numbers in *italics* refer to figures. Page numbers followed by "n" refer to a note on that page.

G. Stevenson Smith is a professor of accounting at West Virginia University. He has a Certificate of Management Accounting and is a CPA. He is also a Certified Cost Analyst. He received a Ph.D. from the University of Arkansas and an M.B.A. from Michigan State University. He has written numerous articles related to governmental accounting topics, accounting education, e-commerce, and managerial issues. His professional experience includes working for the Securities and Exchange Commission in Washington, D.C., as a financial analyst. Dr. Smith is the author of *Accounting for Libraries and Other Not-for-Profit Organizations, Second Edition* (American Library Association, 1999). This reference deals with financial reporting methods for libraries. He has acted as a facilitator and developer of online courses in financial and managerial accounting for several universities and has led numerous seminars related to management issues.